Media Coverage and Political Terrorists

A QUANTITATIVE ANALYSIS

Richard W. Schaffert

New York
Westport, Connecticut
London

Library of Congress Cataloging-in-Publication Data

Schaffert, Richard W.
    Media coverage and political terrorists : a quantitative analysis
  / Richard W. Schaffert.
        p.   cm.
    Includes bibliographical references and index.
    ISBN 0–275–94243–0 (alk. paper)
    1. Terrorism in mass media.   2. Terrorism and mass media.
  3. Terrorism.   I. Title.
  P96.T47S3   1992
  303.6'25—dc20   91–43443

British Library Cataloguing in Publication Data is available.

Library of Congress Catalog Card Number: 91–43443
ISBN: 0–275–94243–0

First published in 1992

Praeger Publishers, One Madison Avenue, New York, NY 10010
An imprint of Greenwood Publishing Group, Inc.

Printed in the United States of America

The paper used in this book complies with the
Permanent Paper Standard issued by the National
Information Standards Organization (Z39.48–1984).

10 9 8 7 6 5 4 3 2 1

To the memory of diplomat William Buckley, educator and good Samaritan William Robertson, and Marine Lieutenant Colonel William Higgins, that their supreme sacrifice shall not be forgotten . . . and to Roswitha, who endured the terror and fought and won a battle in this long and terrible war.

Contents

Tables

Acknowledgments

Special thanks go to my friends and colleagues Professors Raphael Zariski and Ivan Volgyes for their untiring dedication, their professional expertise, and their friendly cooperation while reviewing the manuscript. Professor Susan Welch gave freely of her time and expert advice in the area of quantitative analysis, for which I am most thankful.

The accuracy and the degree of detail of the data base of terrorist atrocities, which forms the basis of this analysis, were enhanced by the superb cooperation of staff members at the Institute for the Study of Conflict in London, the British Embassy and the America House Library in Vienna, the Research Office of the United Nations Organization in Vienna, and the Austrian National Library. I am indebted to them for their selfless contribution of time and expertise.

With gratitude to Erzsébet, whose patience exceeded all expectations.

Introduction

This analysis begins with the derivation of the elements common to terrorist atrocities worldwide, and the examination of those elements, with the objective of formulating a universal basis for the definition of political terrorism.

A review of the literature reveals some of the reasons for the current lack of progress toward a universal definition of political terrorism. For example, a significant portion of the literature labeled "political terrorism" fails to distinguish between the general category of political violence and the subcategory of terrorism.

The analysis proceeds with the investigation of some of the earlier analytical efforts that contributed to the general confusion over the concept of political terrorism. A critique of nonproductive attempts to define political terrorism through the identification of perpetrators and their causes is offered, and an evaluation is made of the usefulness of the many typologies of terrorism that exist in the literature.

An overview of the employment of terrorism as an instrument of politics is presented. Of continuing and current interest is the employment of terrorism by national liberation movements and ideologies. In a world-order system functioning under the threat of nuclear holocaust, a natural progression away from open warfare has precipitated a movement toward state support and sponsorship of international terrorism. The procedures and implications of the employment of terrorism as an instrument of foreign policy are examined by considering the cases of the Soviet Union and Iran.

A significant amount of the literature involves the investigation of the causes of terrorism. Lack of agreement on a definition of the concept of political terrorism has resulted in chaos, whereby acts of terrorism are attributed to literally every known source of political violence. Few have chosen to address the basic question of why a specific individual or group chooses to commit a terrorist atrocity instead of utilizing another form of political protest. A limited discussion focuses directly on the issue of why a decision may be taken to employ terrorism in the pursuit of political goals.

To perform a quantitative analysis of the relationship between media coverage of terrorist atrocities and the success of terrorists, this analysis first identifies and investigates the functions of political terrorism and the applicable functions of the media.

An attempt is made to clarify the nature of the terror that political terrorists seek to impart to a target audience. At issue is the transmission of terrorist violence, inflicted upon symbolic victims, to the target audience by the exploitation of the free press in a democratic society. A clear concept of the relationship among terrorist violence, the media, and the political power of the terrorists is extremely important.

The dependence of international terrorists upon the media to transmit terror is addressed. The effectiveness of the transnational flow of information is equated with the ability of the media to influence the public's perception of terrorism. The relevance of the news media's selection of labels and terminology when covering political terrorism is examined, along with the communicative techniques involved in the intentional or unintentional dissemination of terrorist propaganda.

The tactics that terrorists employ to exploit the press are examined with respect to the vulnerabilities of the Western media.

The responsibilities of a democratic society's media in the reporting of terrorism are emphasized, with attention to the problems of the contagion of terrorist violence, the close association of members of the media with terrorists during the gathering of information, and the tactical errors committed by members of the media on and away from the scene of terrorist atrocities.

A challenge is offered to the general assumption in the literature that the relationship between the media and the terrorists is symbiotic. At issue is whether the benefits derived by both are in balance over the long term.

Prior to embarking on the quantitative phase of analyzing the relationship between media coverage and terrorist success, a review of previous efforts and difficulties in the operationalization of key concepts is undertaken.

The challenge within the quantitative analysis is to conform to accepted research methodologies while overcoming the difficulties of operationalizing and measuring the significant variables in an extensive data base of media coverage and terrorist atrocities. At issue is the selection and investigation of empirical variables that will allow quantification of what is usually described in the literature as the intangible association between media publicity and terrorist success.

Research of problems that can be quantified and analyzed normally yields recommendations as well as conclusions. Alternative resolutions to the problems usually emerge during the analytical process. The problem posed to democratic societies by the exploitation of their media by terrorists is an exception to that generalization.

A pragmatic alternative emerging from the quantitative analysis, which demonstrated a strong positive relationship between media coverage and terrorist success, would be to restrain the media's coverage of terrorists and their atrocities, thereby deterring terrorists by reducing their probability of success. However, alternatives derived by quantitative analysis, much like theoretical considerations, must be viewed in the context of political reality to evaluate their applicability. In a liberal democratic society, complete restraint of the media in the coverage of political terrorism could not be seriously considered. An informed electorate is, of course, vital to the maintenance of a democracy.

It is also apparently not feasible to move to the other theoretical extreme of a media absolutely unconstrained in their coverage of terrorist atrocities. Again, in the context of a democratic society unbridled exploitation of the media by terrorists could result in the eventual destruction of the host democracy.

In an attempt to uncover more realistic concepts for resolving the problem of media exploitation, a cross-national comparison of major democratic nations that have been threatened by contemporary political terrorists is performed. The key factors compared are (1) the historical experience of the state in regard to the nature of the terrorist threat, (2) the counterterror policies that emerged, (3) the role of the media in relation to the terrorist threat and the government's countermeasures, and (4) the resultant relationship among government, media, and citizenry.

The United Kingdom, the Federal Republic of Germany, and Italy offered viable middle-range cases, with significant domestic terrorist threats supported internationally and various levels of media cooperation. The United States offered the extreme case, enduring a significant international threat with a minimal domestic threat and an adversarial media.

A comparison of the experiences of those modern democratic societies in combating political terrorism yields interesting insights into the terrorist exploitation of their media, and shows some of the successful actions taken to minimize that exploitation.

1

In Pursuit of a Definition of Political Terrorism

The operationalization of the concepts employed within a quantitative analysis is a vital and fundamental task with direct effect on the validity and acceptability of the analysis. Normally such operationalization proceeds from a generally accepted definition of concepts and terms. Unfortunately for those who attempt a quantitative analysis of political terrorism, both the concept and the term defy precise definition. As noted by Donna Schlagheck: "Terrorism is now one of the paradoxes of our times. Its threat is as pervasive as nuclear war, but its victims are relatively few in number. . . . Its consequences are widely publicized in excruciating detail. . . . There is no agreement on how to define it."[1] Over 100 definitions of terrorism have been proposed, but none has been universally accepted.[2]

A FRAMEWORK FOR EXAMINING POLITICAL TERRORISM

To establish an orderly process for reviewing the many definitions of political terrorism that exist in the literature, and to identify the key issues in the search for a universally acceptable definition, a simplistic model for the evaluation of social violence in general can be employed. The basic premise can be in the form of the question: "Who is doing what, and why are they doing it?"

It is likely that the perpetrators of violence (who), the method of violence (what), and the goals of the perpetrators (why) can be further considered as organic elements within the general concept of political violence. To adapt this simple model of political violence to political terrorism, (1) the question of who involves identifying the perpetrators of a terrorist act, (2) the question of what involves describing the method of violence that was employed by the perpetrators and (3) the question of why involves investigating the perpetrators' goals.

Focusing on the three organic elements of political violence (who, what, and why) while briefly reviewing a few attempts at defining political terrorism possibly allows one to more fully grasp some of the problems that have resulted in the lack of a universally accepted definition.

PERPETRATORS AS A MISDIRECTED SOURCE OF DEFINITION

Numerous attempts have been made to define political terrorism by reference to the characteristics of its perpetrators. For example, one can critique definitions of political terrorism from the aspect of whether or not they account for terrorism by the state as well as against the state. M. Cherif Bassiouni has noted that the term *terrorism*, with its inception during the French Revolution in the late eighteenth century, initially referred to the modus operandi of a regime that employed terror to subjugate a population. However, it has evolved to normally describe violent attacks by individuals or groups against authority.[3]

The 1937 League of Nations Convention for the Prevention and Punishment of Terrorism apparently rejected the notion that regimes could be the perpetrators of terrorism. It narrowly defined acts of terrorism as "criminal acts directed against a state and intended or calculated to create a state of terror in the minds of particular persons, or a group of persons or the general public."[4] Overly restrictive, the League's definition ignored atrocities committed by regimes against their own citizens—for example, against political opposition or minority groups.

Passage of time, historical evidence of state-employed terrorism such as that demonstrated by Stalin's regime, decolonization that witnessed the emergence of numerous national liberation movements in violent opposition to former rulers, and state-supported terrorism such as that utilized by Iran against its enemies in the Middle East have broadened the views of some governments. As per the U.S. State Department's official definition in 1985, terrorism is "the threat or use of violence for political purposes by individuals or groups whether acting for or in opposition to established governmental authority when such actions are intended to shock, stun, or intimidate a target group wider than the immediate victims."[5]

While considerably expanding the view of who the perpetrators of terrorism might be from that held fifty years earlier, the State Department's definition can be critiqued as showing an originator's temporal bias, which is typical of many definitions, by reference to state-supported terrorism, which was likely perceived as the principal mode of terrorist threat to the United States in 1985.

As noted by Saleem Qureshi, it is sometimes difficult to apply the term *terrorism* to state activities, regardless of the severity of the act:

The violence of the resister is termed "terrorist" whereas that of the regime is the enforcement of the law, and what distinguishes one from the other is the condition of legality. As long as the regime observes these conditions its reprisals against the resisters, no matter how harsh, are excluded from the category of terrorism.[6]

Definitions of political terrorism that have as their basis the issue of the state as the perpetrator of terrorism are scenario-limited, and are consequently unacceptable as a universal definition because of their narrow applicability. Equally as narrow are those definitions that concentrate solely on perpetrators seeking the overthrow of existing governments, which also restricts the usefulness of their explanations to specific incidents. They are, therefore, not applicable to political terrorism in general. For example, Martha Crenshaw's description restricts the meaning of terrorism to a domestic struggle for power: "The core of terrorism is its direct challenge to the state's monopoly on the use of force, its claim to command the loyalty and obedience of its citizens, and hence to its legitimacy."[7]

Efforts to provide an acceptable definition of terrorism by identifying and focusing on the perpetrators, state or otherwise, have apparently proved futile. This was most vividly demonstrated during the early 1970s debate at the United Nations, when the General Assembly considered a draft resolution by the United States against terrorism. From this ill-fated attempt emerged the overused cliché that "one person's terrorist is another's freedom fighter."

METHOD, THE IMPORTANT ELEMENT IN DEFINING POLITICAL TERRORISM

To more rigorously define political terrorism, one can consider that it is not the perpetrators of the act that are at issue but perhaps a more consistent element, such as the method of violence, or nature of the act.

Qureshi's definition has moved away from consideration of the perpetrators of terror to concentrate more on the act itself:

Terrorism is the use of violence in order to induce a state of fear and submission in the victim. The object of terrorism is to secure a change or modification in the behavior of the intended victim himself or to use him as an example for others. The violence of terrorism is the ultimate of coercion, whether actually applied or merely used as a threat. The use of terrorist violence is based on the assumption that the intended victim is unreasonable and incapable of seeing the viewpoint of the terrorist, that the victim cannot be persuaded but only compelled, in a manner by which he has absolutely no choice except to surrender.[8]

Qureshi's concentration on defining political terrorism by the act itself, and its intended results, moves his definition toward broader acceptance. However, he can be criticized as not adequately emphasizing the importance contemporary political terrorists place on the symbolic nature of their victims. In modern times, the victims of a terrorist atrocity seldom are the direct objects of the terrorists' coercion. They most often are only symbols that are related to a more expansive political target that the terrorists wish to intimidate. As per Raymond Aron's observation: "The victim or victims of the actual act of terrorist violence may or may not be the primary target, and the effects of relatively small amounts of violence will tend to be quite disproportionate in terms of the numbers of people terrorised."[9]

Qureshi's definition is further marred by his description of intended victims as being unreasonable and unable to comprehend the viewpoint of the terrorists. This does not seem to apply to that significant portion of contemporary terrorism committed by state-supported terrorist groups against target governments. Their obvious objective has often been a "rational" response by the target government—for example, the withdrawal of the U.S. military presence from Lebanon after the 1983 bombing of the U.S. Marine Corps barracks at the Beirut airport. Perhaps more important, by failing to directly address the crucial issue of the mode of political violence involved in a terrorist atrocity, Qureshi's definition does not contribute to solving the dilemma of one person's terrorist being another's freedom fighter. The method, or mode, of violence involved in the atrocity is of primary importance and can aid in distinguishing terrorism from the other forms of violence that might be employed as instruments of politics.

THE DECIDING ISSUE OF THE METHOD OF VIOLENCE

The late U.S. senator Henry Jackson was among those voicing opposition to a definition of terrorism so meaningless that it could also apply to freedom fighters:

The idea that one person's "terrorist" is another's "freedom fighter" cannot be sanctioned. Freedom fighters or revolutionaries don't blow up buses containing non-combatants; terrorist murderers do. Freedom fighters don't set out to capture and slaughter school children; terrorist murderers do. Freedom fighters don't assassinate innocent businessmen, or hijack and hold hostage innocent men, women, and children; terrorist murderers do. It is a disgrace that democracies would allow the treasured word "freedom" to be associated with acts of terrorists.[10]

Ireland's former minister of posts and telegraphs, Conor Cruise O'Brien, has succinctly stated a segment of the rationale behind the freedom fighter versus terrorist controversy: "Terrorist groups' claims to be liberation movements or groups engaged in 'guerrilla' warfare are attempts to inject terrorist groups with the legitimacy that most contemporary terrorist movements lack."[11]

As the definition of political terrorism progresses from concentration on the perpetrators to consideration of the more definitive element of the act itself, a significant measure of deserved concentration on the methods of terrorists can be noted. British political scientist Paul Wilkinson's definition of political terrorism is as coercive intimidation: "It is the systematic use of murder and destruction, and the threat of murder and destruction in order to terrorise individuals, groups, communities or governments into conceding to the terrorists' political demands."[12]

A distinguished group of Western academicians and government officials meeting at Israel's Johnathan Institute in July 1979 adopted the following definition, which is also apparently based on method: "Terrorism is the deliberate and systematic murder, maiming, and menacing of the innocent to inspire fear for political ends."[13]

THE ABYSS OF LABELING GOALS, AIMS, AND CAUSES AS TERRORISTIC

As with the chaos resulting from the attempt to define terrorism through reference to perpetrators, one should also avoid attempting to use the goals to which perpetrators of political violence allegedly aspire as a means of identifying terrorism. Attempting to refer to the goals, aims, or causes of some violence-perpetrating groups as involving terrorism and others as favoring democracy could lead to as much a quagmire as simply assigning the label of terrorist or freedom fighter.

It seems that a stringent title of "political" can be a universally acceptable label for the goals, aims, or causes of groups perpetrating violence for political purposes, thereby identifying a general characteristic but avoiding the catastrophe that could result if one attempts to refer to a certain goal, aim, or cause as terroristic.

When referring to political terrorism, one distinguishes between atrocities performed by groups or individuals for personal gain and those performed for political gain. Making this distinction acknowledges that the whole of politics includes such far-ranging topics as ideological and ethnic differences. While separating acts of terror for political purposes from acts of terror committed for personal gain appears quite simple, investigation proves it could be difficult. For almost two centuries, nations seeking extradition arrangements have encountered difficulty in agreeing on exactly what constitutes a political crime. Further, recent evidence of cooperation between political terrorists and drug traffickers shows that political and nonpolitical terror may sometimes overlap. However, within the current literature there appears to be relatively little difficulty in making the distinction between political and other forms of terrorism.

Historian Walter Laqueur attempts to bypass the pitfalls of labeling perpetrators and goals, aims, or causes when he argues "terrorism is not an ideology but an insurrectional strategy that can be used by people of very different political convictions...not merely a technique...its philosophy transcends the traditional dividing lines between political doctrine. It is truly all-purpose and value-free."[14]

Unfortunately, labeling political terrorist strategy as "insurrectional" and identifying it as "value-free" apparently limits the universal acceptance of Laqueur's description. For example, it does not apply to one of the most potent terrorist movements of this century—the Iranian-backed movement in the Middle East, which is neither insurrectional in nature nor value-free.

TERRORISM AS A USEFUL CATEGORY OF POLITICAL VIOLENCE

Of utmost importance in Laqueur's observation is the identification of terrorism as a tool of politics that can be used by all. Too often terrorism has been casually noted as an instrument of the weak, with the obvious unstated assumption that stronger groups, perhaps nations, by nature employ more direct and forceful means of violence—for example, limited or total war—to achieve political objectives considered not otherwise available. To associate terrorism with weakness is a crucial error in the study of this form of political violence. As recognized by Schlagheck: "Terrorism is not an instrument solely of the weak; terrorism has often been used by states to govern, and it has become an increasingly common instrument of foreign policy."[15]

Perhaps defining political terrorism, and certainly any analysis proceeding from that definition, can best be undertaken by considering the relationship of terrorism to political violence in general. Harold Nieburg has defined political violence as the perpetration of violence that would "tend to modify the behavior of others in a bargaining situation that has consequences for the social system."[16]

Political violence, and terrorism undertaken as a form of political

violence, should not be considered in isolation. For a broader understanding of the importance of terrorist violence in politics, it should be
considered as a subsystem of the whole of politics. As such, terrorism
shares the general properties of politics. When one considers Harold
Lasswell's description of politics as "who gets what, when, and how,"[17]
then terrorism as an element of that total system becomes a tool for the
creation of political power.

To deny the value of terrorism as a political tool would be to deny
history. In biblical Jerusalem, Sicarii assassinations of Roman soldiers
and officials weakened the resolve of the Roman senate to hold on to
that distant outpost of the empire. Later, the terrorist campaign of Men-
achem Begin et al. brought forth British capitulation of the Palestine
Mandate and the state of Israel. So also did the French finally weaken
before the terrorist assaults of the National Liberation Front (FLN) and
leave Algeria to the Algerians.

In his studies of political conflict within nations, Ted Robert Gurr has
examined the strategies of political violence with regard to the balance
of power. Nearly equal power results in civil war. Coups d'état occur
when governments have less power than those who would take control.
When the government has the most power, then civil disorder and riots
are the prevailing strategy for a violent opposition.[18] While Gurr has
not provided a category for the employment of the strategy of terrorism,
Abraham Miller has noted that a strategy of terror requires a smaller
support base and could logically precede Gurr's category of civil disorder
and riots.[19] One could also assume that terrorism can fit into the system
of domestic politics—and further, into the subsystem of domestic political
violence—as a strategy that, if performed effectively, could lead to other
more potent forms of conflict, with the goal being the derivation of an
increasing level of political power.

This concept of terrorism as a strategy for beginning the struggle for
domestic political power has led some scholars to conclude that it is a
"weapon of the weak," or the "not-yet-strong." This theme prevails in
the earlier literature. However, if one considers the employment of political terrorism internationally by a superpower as a substitute for the
initiation of warfare during times of détente, then the argument that
terror is a weapon only of the weak should be reconsidered.

TERRORISM IS DEFINED BY ITS UNIQUE METHOD
OF VIOLENCE

If one accepts that political terrorism is a tool of politics, and more
specifically one of the many methods of political violence that range
from total war to civil disobedience, then it remains here to identify the
unique characteristics that set terrorism apart from other forms of po-

litical violence. Perhaps within this endeavor also lies the potential for reaching a universally acceptable definition of political terrorism.

The perpetration of violence is the common base for many definitions that attempt to describe the various modes of political terrorism. Whatever the mode—intimidation or coercion, extermination or retaliation—violence is the necessary condition for political terrorism. However, not all political violence is terroristic. For political violence to constitute terroristic violence, the violence must be of a unique form, and here is the point on which so many formal definitions of terrorism falter, and from which the dilemma of terrorist or freedom fighter arises.

Every civilized society has laws defining what modes of violence are to be regarded as criminal, or unacceptable. Almost universally, violent acts such as kidnapping and murder are outlawed. If those unlawful acts of violence are recognized as similar to the modes of violence typically employed by political terrorists, then progress can be made toward a universal definition of political terrorism. Simply stated, the employment of a mode of violence not acceptable to civilized societies helps distinguish political terrorism from other categories of political violence.

While a description of terroristic methods of violence as domestically unlawful could contribute to an acceptable definition of terrorism in democratic Western societies, it is sometimes debated whether such a standard can be applied to fundamentalist Islamic societies, which generally have a different outlook toward the employment of violence. Relatively more violent means of punishment employed by Islamic fundamentalist regimes for transgressors of Koran laws has, perhaps, led some in the West to doubt that agreement on what constitutes terrorist violence could ever be achieved between Judeo-Christian and Islamic societies. However, it should be noted that the Koran classifies such acts as kidnapping and murder as unlawful, in much the same manner as do the criminal codes of Western societies.[20]

INTERNATIONAL AGREEMENT ON ACCEPTABLE POLITICAL VIOLENCE

There is, in fact, precedence for worldwide agreement on "acceptable" forms of political violence. In recent times of rapid decolonization and the movement of the world order toward multipolarity, almost every newly formed state or power group that has emerged from the chaos has expressed an eagerness to embrace the international laws of war. It could be argued that their motivation is, perhaps, based on a desire to internationally demonstrate their degree of civilization and thereby enhance their chances for recognition by others as sovereign states with the potential to become reliable members of the new world order. The international rules of warfare are extensive, and they dictate against such acts as the kidnapping and murder ˜f innocents while making special provisions for noncombatants.[21] Since d. veloped and developing, liberal and authoritarian, states have almost all acknowledged the international rules of war, there exists a precedent whereby a universal understanding of modes of violence can indeed be achieved.

If it can be agreed that political terrorism implies the employment of violence generally unacceptable to the world order and generally unlawful in civilized societies, and if that violence becomes the primary focus for defining terrorism, then the dilemma of who is a freedom fighter and who is a terrorist can be resolved by ignoring the professed goals, aims, or causes of political violence and the identification of perpetrators in favor of considering the methods of violence employed. John Moore insightfully advised at a seminar on terrorism and the media, when addressing the determination of whether a perpetrator of political violence is a freedom fighter or terrorist, "Get away from questioning the justice of the cause.... That is not the issue of low-level violence any more than it is the issue for settings of major conflict.... There are certain kinds of acts of violence that are simply beyond the pale ... acts in which terrorists are engaged today."[22]

In this separation of method of violence from perpetrator and cause, if members of a nation's military are responsible for the murder of innocent civilians in a time of war, then they are war criminals and murderers and should be brought to justice, regardless of the reason why the war is being fought. As a parallel, if members of a political protest group plant a bomb on an airliner and kill innocent people, they are terrorists, murderers, and violators of human rights and should be brought to justice, regardless of their "cause."

In the final analysis, political terrorists should be identified by the nature of the violence they choose to perpetrate, not by their proclaimed cause or the labels they or their opposition may attach to the actions. Within this concept, it is possible to progress toward universal acceptance of a definition of political terrorism.

ATTEMPTING TO EXPLAIN POLITICAL TERRORISM WITH TYPOLOGIES

The literature shows diligent efforts to categorize political terror. Robert Moss has defined acts of political terror with reference to tactics employed. His "offensive terror" category is typically employed by a group to depose a regime and impose its own political beliefs upon a target population. Under "defensive terror" he categorizes those acts that might be perpetrated by partisans against an invader, or by an ethnic community defending its traditions. By "repressive terror" he refers to state or other organized power that attempts to maintain or strengthen its hold over a populace by acts of terror.[23]

While these categories offer an orderly approach to a study of political terrorism, they fall short of contributing to the definition of terrorism. To explain what some act accomplishes, or intends to accomplish, is not to explain how it is accomplished. There are many modes of nonviolent and violent political behavior that could fall within Moss's categories that might not be terroristic. As previously stated, an act of political terrorism should have as its definitional basis the unique mode of violence that places it in the category of terror.

National versus International versus Transnational Terrorism

Attempts abound to clarify the meaning of political terrorism through typologies. Political terrorism is normally categorized as either national or international. National terrorism clearly applies to terrorism within the boundaries of a state: state against populace or a portion thereof, populace or a portion thereof against state, or portions of the populace against each other.

International terrorism typically involves the interests of more than one state. Wilkinson regards terrorism as international when it is "(i) directed at foreigners or foreign targets, (ii) concerted by the governments or factions of more than one state, or (iii) aimed at influencing the policies of a foreign government."[24]

Bassiouni would more simply include in international terrorism all those incidents that are not limited to the internal affairs of individual states.[25] The U.S. Central Intelligence Agency has officially defined international terrorism as:

The threat or use of violence for political purposes when (1) such action is intended to influence the attitude and behavior of a target group wider than its immediate victims, and (2) its ramifications transcend national boundaries (as the result, for example, of the nationality or foreign ties of its perpetrators, its locale, the identity of its institutional or human victims, its declared objectives, or the mechanics of its resolution).[26]

Transnational is another term that has been more recently used to refer to terrorism that is international in nature. The term can be perceived as denoting more action than *international*. *International* seems to imply a state of affairs within global boundaries, whereas *transnational* seems to indicate movement across states' boundaries. Edward Mickolus's significant data base for his quantitative analysis of terrorism, ITERATE, was labeled transnational terrorism, which he defined as:

terrorist action carried out by basically autonomous nonstate actors, whether or not they enjoy some degree of moral and/or material support from sympathetic governments.... The action's ramifications may transcend national boundaries through the nationality or foreign ties of its perpetrators, its location, the nature of its institutional or human victims, or the mechanics of its resolution.[27]

The similarity between Mickolus's transnational and the CIA's international terrorism definitions reflects the frequent interchanging of the terms in the literature despite claims that the two might differ. David Milbank has explained transnational terrorism as that perpetrated by autonomous nonstate actors, while regarding international terrorism as that perpetrated by terrorists under the control of a state.[28]

Categorizing political terrorism as national or international is likely necessary in attempts to determine the sources and effects of terrorism. However, these categories do not assist in defining political terrorism. Varying levels of violence are necessarily involved in the study of both domestic and international politics. Determination of political violence as terroristic remains the basic question of the character of the violence employed. Is it the waging of guerrilla warfare within the rules of war as laid down by civilized societies, or is it the slaughter of unarmed innocents held hostage in an airliner? Both levels of violence fit national or international categorical criterion, but only the latter fits a rigorous definition of political terrorism.

Legitimate or Illegitimate Terror

Political terrorism is frequently categorized as legitimate or illegitimate. From the viewpoint of a government under attack from armed groups within, those groups are obviously illegitimate terrorists. Counterterror tactics taken by the government to end that illegitimate violence would be considered by some as legitimate. When Golda Meir dispatched the *Mivtzan Elohim* (Wrath of God) to hunt down and destroy the Black September terrorists who had massacred the Israeli athletes at the 1972 Munich Olympic Games, the government of Israel regarded it as an act of legitimate "counter" terror. Attacks by the French Resistance against Nazi occupiers during World War II were also categorized by many as legitimate terrorism. However, whether political acts of violence are considered legitimate or illegitimate should be irrespective of whether they are terroristic in nature. Again, only the issue of the mode of violence can place an act into the category of terrorism: it is not dependent on the viewpoint of the perpetrators or the victims, but on the methodology of the attack. To refer to the French Resistance as employing terrorism requires a great deal more investigation. Their targets normally were German soldiers and the materials of Hitler's war machine. They likely did not target the wives or children of German soldiers. By contrast, Ben Bella, with the realization he would never develop an army so strong as to defeat the French in the field, turned to the massacre of French innocents as well as soldiers in his successful terrorist campaign to dislodge French interests from Algeria. Whether viewed as legitimate or illegitimate, to bomb a busload of soldiers carrying out the policies of a hostile government of occupation is apparently within the boundaries of violent behavior accepted by civilized society. To bomb a busload of women and children is apparently not within those boundaries. The latter fits the definition of political terrorism; the first does not.

Overuse of Typologies

Charles Russell, Leon Banker, and Bowman Miller, at the Counterintelligence Directorate of the U.S. Air Force Office of Special Investigations, developed four categories for terrorist groups based on their motivation, constituency, makeup, leadership, size, and outside cooperation: (1) nationalistic or ethnic separatist groups, (2) ideological groups, (3) nihilist groups, and (4) issue-oriented interest groups.[29]

As clearly demonstrated by these categories, the term *terrorism* has become extremely overloaded, covering almost all political violence that is unusual in nature. While categorizations of political violence by objectives, strategies, tactics, and so on provide some analytical tools by which a particular form of violence might be better examined and perhaps understood, they fall short of concentrating on the initial and vital issue of a definition of political terrorism. Such categorization should apparently be preceded by a diligent investigation of what constitutes an act of political terror, and one must look to the character of the violence employed to make that determination.

Motivation for autonomy in Russell, Banker, and Miller's first category does not mean that separatist groups will by nature murder women and children. Upholding an ideology by violence, in their second category, also does not necessarily imply resort to hostage-taking. Perhaps the nihilist groups of their third category would, by nature, perform terrorist atrocities, but it is doubtful that issue-oriented groups of their fourth category would choose to do so. The definition of terroristic violence should remain with the determination of whether the mode of political violence perpetrated is unacceptable within the framework of a civilized international society, and whether it is similar to violence in violation of the customary and conventional laws that bind civilized societies, and therefore an atrocity that can only be defined by the use the of the term *terrorism*.

CONCENTRATION ON THE MODE OF VIOLENCE IS IMPERATIVE

Scholars and statesmen would do well to base their considerations of political terrorism on an initial assessment of what elements constitute an act of political terror. Criteria that Brian Jenkins, Rand Corporation's noted authority on terrorism, has used in his research to classify an act as terroristic include "violence or the threat of violence . . . a crime under municipal law . . . a violation of the laws that govern warfare . . . some political goal . . . effects beyond those on the actual victim."[30]

Most of Jenkins's elements are apparently empirical, could be operationalized, and generally focus on the important potential basis for a universal definition of political terrorism—the nature of the violence employed.

THE ISSUE OF RANDOMNESS

From research and review of definitions for political terrorism, Schlagheck has reported finding common elements that include "the use or threat of violence, unpredictability or randomness, a symbolic target, publicity, and political goals."[31]

While not denying the apparent value of Schlagheck's research, and in particular her analytical approach to the problem of deriving an agreeable definition of political terrorism, one should proceed cautiously in considering the element of unpredictability or randomness as it applies to political terrorism. From the viewpoint of political terrorists, especially those committing the type of international atrocity to be investigated in this analysis, there is nothing "unpredictable" about the violence. Long-term strategies are established and short-term tactics are carefully planned to maximize operational efficiency.

Assuredly, some terrorist groups and individuals are not as highly organized as others. However, as demonstrated by various terrorist groups in West Germany, those that are the most highly organized and most highly skilled survive the longest.[32] One need only consider a simplistic model in which a terrorist wandering through the streets bombing at random would likely encounter law enforcement officials much sooner than a terrorist who planned bombings specifically to avoid an encounter.

If one chooses to examine a specific campaign of political terrorism conducted by an organized group, it soon becomes apparent that there is a distinct plan for the employment of violence, which thus cannot be labeled random or unpredictable.[33] Consider the work done on the Rand Corporation's data bank of terrorist atrocities by R. H. Anderson and James Gillogly, with their development of a model for the prediction of terrorist behavior.[34] Consider the concentration of terrorist hijackings of airliners in the late 1960s, or the terrorist attacks on embassies during 1981, or the priority given by Middle Eastern terrorist groups to the seizing of U.S. hostages in Lebanon. From the viewpoint of the terrorists, their employment of violence cannot be described as unpredictable or random.[35]

It is from the viewpoint of the victim that the unpredictability or randomness referred to by Schlagheck bears consideration. As will be discussed later, the creation of fear is a basic factor in a terrorist campaign. If every individual in a targeted population can be brought to believe that he or she could be the next victim of a terrorist atrocity, then an atmosphere of fear has been created and an important goal of the terrorists has been achieved. One could say that, to the extent that members of a targeted audience feel that it is possible they could be the next victim, then unpredictability or randomness could enter into the definition of terrorism.

Consideration of the phenomenon of unpredictability or randomness in political terrorism is, however, more clearly explained within the concept of a symbolic victim. Among the key characteristics of victim symbology are identification and environment. Unpredictability or randomness, when implying the susceptibility of an individual to terrorist attack, are more closely associated with those characteristics of the symbology of the victim than with the terrorists' tactics for employing violence. When members of a targeted population perceive a remarkable similarity between themselves and those already victimized by terrorists, then the possibility of being the next victim is an important segment of terror. Without the perception of similarity to previous victims, it seems highly debatable that the uncertainty of a terrorist attack contributes to the establishment of an atmosphere of fear throughout a targeted population.

To assume that terrorists employ violence unpredictably or randomly, as indicated by Schlagheck, is likely to be factually inaccurate. While uncertainty of fate is an important consideration in creating fear through terror, it is more appropriately considered within the symbolism of the victim.

SUMMATION

The elements that Schlagheck found common in existing definitions of political terrorism can be condensed as "random violence against symbolic targets possessing publicity value toward the achievement of political goals." Jenkins's criteria for identifying terrorism add the organic element of the mode of violence as a vital determinant for when political violence becomes terroristic.

A synthesis of the efforts of Schlagheck and Jenkins approaches a definition of political terrorism through the combination of the two universally acceptable organic elements of "unacceptable violence" and "political goals," with the violence magnified through the maximization of publicity and focused by the selection of symbolic victims.

If analysts maintain a focus on those basic considerations—unacceptable violence, symbolic victims, maximum publicity, and political goals—while necessarily guiding their analyses to fulfill individual objectives, the results are likely to be acceptable to wider audiences than have been achieved in the past.

Analysts are normally well advised to avoid forming their own definitions for concepts they employ in their analyses. Their products generally prove more useful when definitions employed are universally agreed upon. However, as demonstrated in this chapter, such is not possible in the case of political terrorism. Therefore, to establish the particular basis for this analysis of terrorism, the following definition of political terrorism is generally utilized: "The perpetration of an unacceptable form of violence against symbolic victims to maximize publicity for the attainment of political goals."

The issue of operationalizing the particular category of terrorist violence—hostage taking—upon which this analysis focuses continues in a later chapter.

NOTES

1. Donna Schlagheck, *International Terrorism: An Introduction to the Concepts and Actors* (Lexington, Mass.: Lexington Books, 1988), 1.

2. Alex Schmid, *Political Terrorism: A Research Guide* (New Brunswick, N.J.: Transaction, 1984); cited in Schlagheck, *International Terrorism*, 1.

3. M. Cherif Bassiouni, ed., *International Terrorism and Political Crimes* (Springfield, Ill.: Charles C. Thomas, 1975), 6.

4. Quoted in Saleem Qureshi, "Political Violence in the South Asian Subcontinent," in *International Terrorism: National, Regional and Global Perspectives*, ed. Yonah Alexander (New York: Praeger, 1976), 152.

5. Quoted in Daniel Triesman, *The New Republic* 193 (14 October 1985): 16.

6. Qureshi, "Political Violence in the South Asian Subcontinent," 157.

7. Martha Crenshaw, *Terrorism and International Cooperation* (Boulder: Westview Press, 1989), 59.

8. Qureshi, "Political Violence in the South Asian Subcontinent," 151.

9. Raymond Aron, *Peace and War* (London: Weidenfeld and Nicolson, 1966), 170; cited in Paul Wilkinson, *Terrorism and the Liberal State*, 2d ed. (New York: New York University Press, 1986), 51.

10. Henry Jackson, quoted in George Schultz, "Terrorism: The Challenge to the Democracies," in *Department of State Bulletin* 84, no. 2089 (August 1984): 32.

11. Conor Cruise O'Brien, *Herod: Reflections on Political Violence* (London: Hutchinson, 1978), 72; cited in Juliet Lodge, "Introduction," *Terrorism: A Challenge to the State*, ed. Juliet Lodge (New York: St. Martin's, 1981), 1.

12. Wilkinson, *Terrorism and the Liberal State*, 51.

13. Quoted in Schlagheck, *International Terrorism*, 1.

14. Walter Laqueur, *Terrorism* (London: Weidenfeld and Nicolson, 1977), 4–5; quoted in Lodge, "Introduction," 1.

15. Schlagheck, *International Terrorism*, 13.

16. Harold Nieburg, *Political Violence: The Behavioral Process* (New York: St. Martin's, 1969), 13; quoted in James Miller, "Political Terrorism and Insurgency: An Interrogative Approach," in *Terrorism: Interdisciplinary Perspectives*, eds. Yonah Alexander and Seymour Maxwell Finger (New York: John Jay Press, 1977), 66.

17. From Harold Lasswell, *Politics: Who Gets What, When and How* (New York: Meridian, 1958).

18. Ted Robert Gurr, *Why Men Rebel* (Princeton: Princeton University Press, 1971), 232–73.

19. Abraham Miller, *Terrorism and Hostage Negotiations* (Boulder: Westview Press, 1980), 95.

20. See, for example, John Esposito, *Islam and Politics* (Syracuse: Syracuse University Press, 1984), 1–29.

21. The 1907 Hague Convention ruled against "killing or wounding treacherously." The 1946 Judgment of International Military Tribunal at Nuremburg specified as unacceptable the "taking of hostages." Common Article 3 of the 1949 Geneva Conventions I through IV outlawed "murder, mutilation, cruel treatment and torture . . . taking of hostages . . . outrages upon personal dignity." These, and other, examples of international conventions that identify unacceptable violence can be viewed in Adam Roberts and Richard Guelff, *Documents on the Laws of War*, 2d ed. (Oxford: Clarendon Press, 1989).

22. John Moore, quoted in *Terrorism and the Media in the 1980's*, eds. Sarah Midgley and Virginia Rice (Washington, D.C.: The Media Institute, 1984), 58.

23. Robert Moss, *Urban Guerrillas* (London: Maurice Temple Smith, 1972); cited in Ezzat Fattah, "Terrorist Activities and Terrorist Targets: A Tentative Typology," in *Behavioral and Quantitative Perspectives on Terrorism*, eds. Yonah Alexander and John Gleason (New York: Pergamon Press, 1981), 15–16.

24. Wilkinson, *Terrorism and the Liberal State*, 182.

25. Bassiouni, *International Terrorism and Political Crimes*, 5.

26. National Foreign Assessment Center, Central Intelligence Agency, *International Terrorism in 1977: A Research Paper* (Washington, D.C.: Central Intelligence Agency, RP 78 102554, 1978), 1.

27. Edward Mickolus and Edward Heyman, "Iterate: Monitoring Transnational Terrorism," in *Behavioral and Quantitative Perspectives on Terrorism*, eds. Yonah Alexander and John Gleason (New York: Pergamon Press, 1981), 154.

28. David Milbank, *International and Transnational Terrorism: Diagnosis and Prognosis* (Washington, D.C.: Central Intelligence Agency, PR 76 10030, April 1976).

29. Drawn from Charles Russell, Leon Banker, and Bowman Miller, "Out-Inventing the Terrorist," in *Terrorism: Theory and Practice*, eds. Yonah Alexander, David Carlton, and Paul Wilkinson (Boulder: Westview Press, 1979), 31–32.

30. Brian Jenkins, "Terrorism Prone Countries and Conditions," in *On Terrorism and Combating Terrorism*, ed. Ariel Merari (Frederick, Md.: University Publications of America, 1985), 34.

31. Schlagheck, *International Terrorism*, 13.

32. See, for example, Hans-Josef Horchem, "Political Terrorism—The German Perspective," in *On Terrorism and Combating Terrorism*, ed. Ariel Merari (Frederick, Md.: University Publications of America, 1985), 63–68.

33. See, for example, Brian Jenkins and Janera Johnson, *International Terrorism: A Chronology, 1968–1974* (Santa Monica: Rand Corporation, R–1597-DOS/ARPA, March 1975).

34. R. H. Anderson and J. J. Gillogly, *Rand Intelligent Terminal Agent (R.I.T.A.): Design Philosophy* (Santa Monica: Rand Corporation, R–1809-ARPA, February 1976).

35. Consider, for example, the continuity in terrorist actions demonstrated in the chronologies of events in *Annual of Power and Conflict: 1981–82* (London: The Institute for the Study of Conflict, 1982).

2

Terrorism and Politics

The recorded use of terrorism as an instrument of politics dates to the birth of Christ. As described by Roman historian Flavius Josephus, the Jewish Zealots employed a campaign of terrorism in an effort to force the Romans out of Palestine. Not unlike contemporary threats in the Middle East, the Zealots combined radical religious beliefs with nationalism.[1]

NATIONAL LIBERATION MOVEMENTS AND TERRORISM

From the Jewish Zealots to modern times, nationalism has provided a potent basis for the formulation of political violence leading to campaigns of terror. Frustrated attempts at national autonomy, especially when augmented by fervent religious or ethnic cleavages, foster environments that are favorable for the occurrence of terroristic violence. In such environments, states confront cycles of terror and counterterror, with the dilemma of potential violent political protest whether governments address or ignore separatist demands for autonomy.

However, one should also note that throughout history wars of national liberation and self-determination have been fought by "guerrillas" without recourse to terrorism. Unfortunately, in the literature and in circles where political terrorism is a necessary topic of discussion, many frequently make the mistake of equating terrorism with guerrilla warfare. Wilkinson cautions, "there are quite clear differentiae between the intent, aims and psychological effects of terrorism and those of other forms of violence such as the collective violence of riots and revolutionary uprisings and conventional war."[2] As previously stated, one should proceed cautiously when labeling political violence as terrorism. The repeated theme of this analysis is that terrorism exists only when a unique form of violence, unacceptable to civilized societies, is employed.

Assuredly, some guerrilla movements have at times employed some variety of terror as a weapon. However, terrorist tactics can, and should, be distinguished from guerrilla tactics in general. Wilkinson has provided three basic elements to utilize in examining unconventional warfare to determine whether it is terroristic in nature: "the aims of its perpetrators, their modus operandi in deploying particular forms of violence upon the victims, and the target audience."[3] He urges further examination of the particular form of violence as to whether it (1) is indiscriminate in the selection of victims, (2) appears arbitrary and unpredictable, (3) does not provide for noncombatant status or the other rules of warfare, (4) observes no moral constraints on weaponry or tactics, (5) justifies any means to achieve its ends, (6) regards extreme violence as inspirational and the most effective means available, (7) regards vengeance as a moral necessity, and (8) justifies the use of terror to avoid the greater evil represented by the enemy.[4]

Analysts of political terrorism are well advised to use Wilkinson's descriptive elements when investigating national liberation movements in order to determine whether their active members are guerrillas or terrorists. Such analysis would likely show that some national liberation movements have indeed employed terrorism at various points. However, in only a few instances of a history filled with national liberation movements has the employment of terrorism contributed significantly to successful "liberation." The Irgun and Stern Gang's terror campaign against the British during the Palestine Mandate is the notable exception, along with the limited success of the Palestine Liberation Organization. It can be argued that those successes did not result from the employment of terrorism in isolation, but by its combination with other less violent political endeavors. Those nationalist movements that relied solely or principally on terrorism to achieve their goals have, for the most part, failed. Most notable examples are the Basque Homeland and Freedom (ETA) in Spain and the Provisional Irish Republican Army (PIRA) of Northern Ireland.

An evaluation of the forms of political violence employed by national liberation movements also includes a comparison of the French Resistance during World War II and the later FLN terrorist campaign to "liberate" Algeria. Although German civilians were well within reach of the French underground, they were apparently not normally targeted. France was, of course, eventually liberated and restored as a democratic state, whereas the indiscriminate slaughter of French nationals by Ben Bella's terrorists eventually yielded the undemocratic, despotic state of Algeria. In contrasting terrorist campaigns to national liberation movements, Benjamin Netanyahu has noted that the means employed by terrorists reveal their true objectives: "Those who deliberately butcher women and children do not have liberation in mind.... The choice of means indicates what the true ends are."[5]

IDEOLOGIES AND TERRORISM

Along with the basic human motivations for self-identification and community, beliefs based on social or economic systems, on religions, or on other deeply held convictions have also been identified as sources of political violence that have sometimes led to terrorism. For example, Netanyahu identified Islamic radicalism and communist totalitarianism as two movements that have gained international prominence since World War II while providing a basis for the intensification of terrorism: "Both legitimize unbridled violence in the name of a higher cause, both are profoundly hostile to democracy, and both have found in terrorism an ideal weapon for waging war against it."[6]

While one can accept or reject Netanyahu's observation on the basis of personal convictions and interpretation of evidence, it is instructive to review these two movements as examples of how terrorism can be utilized as a political instrument.

Terrorism and Soviet Foreign Policy

The Soviet Union regularly employed terrorism as an instrument of foreign policy. Extensive evidence has been documented and is available through numerous Western sources.[7] A sharp increase in the level of Soviet-sponsored terrorism began in the 1960s and was the result of a synthesis of several factors. Two of the most important were:

1. Khrushchev's peaceful coexistence, followed by the era of détente, called for low-risk foreign policy alternatives for the global expansion of Soviet influence.

2. The turbulent political atmosphere of the 1960s provided opportunities for the Soviets to disrupt the domestic stability of several Western nations.

Khrushchev's adaptation of the communist ideology at the 20th Party Congress laid the groundwork for a foreign policy that included terrorism as an integrated instrument. Nuclear weapons had negated the inevitability of war, and the communist victory would now be achieved by intensifying the class struggle in capitalist nations, and by worldwide support for every just war of national liberation.[8] The doctrine that developed from Khrushchev's version of the ideology seemed to be directed toward ensuring that both class struggles in the capitalist nations and wars of national liberation in the Third World did, in fact, occur. The violence of terrorism was utilized as a means to bring about the occurrence and/or intensification of those class struggles and those wars of national liberation.

The strategy that evolved for intensifying class struggles proved to be support of whatever violent disruptive forces existed, or could be developed, in targeted capitalist societies. Soviet support, in terms of training and weapons, flowed through surrogates to groups already waging campaigns of political terror against Western regimes. Soviet surrogates sought out, encouraged, organized, trained, and armed violent groups that were spawned by the social conflicts of the 1960s. With peaceful coexistence and the spirit of détente calling for the avoidance of direct confrontation, the Soviets discreetly directed activities through surrogates. Direct control of targeting was neither desired nor required. It was not desired because terrorist violence in the West dare not be attributable to Moscow. It was not required because it was quite sufficient to simply train, organize, and equip the terrorists and allow their innovation to do the rest.[9]

The Soviet strategy for supporting wars of national liberation involved creating a political base for expansion in the target area, then sending aid, advisers, weapons, and money under an elaborate cover of propaganda. Terrorist violence was inflicted to ensure that a sufficient level of conflict arose requiring the prospective client, either the old or the new regime, to request Soviet military assistance. The troops, normally surrogate but sometimes Soviet, were there and ready to assist. The terrorists in these scenarios were normally indigenous groups, but they were trained, equipped, and organized by the Soviets directly or through their surrogates.

Soviet foreign policy and terrorism in the Middle East. The documented evidence shows that the Soviets were often directly involved in training and equipping international terrorists.[10] However, their preferred mode of operation was indirectly through surrogates, and their major effort was through the Palestinians in the Middle East. The Middle East was of vital importance to the Soviets. Proximity to their border invoked national security concerns. Ports and airfields in the Mediterranean area would have greatly enhanced the Warsaw Pact war-fighting capability versus NATO. Further, key members of the NATO alliance depended heavily on the oil resources of the Middle East. The foreign policy instruments of military aid and diplomacy had produced less-than-favorable results with the area's unstable, sometimes erratic Islamic regimes. With Moscow's regional influence apparently based on the oil-rich Arabs' desire for Soviet weapons to oppose the perceived Zionist threat, it was in the Soviet Union's best interests to pursue a foreign policy that would ensure continued fear and hatred between the region's Arabic and Jewish populations. The homeless Palestinians were the precise tool for that task, and extensive Soviet efforts in training and equipping the Palestinians are well documented.[11]

The results of a Soviet foreign policy to create a continued state of low-intensity conflict via Palestinian terrorists were highly successful. In spite of limited U.S. mediation success at Camp David, peace did not come to the Middle East. While the Egyptians became somewhat less hostile and fearful toward Israel, Iraq and Syria, armed with the latest weapons technology, kept the region in a high level of tension. As a bonus for the Soviets, the United States has been forced to pay high economic and political costs for support of Israel. Paradoxically, Israel's reprisals against Soviet-surrogate Palestinian terrorists resulted in the destruction of the adjacent pro-Western state of Lebanon. The Western Judeo-Christian democracies have not been able to cope with the Lebanese situation, and it remains for the Soviets' Islamic client, Syria, to reconstruct the nation in the presence of a strong Iranian-backed terrorist movement.

Coups in South Yemen and Ethiopia allowed Moscow to establish an early military presence that could have ensured wartime control of the Persian Gulf and the eastern approaches to the Suez. When the South Yemen regime embraced communism following the 1978 coup, the Soviets had also successfully encircled conservative Arab states friendly to the United States. Within South Yemen, Soviet terrorist facilities were established that could have threatened the stabilization of the Arab states bordering the Persian Gulf when deemed appropriate by Moscow. International in scope, the South Yemen terrorist facilities were manned by Soviet surrogates from Eastern Europe, Cuba, and Libya, along with thousands of Palestinians.[12]

Soviet foreign policy and terrorism in Western Europe. The Soviets also used Palestinian surrogates effectively throughout Western Europe. Their efficient support of Red Brigades terrorists in Italy in the 1970s almost brought that major NATO member to its knees.[13] Lacking support from Eurocommunists, Moscow developed a Western European network of terrorist groups that proved effective in disrupting the domestic tranquillity of the NATO partners when the Soviet Union deemed it opportune.[14] In the north, Soviet support through Libyan surrogates ensured continued terrorist activities by the Provisional IRA, which tied down thousands of British troops.[15] In the south, the fragile democracy of Spain was challenged by increasingly severe attacks by the Soviet trained and equipped ETA, with Spanish membership in NATO at stake.[16] While Soviet-sponsored terrorism did not threaten the existence of any Western European member of the NATO alliance, the timely employment of terrorism proved more useful to the Soviets in affecting their domestic activity than did the Western European communist parties. Therefore, Soviet employment of terrorism in Western Europe could be viewed as successful in relative terms as to what they achieved through other means.

Soviet foreign policy and terrorism in North Africa. Moscow's bid for ports and airfields in the Mediterranean area was enhanced by its partnership with Libya.[17] Satisfying Qadhafi's desire for military aid resulted in an alliance for terrorism that saw the worldwide deployment of Libyan surrogates as well as development of extensive terrorist facilities in Libya. Qadhafi was most useful in relaying Soviet support to the Muslim rebels in Southeast Asia, especially in the southern Philippines. The vulnerable Philippine democracy was caught between the Communist New People's Army (NPA) in the north and the Muslim separatist rebels in the south, where 85 percent of the Philippine armed forces were often tied down. Obviously the costs to the United States for its Pacific outpost increased considerably.

Libyan support for the Polisario guerrillas was directed toward the gradual replacement of Morocco's regime with one more pro-Soviet.[18] Soviet airfields and ports in Morocco, coupled with facilities in Angola, could create severe difficulties for NATO resupply through central and southern Atlantic sea lanes. A rim of pro-Soviet regimes along the southern shores of the Mediterranean could seriously threaten the southern flank of NATO.

Soviet foreign policy and terrorism south of the Sahara. After their early economic failures in Africa south of the Sahara, the Soviets seemed content to hold on to strategically important Angola while ensuring that Western influence on the continent would be costly. As demonstrated by repeated Western failures in the region, that policy proved successful. Through the African National Congress (ANC) and the South-West Africa People's Organization (SWAPO), the Soviets attempted to develop clients that could eventually come to power in a region from which the United States imports extensive amounts of strategic raw materials. While Moscow politically supported the ANC and SWAPO, Soviet surrogates trained and equipped their armed terrorist branches.[19]

Soviet surrogates in the Western Hemisphere. Keenly aware of both sides of the balance-of-power equation, the Soviets adroitly targeted for destabilization those areas with the highest potential cost for the opposing superpower. The Soviets' first client in the Western Hemisphere, Cuba, proved to be extremely costly, and apparently discouraged them from fully supporting another. Moscow instead discounted part of the expense of Cuba by utilizing Castro's armed forces and intelligence services. Under KGB tutelage, an impressive number of international terrorists graduated from Castro's terrorist training facilities. Their exploits and successes throughout the Caribbean, Central and South America, and Western Europe are well documented.[20] While the United States obviously pursued its role as the major regional power, Soviet-orchestrated destabilization of the southern half of the Western Hemisphere exacted a heavy political and economic toll on Washington.

The lack of a challenge to Soviet-sponsored terrorism. Ample evidence shows that Moscow did not always succeed in disguising its support for terrorism. Documents captured in Lebanon and uncovered in Western Europe, along with numerous Western intelligence reports, clearly show the roots of international terrorism reaching deep into the Soviet Union.[21] The question remains why the Western powers did not call more attention to this obvious violation of the principles of peaceful coexistence and the spirit of détente. For Western European regimes, the answer was simple and direct: the Soviets had skillfully woven a strong Arab participation into their terrorist network. Even though Western European authorities often apprehended Moscow's surrogate terrorists, they normally stopped short of effective punitive measures for fear of provoking those Islamic Arab nations upon whom they were energy-dependent. In the case of the United States, the Soviet support of international terrorism was ignored by an American regime, media, and public interested in not disturbing the era of détente.

By discreet employment of surrogates, and by agreeing to a few antiterrorist treaties of common economic interest, such as the prevention of hijackings, the Soviets were able to maintain a lofty separation between their status as a superpower and the reality of their perpetration of terrorist violence at the international level.

Islam and Terrorism

Muslims constitute one-seventh of the world's population, are a majority in some forty-three countries, and are a significant minority in others. There is generally little popular awareness in the West of the basic tenets of Islam, and only minimal appreciation of the role of Islam in politics, law, and society.

For Americans, the activities of Islam in Iran and elsewhere in the Middle East are in contrast to at least three American traditions and beliefs:

1. The separation of religion and politics, basic to the U.S. version of democracy, is challenged by Islam's combination of church and state.
2. Americans tend to believe that Islam has been a barrier to socioeconomic progress in Islamic countries.
3. Americans tend to believe that secular nationalism is a stage through which

developing nations must pass, and, at least in some Muslim states, Islam has not been overpowered by secularism.[22]

The West is traditionally viewed by fundamentalist Muslims as responsible for the downfall of Islam. The recent resurgence of Islamic fundamentalism has given new life to a radical version of the faith that partitions the world into Muslims and infidels, and calls for Muslims to convert the infidels to Islam, to subjugate them, or to destroy them. Contemporary terrorism has given that resurgence a means of radical expression.

Islam is a politicized religion. Muhammad was a ruler as well as a religious leader, promulgating laws while enforcing and adjudicating them, levying taxes and raising armies and making war and peace. All of those functions have a part in the *Quran* (Koran), the Holy Law of Islam.

Within Islamic law, tradition, and history, violence has two forms: (1) conflict against external enemies and (2) conflict against internal enemies. The conflict against external enemies is the violent struggle between the worlds of Islam and the infidels. It can be ended only by the death, conversion, or subjugation of the unbelievers. This external conflict is conducted by rules of war contained in Islamic law, which, at least by some interpretations, do not condone terrorist atrocities.[23]

The internal conflict involves the use of violence to defend God's state against those who have violated it. This was demonstrated in the seventh century when the third caliph of Islam, the Caliph Uthman, was killed by the Shiite faction. They regarded the Caliph as a tyrant in violation of God's law, and his execution as the will of God. The Sunni faction regarded the Shiites as murderers that should be prosecuted under the law. Out of this internal conflict emerged Shiite radical groups. They combine Islam and terrorism in a tradition that began with the eleventh-century Assassins in the north of Iran. Shiites under the leadership of Hasan-i Sabbah were dedicated to the killing of the enemies of Islam.

The terrorism of the Shiites has endured for centuries, expressing the frustrations within a society undergoing dramatic change. It terrorized many regimes, and its offspring has now emerged in the Middle East as perhaps the most important terrorist threat of this century. The same tradition of violence and terror is continued today by the followers of the late Ayatollah Khomeini: "God is our goal, the Prophet is our leader. The Koran is our Constitution, struggle is our way. Death in the service of God is the loftiest of our wishes. God is great, God is great."[24]

A predecessor of Khomeini led the Shiite Muslim Fedayeen-i Islam in terrorist attacks against the Russians and the British in Iran in the late nineteenth century. Their descendants attempted to assassinate the Shah in 1948, and later provided the core around which the Ayatollah

Khomeini grouped his followers in their successful revolution to return fundamental Islam to Iran.

The martyrdom of Caliph Ali's son, Husayn, at Karbala in A.D. 680, after an unsuccessful Shiite rebellion against the Umayyad Caliph Yazid, was the paradigm for the 1970s revolution. Shiism provided the ideological framework and Ali Shariati (1933–1977) was the ideologue. The mosques provided the focus, and Khomeini was the spokesman.[25]

Shiite Islam is a religion of protest. "To kill and get killed for Allah, that's the message of Ruhollah."[26] As explained by Schlagheck, in a religious society where crime is punished by amputation and stoning, "it is consistent with Shiite beliefs to use violence, physical struggles, jihad, martyrdom, and even death to combat the enemies of Islam."[27]

The Ayatollah's followers view Western influence as the major enemy of Islam. They firmly believe that they are emerging from an era in which their culture and values were corrupted by Western infidels. Their defense of Islam involves the destruction of the Western influence, by whatever means available. One of those principal means has clearly been the formation and support of terrorist groups to promote the violent Shiite version of Islam throughout the Middle East.

The employment of terrorism within and outside of Iran has become a trademark of Khomeini's revolution. In 1981 Khomeini followers liquidated the Marxist Mujahdeen opposition in Iran by killing more than six thousand of its members. In camps in Qom and Tehran, the regime began the training of thousands of *entaharis* (commandos) for suicide attacks. Fundamentalist groups in the Philippines, Malaysia, Turkey, and Pakistan, as well as those in the Middle East, were recipients of a massive propaganda campaign. Egypt's President Anwar Sadat was assassinated by followers of the Ayatollah. When the 1982 Israeli invasion of Lebanon produced a power vacuum and chaos, hundreds of Iran's Revolutionary Guards were sent into the Bekaa Valley to organize and train Shiite terrorist groups, among those the Islamic Jihad, the Islamic Amal, Hizballah, and Al Da'awa.[28] By 1983, the capability of those groups was being demonstrated by the suicide bombings of the U.S. embassy in Beirut and the U.S. Marine Corps barracks at the Beirut airport, as well as attacks on French military installations. In 1984, Islamic fundamentalist terrorist tactics were expanded to include hostage taking, and in 1985 terrorists hijacked TWA Flight 847. After Islamic fundamentalist terrorists kidnapped and tortured to death the U.S. embassy's political attaché, William Buckley, the Reagan administration made secret arms sales to Iran that led to the release of two other hostages. After the disclosure of the Iran-*contra* affair, the kidnappings continued.

The terror campaign of the Islamic fundamentalists in Lebanon could be judged a success, with the withdrawal of Western military forces and the sharp reduction of Western influence. Although Lebanon today is essentially destroyed and can no longer effectively function as a state, the Shiite factions in Lebanon are in a considerably stronger position than are their Christian or other Islamic sect competitors.

Threatened by the exportation of Khomeini's revolution, other Arab regimes in the Middle East must deal with instability from within and terrorism from without. As per John Esposito's conclusion: "To the extent that incumbent governments fail to satisfy the political and economic needs of their societies and to pursue a path of modernization which is sensitive to their Islamic heritage, they will remain in a precarious position in which stability is based more often than not on authoritarian rule and force."[29]

The Ayatollah Khomeini's plan for the escalation of terror. The escalation of Iranian-sponsored terrorism in the Middle East is examined in a recent academic publication that includes a document, reportedly smuggled out of Iran to Britain, containing the classified minutes of a 26 May 1984 meeting of Iranian government leaders, wherein they decided upon the creation of a brigade-size terrorist unit to attack targets throughout the Middle East.[30]

The Ayatollah Khomeini's comments to the meeting reportedly included: All the rulers of Islamic countries are servants of foreigners . . . and have left the entire Islamic heritage in the hands of foreigners. . . . We have to spread Islam everywhere, and in this path we have given a great deal of blood, and we will give more . . . act according to your religious duties. Whatever is necessary to destroy them must be carried out.[31]

Remarks in the document by the Iranian Minister for National Guidance included: "It is not possible for us to directly confront this enormous force that is supported by the superpowers. . . . It has been decided that the strike force which at present is composed of a few groups of 10–20 people each, who are currently serving in the Lebanon should be increased to the size of a brigade."[32]

Remarks by the shadowy leader of the terrorist brigade, Mirhashem, included:

We have at present a number of dedicated groups . . . who have, to the outside world, become known as suicide groups. These groups . . . are by themselves inadequate. . . . It has been decided to select dedicated religious and fully committed candidates from all combat organisations . . . for carrying out unconventional warfare in enemy territory. . . . The target countries are . . . Saudi Arabia, Kuwait, United Arab Emirates and Bahrain . . . Hashamite Jordan . . . France and other countries who will try and confront the Islamic Republic. . . . There is no way that we can bring them to their knees unless we are able to inflict relentless blows on them from within.[33]

A few months after the Iranian regime's conference on escalating terrorism, an "open letter" appeared that apparently constituted the operational charter of Hizballah.[34] Hizballah emphatically claimed to be directly linked to and receive guidance from Iran. It claimed responsibility for destroying the Marine Corps barracks at the Beirut airport, and included the United States, NATO, and France in its list of enemies, while calling for the "obliteration" of Israel.

In the year following the Tehran decision to expand its sponsorship of terrorism, Shiites operating out of Lebanon began to imitate George Habash's Popular Front for the Liberation of Palestine (PFLP). They perpetrated the hijacking of TWA Flight 847 in June 1985, and blew up a Jordanian airliner at Beirut in the summer. Tehran's Islamic Jihad in Lebanon also sent messages to the U.S., British, and French embassies in Cairo and Jakarta warning of retaliatory attacks against their embassies, diplomats, citizens, and property throughout the world for their participation in a multinational force in Beirut.[35]

Addressing the Fletcher School of Law and Diplomacy in 1985, CIA Director William Casey identified the goals and intensity of Iran's sponsorship of international terrorism: "Tehran uses terrorism as a major element of its ongoing campaign to export the Iranian revolution throughout the Muslim world and to reduce Western influence.... In 1983 we identified as many as 50 terrorist attacks with a confirmed or suspected Iranian involvement.... We believe that agents working out of Iranian Embassies and Islamic cultural or student centers in several European nations will continue to attempt operations in Western Europe in the near future."[36]

Tehran and the international network of terror. While the Iranian regime has capitalized on the expertise of Shiite terrorist groups already in existence in Lebanon, it remains to be seen if it can develop a training infrastructure and organization as efficient as that which the Soviets developed with Palestinian elements. For example, on 23 May 1990, the nations of North and South Yemen merged to re-form a united Yemeni state. During the twenty-seven years of separation, the Marxist government in the south had suffered from an increasingly difficult economic situation. Pressure from Arab neighbors to oust the Soviet influence was sufficient by May 1990 to provide a unanimous vote by the South Yemen legislative body to merge with the North. North Yemen has moved more toward fundamentalist Islam in the last few years, and the acceptance by the South to merge was not unanimous because of the recognition of women's rights, which had emerged under the Marxist regime. Whether the terrorist training facilities of South Yemen, which had accommodated the Palestinians and the international network, will now become facilities for the training of radical Shiite groups is a question of some concern to moderate Arab neighbors as well as to Western interests in the Middle East.

Tehran's motivation for the sponsorship of international terrorism differs considerably from that of Moscow's in the 1960s. However, if it is able to develop a network at the same pace as the Soviets, then the 1990s could see the escalation of an already severe problem in the Middle East. As per the preceding quote from the former director of the Central Intelligence Agency, it would seem that the Iranians already have the nucleus of an international terrorist organization in place in Western Europe. Also, Iranian leaders were quoted as saying that "one thousand suicide bombers poised to strike were in the United States."[37]

STATE SPONSORSHIP AND SUPPORT OF INTERNATIONAL TERRORISM

During the eras of peaceful coexistence and détente, states desiring to employ political violence apparently sometimes chose to utilize a discreet mode of terroristic violence rather than to commit directly to warfare by proxy. Neil Livingstone and Terrell Arnold have outlined the advantages of terrorism as a political instrument for both weak and powerful states:

Small, weak states have discovered that it can greatly increase their political clout, and plagued as they are by resource shortages, they are not likely to abandon terrorism as a political and military tool. Larger, stronger states, by contrast, have discovered that terrorist proxies can help them achieve their national objectives without the risk attendant to other forms of warfare and without the protracted delays characteristic of the bargaining table.[38]

The violence perpetrated by a state's surrogate terrorists is designed to create an atmosphere of fear in a target population, with the intent of forcing the target government to pursue a course of action favorable to the state sponsoring and/or supporting the attack. Terrorism as defined in this analysis—the employment of a unique form of political violence—is precisely the instrument to elicit such a response. The atrocity committed is of a horrifying nature and attracts the international media. The media coverage, utilizing modern technology, is so spectacular and intense that the desired goal of creating an atmosphere of fear in the target population is quickly and efficiently achieved. If the target government does not select the response option desired by the sponsoring/supporting state, another atrocity is perpetrated. The atrocities might be short-lived and intense—like the 1983 Iran-sponsored bombing of the U.S. Marine barracks at the Beirut airport, which prompted the withdrawal of U.S. military forces from Lebanon—or they may be of a continuing agonizing nature—like the long ordeal of the Western hostages seized in Lebanon by Iran-sponsored groups attempting to bring external pressure upon Western governments for various concessions.

United States Secretary of State George Shultz addressed the challenge of state-supported terrorism in 1984 at the Johnathan Institute's second Conference on International Terrorism in Jerusalem: "Terrorists and those who support them have definite goals; terrorist violence is the means of attaining those goals. Our response must be two fold: we must deny them the means but above all we must deny them their goals.... In many countries, terrorism would long since have passed away had it not been for significant support from outside."[39]

Sponsorship or Support

Scholars and politicians alike use the terms *sponsorship* and *support* interchangeably when addressing state involvement in international terrorism. More rigorously examined, support of terrorism indicates actions on behalf of a state to provide a means of support to an existing group of terrorists. *Sponsorship* indicates a deeper relationship with the state in the formation and organization of the group itself, as well as further support. So defined, the term *support* apparently applies to Moscow's actions on behalf of those terrorist groups in Western Europe that emerged during the turbulence of the 1960s. The term *sponsorship* could be exemplified by the actions of Tehran, wherein it has taken an active part in the formulation and organization of terrorist groups in Lebanon and throughout the Middle East.

Conclusions about State Support and Sponsorship of Terrorism

> Truth, mutual trust, serious and strict solidarity exists only amongst a dozen or so individuals who form the sanctus sanctorum of the society. All the others must serve as blind tools, exploitable material in the hands of these dozen men with real solidarity.
>
> Bakunin, Letter to Alfred Talandier

The application of the full force of available military power as an instrument of politics becomes necessarily constrained within a world system where nuclear weapons are available. War as an option for resolving political confrontations may become further unlikely as technological advances make nuclear weapons even more effective, and more states become members of the nuclear weapons club. Michael Mandelbaum has postulated that, the more heavily armed each side is, the more deadly would be the war, and perhaps the less likely that it would be risked.[40]

The first forty years of a world system dominated by the threat of nuclear holocaust witnessed the increasing employment of low levels of violence, often perpetrated through surrogates, by states intent upon expanding their influence upon the world order. As recognized by Richard Feinberg, the developing world has proved to be a fertile, alternative battleground where the Great Powers can wage a shadow war by proxy, and where each can seek to spread its own influence and deny or disrupt its opponent's ambitions.[41] Both democratic and authoritarian states have conducted warfare by proxy in attempts to dominate lesser-developed regions—for example, the United States and the *contras* in Nicaragua, and the Soviet Union and Cuban troops in Angola. As the states in lesser-developed regions become more developed and move into alliances with stronger states, or form coalitions of their own, the prospects of success through proxy warfare become less. For example, the ASEAN pact served to lessen the Muslim separatist threat to the Philippines, as Malaysian cooperation contributed to the disruption of Qadhafi's material support of the separatist rebels on Mindanao. Perhaps more important, technological advances in weaponry have degraded the ability to prevent escalation of proxy war to general war, and states contemplating proxy warfare face increased risks of losing control of the situation. For example, as demonstrated by Saddam Hussein's SCUD missile attacks on Israel during the Persian Gulf conflict, the possession of long-range weapons of mass destruction by Third World nations seems to pose significant problems in constraining conflicts to local areas.

With total war becoming unthinkable, and proxy warfare increasingly risky and unproductive, the eras of peaceful coexistence and détente have seen the implementation of terrorism as an important instrument of international politics. By nature of its execution and strategy, political terrorism, rigorously defined, is useful only against liberal societies. Its effectiveness as a political instrument depends upon its ability to create an atmosphere of fear within a target population to the extent that the population will force the target government to follow a course of action desired by the state sponsoring or supporting the perpetrator.

The creation of an atmosphere of fear has, in the last thirty years, depended on the media as the instrument through which the terror of atrocities is transferred to a target population. With the media's technological capability to reach and penetrate a target audience increasing rapidly and with the media's potential for exploitation by international terrorists, the increasing efficiency of terrorism as a political instrument can be expected to become even more attractive for state sponsorship and support.

As the liberalization progresses of states and regions formerly closed by communism, the field for possible political terrorism will increase proportionally. The old hatreds of the early 1900s are already emerging in Eastern Europe. While those nations, and the nationalistic groups within them, are not immediately militarily capable of making demands upon their neighbors, the appeal of sponsoring campaigns of terror in support of their politics could likely be very tempting. Almost all of them had apparats employed by the Soviets to train, equip, and support their surrogate terrorists.[42] They could again be put into operation for nationalistic or other causes.

SUMMATION

The employment of terrorism as an instrument of politics began in biblical times. In recent decades, it has been employed principally in support of nationalism, ideologies, and religious radicalism. During eras of peaceful coexistence and détente, it has been supported by developed states as a means of political violence short of warfare, and sponsored by developing states as a means of achieving political successes against more powerful opponents. Under the constraint of nuclear weapons, with the efficiency of political terrorism increasing and its range of applicability widening, it can be expected that some states may choose to employ or perhaps to increase their sponsorship and support of international terrorism.

NOTES

1. For a review of Zealot terrorism see Donna Schlagheck, *International Terrorism: An Introduction to the Concepts and Actors* (Lexington, Mass.: Lexington Books, 1988), 15–18. For an authoritative study on the Zionist movement and terrorism see J. Bowyer Bell, *Terror out of Zion: Irgun Zvai Leumi, LEHI, and the Palestine Underground, 1929–1949* (New York: St. Martin's, 1977). An interesting view of religion and Palestinian terrorism is presented in Nels Johnson, *Islam and the Politics of Meaning in Palestinian Nationalism* (London: Kegan Paul, 1982).

2. Paul Wilkinson, *Terrorism and the Liberal State*, 2d ed. (New York: New York University Press, 1986), x.

3. Ibid., 54.

4. Ibid., 54–56.

5. Benjamin Netanyahu, "Defining Terrorism," in *Terrorism: How the West Can Win*, ed. Benjamin Netanyahu (New York: Farrar, Straus, Giroux, 1986), 12.

6. Ibid.

7. For a listing of Moscow's general goals for the employment of terrorism see Ray Cline and Yonah Alexander, *Terrorism: The Soviet Connection* (New York: Crane, Russak, 1984), 6–8. For a description of the Soviet employment of terrorism as an instrument of politics see *Terrorism in Europe*, eds. Yonah Alexander and Kenneth Myers (London: Croom Helm, 1982).

8. Nikita Khrushchev, from speech to the 20th CPSU Congress, February 1956; quoted in Cline and Alexander, *Terrorism: The Soviet Connection*, 10.

9. In a 6 January 1961 speech to the Higher Party Schools attached to the Central Committee, Khrushchev outlined the opportunities to destabilize pro-Western governments in Third World nations by training and arming communist underground elements for terrorist activities. See Cline and Alexander, *Terrorism: The Soviet Connection*, 11. For general information on Soviet training of terrorists see Robert Friedlander, *Terror—Violence: Aspects of Social Control* (New York: Oceana Publications, 1983), 173; Central Intelligence Agency, *International and Transnational Terrorism* (Washington, D.C.: GPO, April 1976); and U.S. Congress, Senate Foreign Relations Committee, *Hearings on International Terrorism*, 95th Cong., 1st sess., 19 September 1977. For a general description of Soviet support for terrorists see Yuri Andropov, *Speeches and Writings* (New York: Pergamon Press, 1983), 31; and U.S. Congress, Senate Committee on the Judiciary, Subcommittee on Security and Terrorism, *Hearings on Historical Antecedents of Soviet Terrorism*, 97th Cong., 1st sess., 11–12 June 1981.

10. See, for example, Central Intelligence Agency, *International and Transnational Terrorism*, 20; Cline and Alexander, *Terrorism: The Soviet Connection*, 55–73; and documentation of a meeting of Yasser Arafat and Palestinian terrorist leaders with Soviet Foreign Minister Gromyko and various Soviet authorities in 1979, in *Hydra of Carnage*, eds. Uri Ra'anan, Robert Pfaltzgraff, Jr., Richard Shultz, Ernst Halprin, and Igor Lukes (Lexington, Mass.: Lexington Books, 1986), 499–512.

11. See, for example, Yonah Alexander, "Some Soviet-PLO Linkages," *Middle East Review* 14 (Spring-Summer, 1982): 65; documents exhibited in Cline and Alexander, *Terrorism: The Soviet Connection*, 81–140; and documents exhibited in Ra'anan et al., *Hydra of Carnage*, 531–32.

12. See, for example, *Congressional Record*, 26 April 1978, S–6426; Cline and Alexander, *Terrorism: The Soviet Connection*, 67–68; *Rheinplatz* (Ludwigshafen), 24 August 1978; and *Elseviers Magazine* (Amsterdam), 1 September 1979.

13. For reports on Soviet training and equipping of the Red Brigades see Vittorfranco Pisano, *Contemporary Italian Terrorism: Analysis and Countermeasures* (Washington, D.C.: Law Library, Library of Congress, 1979). For information on the passing of Soviet arms through the PLO to the Red Brigades see "Document of an Italian Appellate Court," in Ra'anan et al., *Hydra of Carnage*, 584–86. For reports of other Soviet support for the Red Brigades see *Il Giornale Nuovo* (Milan), 11 January 1980; and *Corriere della Sera* (Milan), 16 April 1980.

14. See, for example, Daniel Seligman, "Communism's Crisis of Authority," *Fortune* 93, no. 2 (February 1976): 92–95, 168; and Yonah Alexander, "International Network of Terrorism," in *Political Terrorism and Energy*, eds. Yonah Alexander and Charles Ebinger (New York: Praeger, 1982), 39–64.

15. For information on PIRA training by the PLO see, for example, Cline and Alexander, *Terrorism: The Soviet Connection*, 62–67. For reports on Soviet arms shipments to the PIRA see, for example, Maria McGuire, *To Take Arms: A Year in the Provisional IRA* (London: Macmillan, 1973), 37–68; *Daily Mail* (London), 2 April 1973; and John Barron, *KGB: The Secret Work of Soviet Secret Agents* (New York: Bantam Books, 1974), 346–48.

16. For information on Soviet bloc and Palestinian support of the ETA see,

for example, Cline and Alexander, *Terrorism: The Soviet Connection*, 63; Francisco Ortzi, *Historia de Euskadi* (Barcelona: Ruedo Iberico, 1978), 383–91; Jose Portell, *Los Hombres de ETA* (Barcelona: Dopesa, 1977), 88; *Cambio 16* (Madrid), 24 November 1978; and *El Pais* (Madrid), 23 January 1979.

17. For a description of Libya's involvement with the Soviets and with international terrorism see, for example, Brian Crozier, "Libya's Foreign Adventures," *Conflict Studies*, no. 41 (London: Institute for the Study of Conflict, 1973).

18. *Defense and Foreign Affairs Weekly* 14 (April 4–10, 1983), 4–5; cited in Cline and Alexander, *Terrorism: The Soviet Connection*, 68–69.

19. See, for example, remarks by Chairman Jerimiah Denton, U.S. Congress, Senate Committee on the Judiciary, Subcommittee on Security and Terrorism, *Hearings on International Terrorism*, 98th Cong., 1st sess., 2 February 1983, 7; cited in Cline and Alexander, *Terrorism: The Soviet Connection*, 61–62.

20. For a review of the development of Cuban and Soviet relations and the Cuban involvement in international terrorism see, for example, Brian Crozier, "The Surrogate Forces of the Soviet Union," *Conflict Studies*, no. 92 (London: Institute for the Study of Conflict, 1978); *Annual of Power and Conflict: 1978–79* (London: Institute for the Study of Conflict, 1979), 5, 375–76; Cline and Alexander, *Terrorism: The Soviet Connection*, 71–73; Suzanne Labin, *La Violence Politique* (Paris: France-Empire, 1978), 130; Jacques Kaufmann, *L'Internationale Terroriste* (Paris: Librairie Plon, 1976), 277; David Anable, "Terrorism: How a handful of radical states keeps it in business," *Christian Science Monitor*, 15 March 1977, 14–15; and *Elseviers Magazine* (Amsterdam), 1 September 1979.

21. For one of the most encompassing publications on the subject see Cline and Alexander, *Terrorism: The Soviet Connection*.

22. Drawn from John Esposito, *Islam and Politics* (Syracuse: Syracuse University Press, 1984), xii. For a comparison between Islam and Western democracy see *The Politics of Islamic Reassertion*, ed. Mohammed Ayoob (New York: St. Martin's, 1981).

23. For an interpretation of Islamic law in various Arab states see Esposito, *Islam and Politics*, 94–151.

24. R. Hrair Dekmejian, *Islam on Revolution* (Syracuse, N.Y.: Syracuse University Press, 1985), 58; quoted in Schlagheck, *International Terrorism*, 57.

25. For a condensed review of the Islamic revolution see Esposito, *Islam and Politics*, 190–94.

26. Amir Taheri, *The Spirit of Allah: Khomeini and the Islamic Revolution* (Bethesda, Md.: Adler & Adler, 1986), 32; quoted in Schlagheck, *International Terrorism*, 57.

27. Schlagheck, *International Terrorism*, 58.

28. For a summation of Iran's involvement in international terrorism since the Khomeini revolution see Ra'anan et al., *Hydra of Carnage*, 480–87.

29. Esposito, *Islam and Politics*, 239.

30. Ra'anan et al., *Hydra of Carnage*, 480.

31. Ayatollah Khomeini, quoted in ibid., 482.

32. Iranian Minister for National Guidance, quoted in ibid., 483.

33. Mirhashem, quoted in ibid., 483–86.

34. Joint Publications Research Service, *Near East/South Asia Report* (19 April 1985); cited in ibid., 488.

35. Wilkinson, *Terrorism and the Liberal State*, 278.

36. William Casey, "International Terrorism: Potent Challenge to American Intelligence," *Vital Speeches of the Day* 51, no. 23 (15 September 1985): 713.

37. Quoted in Neil Livingstone and Terrell Arnold, "Democracy under Attack," in *Fighting Back: Winning the War against Terrorism*, eds. Neil Livingstone and Terrell Arnold (Lexington, Mass.: D. C. Heath, 1986), 2.

38. Ibid., 5.

39. George Shultz, "Terrorism: The Challenge to the Democracies," in *Department of State Bulletin* 84, no. 2089 (August 1984): 31–34.

40. For an examination of the likelihood of nuclear war see Michael Mandelbaum, *The Nuclear Future* (Ithaca, New York: Cornell University Press, 1983).

41. For a detailed examination of conflict in the Third World during the cold war years see Richard Feinberg, *The Intemperate Zone: The Third World Challenge to U.S. Foreign Policy* (New York: Norton, 1983).

42. For specifics on the operations of Eastern bloc international terrorist training organizations see, for example, the testimony of defecting Czech General Jan Senja in Ra'anan et al., *Hydra of Carnage*, 570–78; documents showing connections between the PLO and Eastern bloc states in Ra'anan et al., *Hydra of Carnage*, 544–49; and documents on terrorist training in Eastern bloc states in Cline and Alexander, *Terrorism: The Soviet Connection*, 121, 125.

3

The Sources of Political Terrorism

The study of the phenomenon of political terrorism has generally been concentrated on its sources. Most of the effort apparently suffers from the lack of a rigorously defined concept of terrorism. If the principal criterion for terrorism advocated by this analysis—the employment of a unique form of unacceptable violence—is applied to that research, then much of it could be recategorized as identifying the basic sources of political violence in general but not the specific sources of terrorism.

A significant amount of the effort to determine the sources of terrorism is also heavily scenario-dependent and loses meaning and importance over time. For example, Russell, Banker, and Miller have observed that, for the traditional analyst: "The roots of modern terrorism . . . appear to lie largely in the rising tide of student and radical unrest so evident in most nations of the world during the early 1960s."[1] They further indicate that "almost all terrorist groups active today either find or rationalize their raison d'être in Marxist ideology or anarchist schools of thought."[2]

While factors like ideologies and the contagion of unrest of the 1960s could be considered sources of political protest and violence, it is not at all clear why such factors should necessarily lead to terrorist atrocities. Further, such scenario-dependent explanations have not withstood the test of even a relatively short period of time. Simultaneous with Russell, Banker, and Miller's publication, the Ayatollah Khomeini's revolution was rendering incomplete any explanation of the sources of political violence and terrorism that did not include reference to state sponsorship and radical religious beliefs. Those factors are, perhaps, also scenario-dependent and could eventually disappear from the world system.

CAUSAL FACTORS OR OPERATIONAL CONSIDERATIONS

Within the extensive literature directed at the causes or sources of terrorism (which could usually be more correctly termed an identification of the sources of political violence in general), there exists a framework wherein an attempt is made to analyze the sources of terrorism by reference to a set of factors that facilitate the employment of terrorism. Those considerations are, in reality, operational factors and not causal or source factors.

For example, Wilkinson has attempted to attribute the causes of terrorism to what are mostly operational considerations. He has reported finding wide agreement among students of terrorism with what he labels its underlying causes:[3]

1. Success in gaining short-term objectives has encouraged emulation.
2. Emulation has been facilitated by diffusion of information about techniques, tactics, and weaponry.
3. The scale, complexity, and vulnerability of international communications have made the terrorists more mobile and potentially more dangerous.
4. The worldwide development of mass media with international news coverage has vastly increased the terrorists' opportunity and appetite for publicity.
5. An international world order, where major nuclear powers attempt to avoid armed conflict, lest it should escalate and disrupt the nuclear balance and détente, is conducive to terrorism and other forms of unconventional warfare.
6. Terrorism as a method of unconventional war by proxy has been energetically promoted by a wide variety of states.

While it could be agreed that Wilkinson's observations have general acceptance as common characteristics of contemporary terrorism, it is doubtful that they are the "underlying causes." Emulation, dissemination of information, advances in technology, availability of publicity, warfare by proxy, and state sponsorship are all operational considerations that can nurture and encourage the expansion of terrorism; however, with the exception of publicity, they lack the power to explain why any certain group or individual would decide to commit a terrorist atrocity instead of employing another mode of political protest or violence.

POLITICAL MOTIVATION AS A CAUSAL FACTOR

Bassiouni contributes the following toward a determination of the basic causes of terroristic forms of violence, formulated by categories of terrorists based on their particular motivations: (1) participating in separatist movements emanating from racial, religious, or language cleavages, (2) attempting to change national economic, social, or political structures, (3) employing violence to propagandize causes, and (4) seeking power to support an ideology.[4]

Bassiouni's categories illuminate the sources of political violence in general and could prove useful in a quantitative analysis of which category of political violence most likely employs terrorist atrocities. However, a process of categorization cannot account for the ultimate decision by one group to commit a terrorist atrocity while another group chooses to stage a protest demonstration and another group initiates guerrilla warfare.

WORLD SYSTEM ANALYSIS OF THE SOURCES OF TERRORISM

A leading authority on terrorism, Yonah Alexander, has approached the determination of the sources of terrorism by identifying factors to be included in the reasons why the level of nonstate violence remains high: "disagreement about who is a terrorist, lack of understanding of the causes of terrorism, the support of terrorism by some states, the existence of an international network of terrorism, the politicization of religion, double standards of morality, loss of resolve by governments, weak punishment of terrorists, flouting of world law, the roles of the mass media."[5]

Alexander's factors are apparently a combination of basic sources of political violence in general and some operational considerations for political terrorism. While explaining why terrorism has flourished in the modern world system, these factors—with again perhaps the exception of the role of the media—also fail to distinguish why some perpetrators of political violence choose to commit terrorist atrocities while others do not.

SUMMARIZING THE LITERATURE ON THE CAUSES OR SOURCES OF TERRORISM

In a useful compilation, Jenkins identified fourteen hypotheses, in five categories, that have been offered in the literature to explain why some countries seem to have higher levels of terrorism than others. This compilation also serves to assemble the majority of rationales expressed as to the causes or sources of terrorism.

Included in the political category are the views that a repressive government leads to terrorism—or the opposite, that democratic societies with their free press produce terrorism. Other political hypotheses focus on communist nations' employment of terrorism against democracies, the concept that communism has become too conservative for left-wing radicals, or that international terrorism has its roots in the Palestinian problem.

The historical category hypotheses view terrorism as the result of ethnic or ideological cleavages, or perhaps it stems from discredited regimes who lose their "moral authority," or maybe it is the natural result of a historical tendency toward anarchy.

Economic growth, economic stagnation, and affluence were all hypothesized as causes of terrorism within Jenkins's economic category. Within the social and demographic categories, hypotheses considered the process of urbanization, the loss of morality, and the weakening of family, church, and state as contributing to terrorism, as well as the "prolonged adolescence" that is apparently characteristic of affluent nations.[6]

Jenkins has offered an insightful and worthy critique of each of the hypotheses. Most are proved to be incomplete as explanations of terrorism. For example, if political terrorism is the product of affluence, then Switzerland, Japan, and the Scandinavian countries should have experienced similar levels of terrorism as the United States and West Germany. Similarly, if terrorism is the violent expression of legitimate grievances against a repressive government, then terrorism should have been rampant in the Soviet Union.

Jenkins's rather light treatment of the hypothesis of a free press as a source of terrorism is disappointing. Unfortunately, he has failed to investigate in sufficient detail why some particular individuals or groups involved in violent political activities choose to commit terrorist atrocities instead of employing other modes of violence. It can be argued that political violence becomes terroristic in nature when the perpetrators perceive a need for increased publicity to achieve their goals. Barring the possibility of a future terrorist atrocity involving mass destruction, terrorist atrocities are not normally of a magnitude that can bring about a change in the (im)balance of physical power between political terrorists and their target governments; the massacre of 300 innocents in an airliner or the taking of a dozen hostages is not likely to change the power equation. But as will be demonstrated later in a discussion on fear and terrorist atrocities, the decision to select terroristic violence as a political weapon is likely based on the desire for increased publicity, domestically, internationally, or both.

The many hypotheses that Jenkins has identified demonstrate the considerable thought and innovative approaches that have been applied to determining the causes or sources of political terrorism. However, with the exception of publicity, most appear to have merit in determining only the causes or sources of political violence. It is quite clear that what is lacking is the recognition that terrorism is a special subcategory of unique violence within the general category of political violence. Determining the causes or sources of terrorism need not concern a review of all the possible origins of political discontent. The question is more directly: Why do some groups or individuals choose to commit terrorist atrocities as a form of political violence while others do not? If one utilizes the framework of this analysis—that political terrorism is defined by a unique form of unacceptable violence—it is not difficult to focus directly on that revealing question.

PUBLICITY, AN UNDERLYING FACTOR IN CHOOSING TERRORISM

Almost all the aforementioned factors that have been identified as contributing to terrorism actually contribute to political violence in general. To focus on the issue of terrorist violence, one considers such questions as why the participants in the Watts riots and similar civil rights violence in the United States in the 1960s did not resort to terrorism, or why the 1990 revolutionaries in Liberia did not find it necessary to commit terrorist atrocities. One looks at why the PIRA in the United Kingdom, the ETA in Spain, the Red Brigades in Italy, and the Red Army Faction (RAF) in West Germany chose to become perpetrators of terrorism early in their political protests. The classic question is, of course, why certain Palestinian elements chose to concentrate on terrorism after the 1967 war. One answer seems to dominate over all other considerations: When those involved in the perpetration of political violence believe that success lies primarily in the ability to widely communicate their cause to others, and the media are not already performing that task (over which they hold a monopoly), then those individuals or groups will be tempted to commit terrorist atrocities to attract the media. Herein lies the basic reason for employment of the unique form of unacceptable political violence correctly classified as terroristic.

To obtain valid and meaningful results from a search for the source of political terrorism, one is well advised to first proceed with an examination of how political terrorism functions, the topic of the next chapter. Understanding the processes involved in striking terror into the hearts and minds of a target population also reveals the rationale for its employment, and hence the true source of its being.

NOTES

1. Charles Russell, Leon Banker, and Bowman Miller, "Out-Inventing the Terrorist," in *Terrorism: Theory and Practice*, eds. Yonah Alexander, David Carlton, and Paul Wilkinson (Boulder: Westview Press, 1979), 4.
2. Ibid., 8.

3. Paul Wilkinson, "Terrorism versus Liberal Democracy: The Problem of Response," *Conflict Studies*, no. 67 (London: Institute for the Study of Conflict, 1976).

4. Drawn from remarks by M. Cherif Bassiouni, in *The Media and Terrorism: A Seminar Sponsored by the Chicago Sun-Times and Chicago Daily News* (Chicago: Field Enterprises Inc., 1977), 6; cited in a report to the National News Council, "Paper on Terrorism," in *Terrorism, the Media, and the Law*, ed. Abraham Miller (Dobbs Ferry, N.Y.: Transnational Publishers, 1982), 135.

5. Yonah Alexander, "Terrorism and the Media: Some Considerations," in *Terrorism: Theory and Practice*, eds. Yonah Alexander, David Carlton, and Paul Wilkinson (Boulder: Westview Press, 1979), 160.

6. Drawn from Brian Jenkins, "Terrorism Prone Countries and Conditions," in *On Terrorism and Combating Terrorism*, ed. Ariel Merari (Frederick, Md.: University Publications of America, 1985), 28–32.

4

The Functioning of Political Terrorism

With an awareness of the numerous and widely varied sources of political violence, one should proceed cautiously to consider more narrowly why some individuals or groups choose terrorism as a form of political violence. A clear concept of what constitutes terror and how terrorism functions must be obtained at the onset. To illustrate, terror is a superlative form of fear, and fear is a human emotion that pertains only to the living. The helpless victims who were massacred by the Abu Nidal group at the Vienna and Rome airports in December 1985 were not terrorized. They were simply murdered. Those who survived the massacre, either physically present at the airports or miles away learning of the atrocities through media depictions, were those who were perhaps terrorized.

DISTINGUISHING BETWEEN THE VICTIMS AND THE TARGETS OF TERRORISM

While the above illustration is overly simplistic, one is well advised to approach the study of political terrorism by recognizing that the "victims" of political terrorist atrocities are not normally the "targets." Herein lies an important distinguishing feature that separates political terrorism from other forms of terror such as psychopathic.

The psychopath's victim is likely to be first terrorized and then killed, and is the principal object of the psychopath's atrocity. The terrorizing and elimination of the victim is both method and goal.

In contrast, the political terrorist's victim is symbolic. A victim is chosen who is representative of a target group that is strategically involved in the terrorist's political goals. When the Iranian-backed hijackers of TWA Flight 847 beat and killed U.S. serviceman Robert Stethem and threw his body on the tarmac at the Beirut airport, his death was not a direct objective of the terrorists. His demise was not their goal; rather, their goal was the elimination of U.S. influence in the Middle East in general and Lebanon in particular. Stethem was their victim, but not their target. Their target was the American public who observed the atrocity through the international media. The strategy for their target selection was based on the notion that the American public had the power to force a change in the Reagan administration's foreign policy for the Middle East and Lebanon.

TRANSMITTING THE TERROR OF THE ATROCITY TO THE TARGET

Obviously those present in the Vienna and Rome airport terminals during the Abu Nidal group's shooting and grenade explosions were more "terrorized" than those who later witnessed the atrocities through the international media. Further, of those learning of the atrocities through the media, it is likely that only those who were considering international travel, personally or by friends or associates, experienced some degree of fear. The association between the symbolic victim and the target audience is indeed a critical aspect of political terrorism effectiveness. However, regardless of the degree of association, a means of transmission must exist to make the target audience aware of what has happened before an atmosphere of fear can be created. Those who might not yet have heard of an atrocity are in no way terrorized by it. Given that one understands the basic rationale for the terrorist's tactical selection of a symbolic victim associated with the strategic target audience, the next item for consideration is how the terrorist transmits the terror of the violence perpetrated on the victim to the target group.

The focus of this analysis is necessarily the perpetration of political terrorism by groups and individuals not in power. However, it may be instructive to deviate briefly and consider how the transmission of terror as a superlative form of fear might be accomplished by a regime. For this examination, a regime is considered to be a government in power that has at its disposal all the forms of physical force normally associated with that position. It seems that the characteristics of the target population are a primary determinant in a regime's selection of the most efficient method of transmitting terror. For example, if the target population consists only of a few closely associated individuals—say, the

Charter 77 group in Czechoslovakia in the recent past—the persecution of one of them at the hands of the regime normally becomes immediately known to them all. Obviously, in such controlled circumstances, transmission of terror to the members of a small target population is not difficult to achieve and publicity is not a factor. In fact, regimes employing terrorism may choose to keep it a secret from the general population.

But if the target population is not closely associated—for example, when it constitutes the entire population of a state—a regime like Stalin's may choose to employ public processes of terror, such as trials and executions. Others, like some authoritarian regimes in Latin America, may choose to terrorize their political opposition through secret terrorist organizations. If such methods are employed, then publicity also becomes an important consideration to transmit the desired level of terror to the general target population.

However, the focus of this analysis is on political terrorists not in power, and the transmission of terror to a target population is then from a much different perspective. Normally the target populations are large and not especially closely associated. Through the perpetration of a violent atrocity on a symbolic victim, modern terrorists attempt to create an atmosphere of fear and then adroitly manipulate that atmosphere to influence the political behavior of the target population. If successful, such atrocities can bestow upon terrorists a capability to influence behavior that is extensively disproportionate to their actual political power.

To be effective in a political sense, the fear generated by the transmission of terror must, in turn, produce a level of intimidation in the target population sufficient to elicit the response desired by the terrorists. As noted by Sam Sarkesian, terrorism "is the creation of fear in a population in order to force the existing system to respond to the terrorists' demands and/or objectives."[1]

THE UNIQUE CHARACTERISTIC OF
TERRORIST VIOLENCE

To achieve effective distribution of terror to a target population, the violence used to create the atmosphere of fear must be perceived as a threat to each member of the population. Violence in general has a unique quality that provides for such a perception. As highlighted by Hannah Arendt, violence is unpredictable.[2] Within a political environment, strength, force, and power can all be exerted with a certain measure of predictability of results, whereas the application of violence produces results that cannot be predetermined.

Louis Beres explains that the unpredictability of results from the application of violence creates an atmosphere dominated by fate. It "creates a devastating aura of uncertainty, one in which the hegemony of means over ends may paralyze the will of potential opponents."[3] Within an aura of uncertainty dominated by fate and based upon violence, political terrorism, according to Beres, interestingly broadens its role as "an improvement upon war as the ultima ratio in world affairs, a strategy whereby the weak become effectual participants on the global stage."[4] While state sponsorship and support of terrorism seem to weaken Beres's argument for what might also be termed a possible "tyranny of the minority in the world order through terrorism," his observation has strong merit. Terrorist atrocities, wherein the violence has been effectively transmitted to the target population and an aura of fear created, can yield disproportionate political power to the perpetrators and, in some instances, to their sponsors and supporters.

The purpose of violence for political terrorism is then as cited by the ancient Chinese proverb: "Kill one, frighten ten thousand." Or, as modified and updated by Jenkins, "The terrorist wants a lot of people watching rather than a lot of people dead."[5]

A CONCEPT OF TERRORIST VIOLENCE, POLITICAL POWER, AND THE MEDIA

Arendt's seminal work on political violence was oriented toward the employment of violence by totalitarian regimes. In that context, she made the observation: "Power and violence are opposites; where the one rules absolutely, the other is absent."[6] There appears to be an interesting application of a somewhat parallel concept within contemporary political terrorism. One can postulate that the political power of terrorists is enhanced by the publicity they receive from the media. When that power is decreased by media disregard for their latest efforts, terrorists are prone to increase the level of violence, thereby increasing the media coverage with the hope of again increasing their political power. If this concept holds, then terrorist violence should also decrease as a terrorist group gains a level of political power that they perceive as sufficient. The precise phenomenon that demonstrates the accuracy of this hypothesis is, of course, the history of the Palestine Liberation Organization.

TERRORIST DEPENDENCY ON THE MEDIA FOR THE TRANSMISSION OF TERROR

In the modern world, international political terrorists have few problems and little difficulty in selecting a suitable symbolic and vulnerable victim and in committing an atrocity with a level of violence that can create fear in their target population, provided the violence of the atrocity is effectively transmitted. Therein lies the challenge for today's political terrorists. Terrorists do not have a self-contained capability to transmit the violent terror of an atrocity to their target population. Even with all the wonders of modern science available to them, contemporary political terrorists must rely on the powerful monopolistic resources of the media to transmit the terror of their violence. On some occasions terrorist groups have seized broadcast facilities. Terrorist demands often include publicity, and recently some terrorist groups have facilitated the transmitting of their violence through homemade videos, taped as their atrocity is being committed. However, it remains for the media to transmit effectively the terror of violence for terrorists. Only that worldwide network can sufficiently penetrate the very large audiences normally the targets of modern political terrorists.

While acknowledging the diversity of the "motivations, ideologies, and allegiances" held by various terrorist organizations, hostage negotiations expert Abraham Miller has identified specific elements that are emphasized by all political terrorists. Among those common elements, Miller includes "exploitation of the media to publicize their cause."[7]

One can also observe that terrorist exploitation of the media reflects, in reality, a dependence upon the media for the transmission of terrorist violence to the target population. To once again oversimplify, if one does not know of a terrorist atrocity, one is in no way terrorized by it. Political terrorism as it is now practiced by international terrorists is above all dependent on the media for the transmission of terror. Without the media there is no terror, only murder and mayhem. Exceptions, of course, might be a few terrorized eyewitnesses who survive the atrocity.

CRITIQUE OF A VIEW THAT ALL TERRORISM IS NOT DEPENDENT UPON THE MEDIA

Journalist Charles Krauthammer disagrees with the above observations. He cautions that not all terrorism is dependent on the media. He separates terrorist events into three categories, with differing needs for the media:[8]

1. Assassination: the goal is to eliminate a politically important person, with publicity not desired by the assassin.
2. Attacks upon a specifically targeted group: the goal is to demoralize a group identified as the enemy, with the attacks independent of the media.
3. Random attacks to publicize political grievances: the target population is the world, and media coverage is a vital necessity.

If one holds to a rigorous definition of political terrorism, Krautham-mer's assassination category—with the objective of eliminating a specific political actor—is not an act of terrorism. No one is terrorized; the victim is also the target, and with the killing the political goal is achieved. Certainly this is a category of political violence, but it is not the category of terrorism because terror is not involved. Krauthammer has made the debatable assumption, as have so many others, that assassination and terrorism are synonymous. Depending upon the rigor of one's definition of political terrorism, this assumption may not necessarily hold. Unfor-tunately overuse of the term *assassination*, as with overuse of the term *terrorism*, has led to an extreme vagueness about what is really involved. Members of the media frequently use the term *assassination* to describe any killing of an individual that has political overtones, and that usage is also unfortunately often employed by others.

Certainly assassination—where, by definition, the goal is the elimi-nation of a politically important personage—is not terrorism in the pure sense of the word. As per the rigorous definition of terrorism offered in this analysis, terrorist victims have only symbolic value; as individuals they lack political importance.

Krauthammer's second argument—that the terrorization of a certain group of persons with the intent to demoralize that particular group does not require media publicity—is scenario-oriented and has limited applicability. Unless the target group is extremely small and in close contact, one must question how the murder or kidnapping of one of them could possibly terrorize the others unless the media publicize the event. The need for publicity for this category becomes identical with Krauthammer's third category, which he has so eloquently described: "This is where terrorists' utter dependence on the media begins."[9] This general situation describes the overwhelming majority of international terrorist activities in the contemporary world.

As is recognized by literally everyone with access to independent radio, television, or printed matter, terrorists obviously have access to the me-dia. Yonah Alexander and Seymour Maxwell Finger have noted, "as the world is shrinking through the revolution in communications, terrorists are assured extensive publicity for their wanton acts and enunciated causes.... The immediacy and diffusion of acts of terror through the electronic media have consequently produced great psychological effects."[10]

To proceed with the examination of the functions of political terror-ism, one must consider if the transmission of terrorist violence by the media actually produces results for the terrorists, as indicated by Alex-ander and Finger's preceding statement. The next chapter investigates whether political power can actually be achieved through the employ-ment of terror.

NOTES

1. Sam Sarkesian, "Defensive Responses," in *Hydra of Carnage*, eds. Uri Ra'anan, Robert Pfaltzgraff, Jr., Richard Shultz, Ernst Halperin, and Igor Lukes (Lexington, Mass.: Lexington Books, 1986), 203.

2. Hannah Arendt, *On Violence* (New York: Harcourt, Brace & World, 1970), 5.

3. Louis Beres, *Terrorism and Global Security: The Nuclear Threat* (Boulder: Westview Press, 1979), 8.

4. Ibid.

5. Brian Jenkins, "International Terrorism: A Balance Sheet," *Survival* 17, no. 4 (July-August 1975): 158; quoted in Neil Livingstone, "Terrorism and the Media Revolution," in *Fighting Back: Winning the War against Terrorism*, eds. Neil Livingstone and Terrell Arnold (Lexington, Mass.: D. C. Heath, 1986), 216.

6. Arendt, *On Violence*, 56.

7. Abraham Miller, "Terrorism, the Media, and Law Enforcement: An Introduction and Overview," in *Terrorism, the Media, and the Law*, ed. Abraham Miller (Dobbs Ferry, N.Y.: Transnational Publishers, 1982), 1.

8. Drawn from Charles Krauthammer, "Terrorism and the Media: A Discussion," *Terrorism, The Reference Shelf*, ed. Steven Anzovin, vol. 158, no. 3 (New York: H. W. Wilson, 1986), 98.

9. Ibid.

10. Yonah Alexander and Seymour Maxwell Finger, "Introduction," in *Terrorism: Interdisciplinary Perspectives*, eds. Yonah Alexander and Seymour Maxwell Finger (New York: John Jay Press, 1977), xii.

5

The Transmission of Terror and Its Translation into Political Power

To postulate terrorist dependency upon the media to transfer the terror of an atrocity to a target population is to assume that the media can, in fact, effectively transmit information. Evaluations of this assumption cross disciplinary lines and have been performed by a wide range of social scientists. Within the discipline of political science, the effort has generally focused on the ability of the media to influence public attitudes and opinions in terms of domestic political issues. There is a marked lack of construct validity between the general topics analyzed in those studies and international terrorism. One must proceed cautiously if an attempt is made to relate the results of those studies to the specific question of whether the media can instill a feeling of fear in an audience through coverage of terrorist atrocities.

STUDIES OF MEDIA INFLUENCE AND GENERAL MASS-MEDIA THEORIES

General theories on the effect of the mass media on their consumers—agenda setting, direct impact, two-step flow of communication, and uses and gratification—argue that personal attitudes and opinions are not changed by exposure to the mass media. On the contrary, Hillel Nossek has reported that "both psychological and sociological research have found that the effect of the mass media is to strengthen existing attitudes and opinions."[1]

However, it is imperative to note that the focus and function of terrorism is the creation of an atmosphere of fear. As one of the most basic human emotions, fear can be perceived as preceding the more sophisticated human responses such as the formation of political attitudes and opinions. Whether a state of fear, once created, leads to a change of attitudes or opinions would necessarily depend on its intensity and duration.

A target population's association with a terrorist's symbolic victim leads to the conviction that such a misfortune could also befall each of them personally. As per the general theories of mass media influence on consumers, when a target population consumes the end product of the mass media's coverage of a terrorist atrocity, the feeling that each could become a victim and suffer such an atrocity is reinforced.

That media coverage of terrorism is absorbed by the public is apparently a matter of general agreement. Empirical proof is afforded by mid–1970s public opinion polls by Yankelovich, Shelly, & White, Inc. Shortly after Yasser Arafat's appearance at the U.N. General Assembly in November 1974, their poll found that 52 percent of the American public had heard of the Palestine Liberation Organization (PLO). One year later, with increased media attention precipitated by the U.N. Security Council's invitation to Arafat to participate in Middle East debates, a follow-up poll showed 63 percent recognized the PLO.[2]

Empirical evidence of public formation of, and changes in, attitudes and opinions based on media coverage of terrorism was documented during the 2 December 1975 South Moluccan terrorist hijacking of the Netherlands intercity train from Groninggen to Amsterdam near the village of Beilen. The terrorists took more than seventy hostages. The engineer and a soldier were murdered during the take-over. The train was surrounded by Netherlands police and military personnel. During the first day, three women and a child were released to deliver the terrorists' demands, which included an aircraft for safe passage, publication in all Netherlands newspapers and the broadcasting on television of South Moluccan grievances, a televised interview of South Moluccan community leaders, a conference between Indonesia and the South Moluccan exiled governments, and the presentation of the South Moluccan issue to the United Nations. Later on the first day, six hostages escaped. On the second day, seventeen hostages escaped and another was released with an additional terrorist demand for the release of all South Moluccan prisoners from Netherlands jails and an ultimatum for the Netherlands government to meet all demands before the end of that day. The ultimatum expired without concessions and the terrorists killed a hostage. On the fourth day, an explosion on the train injured three hostages and one terrorist, all of whom were taken to Netherlands hospitals. On the fifth day, the terrorists dropped their demand for safe passage, with the Netherlands government maintaining their no-concessions stance. Negotiators secured the release of two elderly hostages and a telegram was sent to the U.N. Secretary General asking for consideration of the South Moluccan claims. Negotiators also requested International Red Cross assistance. On the twelfth day, the terrorists surrendered.

During the siege of the train, and another later train hijacking simultaneous with the seizing of the Indonesian consulate building, there was an abundance of media coverage. Local radio and television reporting was especially intense. The Netherlands public responded to the coverage. A South Moluccan was beaten at the Amsterdam train station, and two others were thrown off a stationary train in Rotterdam while transport workers protested against carrying South Moluccans on their trains. In Rotterdam, petitions were circulated to demand stiffer sentences for terrorism. Polls showed that 63 percent approved of the government's no-concessions policy. Initially, 41 percent believed the terrorists deserved understanding while 44 percent said they did not. That ratio later changed when the South Moluccans took schoolchildren hostage at Bovensmilde. After that attack, only 27 percent believed the terrorists deserved understanding with 67 percent saying that they did not.[3]

While receiving extensive publicity, this incident also uniquely included polls that measured the public's formation and changes of attitudes. It clearly showed that media coverage of terrorist events is absorbed and processed by the public. Unfortunately for the South Moluccan terrorists, they failed to win support from major powers or from public opinion. As noted by Laqueur, "They are the proletariat of the terrorist world."[4]

Within the framework of political terrorism, the study of the effect of mass media on consumers primarily involves the capability of the media to generate a flow of information of sufficient intensity to create fear. A follow-on consideration is whether that flow is of sufficient intensity and duration to create a level of fear that leads to a change in attitudes and opinions.

In sum, terrorism involves fear, and fear is one of the highly motivational forces in the universe. When the media become involved by reporting the violence of a terrorist atrocity, they serve as transmitters of fear from the symbolic victim to the target audience. When the transmission of that fear is intense and of a significant duration, the attitudes and opinions of the target audience could likely be influenced.

THE TRANSNATIONAL FLOW OF INFORMATION AND POLITICAL VIOLENCE

In regard to political violence in general, media functions include far more than just transmitting fear to terrorist targets. One of the key characteristics of the modern media is their dispersion of an abundance of information worldwide with such rapidity that it allows societies to closely observe others in "real time." Amy Sands Redlick, of the U.S. Office of the Special Assistant to the Secretary of State and Coordinator of Activities to Combat Terrorism, has labeled this communications phenomenon a "transnational flow," and has examined its relationship to terrorism. She believes that the structure of the transnational flow of information may "cause attitudinal changes, such as changes in frame of reference, perceptions, and mood"; and further that "external information may shape the strategy, tactics, and ideology of the groups involved in a conflict."[5] Joseph Nye and Robert Keohane have observed that: "By facilitating the flow of ideas modern communications have also increased intersocietal sensitivity."[6]

Redlick views two factors as the determinants of a society's sensitivity to the flow of external information: (1) the structure and stability of the society that determine its accessibility and vulnerability, and (2) the identification of the society with the outside force.[7] She hypothesizes that the transnational flow of information "may be a catalyst to the outbreak and development of terrorism in tense situations," and "can activate and then reinforce violent tendencies within an individual or community."[8]

Certainly Redlick's observation, that the "thoughts and actions of radicals" have so influenced modern societies that violence and revolution have been given an "aura of legitimacy,"[9] depends on the capabilities of the modern media to transmit those thoughts and portray those actions worldwide.

The transnational flow of information has apparently provided an international atmosphere wherein, according to J. Bowyer Bell, "rebels everywhere feel a solidarity with others waging armed struggle against colonialism or neoimperialism. . . . It has become far more alluring for the frantic few to appear on the world stage of television than remain obscure guerrillas of the bush."[10] Redlick emphasizes that by making "the revolutions, liberation struggles, and terrorist attacks so widely known and honored, the transnational flow of information has contributed to the creation of an atmosphere in which violence, especially terrorism, appears justifiable and acceptable."[11]

The noted journalist and author on terrorism Claire Sterling apparently holds the same perception of this "atmosphere" in her description of the attempted assassination of the Pope: "The world had become so inured to terrorism that this was the most acceptable method by which the Soviet Union could physically eliminate the Polish Pope."[12]

Those who doubt the authenticity of Sterling's remarks can consider the results of years of investigation by Italian Judge Ilario Martella. His evidence reportedly indicates that the Soviets had given the task of assassinating the Pope to Bulgaria.[13] The Bulgarians had reportedly assigned the task to a Turkish terrorist group called the Turkish Mafia, which they subsidized, sponsored, and directed. Professional killer Mehmet Ali Agca of the Turkish Mafia was given the assignment to murder the Pope. While the operational planning was left to Agca and his accomplice, Oral Celik of the Turkish Gray Wolves terrorist group, a Bulgarian secret service official (the treasurer of the Bulgarian embassy in Rome) promised them that, "Bulgaria would put up the money, provide the escape route by means of an international truck, and arrange for sanctuary."[14] The two assassins were to receive weapons, intelligence, money, and safe houses from Gray Wolves contacts in Western Europe while planning the murder.

The modern transnational flow of information has provided an atmosphere for the contagion of terrorism and acceptance of increasing political violence that could endanger governments. Cynthia Enloe has indicated that the capabilities of governments to respond to these dangers have been simultaneously eroded: "Modern change is noted for its rapidity, due to faster communications and tighter functional interdependence. Modern change is international, hard to confine within geographical limits. These qualities make it difficult to deal with an issue or group in a vacuum or for its own sake."[15]

Certainly the "contagion" of terrorism through the media is a very important consideration. Those who criticize the media for their role in that regard are supported by Gurr's observation:

A community may have a nonviolent tradition itself, but if its members see similar groups elsewhere making gains through political violence they are likely to see utilitarian justifications for violent tactics for themselves. In the modern world this demonstration effect of one group's successful use of violence can have almost simultaneous, worldwide consequences.[16]

Karl Deutsch has also noted that the dramatic increase in terrorist incidents must be at least partly linked to the international flow of information. Perpetrators of terrorist violence have received significant publicity and even sympathy, while other groups have been inspired to attempt similar activities.[17]

What Redlick has labeled as the "demonstration effect"[18] can be detected by consideration of a series of events involving hostage-taking in the United States during the month of February 1977: (1) a Vietnam veteran barricaded himself in a Silver Springs, Maryland, bank; (2) a customer held hostage an executive of a mortgage firm that had foreclosed on him; (3) a young weightlifter barricaded himself in the warehouse where he had lost his job and killed five persons; (4) a black man sought to publicize the deprivations experienced by blacks by holding a hostage in Cleveland; and (5) the Hanafi Muslims started a media extravaganza when they occupied three buildings in Washington, D.C., and held several hostages.

Redlick offers the Quebec National Liberation Front (FLQ) as an example of the influence of the modern transnational flow of information on terrorism. Apparently the FLQ duplicated the cell organization and bombing techniques of the Algerian FLN, and later patterned their kidnappings after the Uruguayan Tupamaros.[19] She concludes that the transnational flow of information can benefit terrorists in four principal ways: (1) draw attention to the perpetrators and their cause, (2) expose societies to information that could inspire and legitimize violence, (3) distribute technological knowledge and ideological justification to potential terrorists, and (4) increase the contagion effect by publicizing successful terrorist attacks.[20]

In sum, the modern media can effectively transmit to a world audience the violence of a terrorist atrocity. To the extent that individuals in targeted population groups may sense an association with the terrorists' victims, an atmosphere of fear can be created that can lead to changes in beliefs and attitudes. Further, the modern media have the capability to provide a transnational flow of information with such volume and rapidity that individuals and groups prone to political violence can draw upon the activities and experiences of others to initiate their own style of violence.

TRANSFORMING TERROR INTO POLITICAL POWER

With the extraordinary information flow available through the modern media, those seeking to transmit terror apparently need be concerned only with committing an atrocity of sufficient violence and horror to attract the media. At such moments as when Pan Am Flight 103 exploded from a terrorist bomb over Scotland, there is no denying that terrorists can seize the public agenda almost at will, albeit only with the added value that media coverage bestows upon their violence.

However, to translate terror into political power, to succeed in employing terror as a tactic within a strategy of political conflict, terrorists must not only be able to momentarily seize the public agenda, but also have the capability to control it. This involves melding terror tactics with political objectives. Numerous examples are available to demonstrate the capabilities of terrorists and their sponsors to succeed at this task.

Black September not only put the Palestinian cause on the public agenda at the 1972 Munich Olympics; it also gained a measure of control over that agenda. Prior to the massacre of the nine Israeli athletes, Egypt had initiated peace proposals with Israel through West Germany. With Black September holding the Israeli athletes hostage in Munich, the West Germans requested that Egypt take part in negotiations with the terrorists. The Egyptian refusal irritated the West German authorities and the peace initiative was lost.[21] Black September had successfully controlled the public agenda. The PLO was handed a political victory through this ultra-terrorist group, which had been formed after King Hussein's military forces had massacred the Fatah at its strongholds in Jordan in September 1970. A mastermind of the Munich Olympic massacre, Abou Daoud, was later captured in France. Dependent on Arab oil for 85 percent of their energy supply, and with a strong desire to sell military equipment to Arab nations, the French released Daoud and gave him safe conduct.[22] National interests apparently prevailed over considerations for containing international terrorism.

When Egyptian President Anwar Sadat made known his desire to visit Israel, the question of the PLO's involvement in any peace negotiations was again a key issue. Moderates within the PLO had been searching for a basis for negotiations with Israel through their representative in London, Said Hammami. Fearing a weakening of the PLO resolve, Abu Nidal of the rejectionist front had Hammami murdered in London on 4 January 1978.[23] The public agenda was controlled by Abu Nidal, as the moderate factions within the PLO were constrained from encouraging Sadat's peace initiatives.

In March 1978, just prior to Prime Minister Begin's departure for Washington for talks with President Carter over President Sadat's peace initiatives, Yasser Arafat's Fatah began random attacks on Israeli motorists north of Tel Aviv with the hijacking of two tourist buses and the killing of thirty civilians, including children.[24] The atrocities were apparently a demonstration of the PLO's hard-line position. The Israelis retaliated with attacks on PLO positions in southern Lebanon. While the Camp David peace accords were finally achieved, Israel's 1978 success in attacking the Fatah through United Nations observer positions preceded the ultimate Israeli invasion of Lebanon in 1982.

While the Israeli invasion destroyed the military capability of the PLO, the PLO's demonstrated ability to control the public agenda through terrorism had already contributed in no small way to its acceptance by Arab leaders as the representative of the Palestinian people—and, eventually, to the special status which it was accorded at the United Nations.

The saga of the Western hostages in Lebanon, which began in 1984, clearly demonstrates how terrorist groups can use the media to seize the public agenda almost at will. When the 100-hour Persian Gulf war drew to a close, America's president George Bush appeared to be in a most powerful position to influence Middle East politics. Having forged a coalition of Western and Arab military forces (which would not have seemed possible only a short time earlier), and simultaneously employed U.S. weapons to defend Israel, he appeared to be making substantial progress in moving toward a peace settlement in the Middle East. With at least a portion of the Arab population of the area grateful for the liberation of Kuwait, and the Israeli people thankful for America's defense of their cities against Saddam Hussein's SCUD missiles, President Bush was also enjoying extreme popularity at home. It would be difficult to construct a more favorable scenario for strengthening U.S. influence in the region.

Unfortunately, President Bush's efforts for peace talks were promptly derogated by yet another exploitation of the Western hostages held by Islamic terrorist groups in Lebanon. Employing the same tactics used during the 1985 hijacking of TWA Flight 847, the terrorists offered to trade hostages for prisoners held by the Israeli government. Apparently of particular importance among those in Israeli jails was the Islamic leader Sheik Obeid, who was captured by the Israelis after his alleged involvement with the murder of an officer of the U.N. peacekeeping force in southern Lebanon, U.S. Marine Lieutenant Colonel William R. Higgins.[25]

The exchange of nine Western hostages and seven missing Israeli soldiers for about 400 prisoners in Israeli jails became a topic for discussion in 1987. When the Islamic terrorists and their Iranian supporters deemed it necessary to disrupt the political scene in the Middle East (and strengthen Arab unity while weakening the ties between the American public and Israel), the Western hostages were put on the world stage with the suggestion of a possible release. As per the 1985 TWA hijacking, the U.S. news media were quick to respond. Interviews with hostages' friends and relatives dominated newscasts, and the situation was analyzed again and again by media experts. Unfortunately the perception that was sometimes imparted by U.S. media personalities seemed to be exactly that desired by the terrorists and their supporters. For example, on the "Today" show on the morning of 8 August 1991, the commentator referred to the possibility of an exchange as the swapping of the terrorists' hostages for the Israeli-held "hostages." Evidently more than just an inadvertent error, the key words of "hostages held by Israel" were used again by the commentator on the "NBC Evening News" on 15 August. The unfavorable and discrediting perception of the duly-elected government of Israel imparted to the American public by such newscasts most likely fulfilled one of the terrorists' goals.

As demonstrated by the events of 1991, it seems readily apparent that, through the Western media, a relatively small group of terrorists can command the attention of the secretary general of the United Nations and weaken the political strategies of a superpower. It seems undeniable that terrorism in the Middle East has been translated into political power, and the principal mode of translation has been the media.

SUMMATION

During the coverage of a terrorist atrocity, the media serve as the transmitters of fear from the victims to the target audience. To the extent that fear provides a basic motivation for human responses, the attitudes and opinions of the target audience can be influenced.

The modern media provide a transnational flow of information with sufficient volume and rapidity to influence groups and individuals prone to political violence to attempt to imitate or emulate terrorists.

In order to convert political terrorism into political power, terrorists must be able to seize the public agenda. Through adroit exploitation of media coverage, terrorist groups have demonstrated that capability.

As one proceeds with the examination of the media's role in transferring terror from symbolic victim to target audience, it becomes important to investigate the peculiarities of the modern media that allow terrorists to coordinate atrocities and achieve objectives. This is the subject of the next chapter.

NOTES

1. Hillel Nossek, "The Impact of Mass Media on Terrorists, Supporters, and the Public at Large," in *On Terrorism and Combating Terrorism*, ed. Ariel Merari (Frederick, Md.: University Publications of America, 1985), 89.

2. As reported in Yonah Alexander, "Terrorism and the Media: Some Considerations," in *Terrorism: Theory and Practice*, eds. Yonah Alexander, David Carlton, and Paul Wilkinson (Boulder: Westview Press, 1979), 162–63.

3. Polls cited in Valentine Herman and Rob van der Laan Bouma, "Nationalists without a Nation: South Moluccan Terrorism in the Netherlands," in *Terrorism: A Challenge to the State*, ed. Juliet Lodge (New York: St. Martin's, 1981), 136.

4. Walter Laqueur, "Terrorism—A Balance Sheet," in *The Terrorism Reader: A Historical Anthology*, ed. Walter Laqueur (Philadelphia: Temple University Press, 1978), 259.

5. Amy Sands Redlick, "The Transnational Flow of Information as a Cause of Terrorism," in *Terrorism: Theory and Practice*, eds. Yonah Alexander, David Carlton, and Paul Wilkinson (Boulder: Westview Press, 1979), 73.

6. Joseph Nye and Robert Keohane, eds., *Transnational Relations and World Politics* (Cambridge, Mass.: Harvard University Press, 1972), 376.

7. Redlick, "The Transnational Flow of Information as a Cause of Terrorism," 80–82. See also Karl Deutsch, *Nationalism and Social Communication: An Inquiry into the Foundation of Nationality* (Cambridge, Mass.: The MIT Press, 1953), 60–80, for more information on the effect of similarities between two societies on the flow of information between them.

8. Redlick, "The Transnational Flow of Information as a Cause of Terrorism," 74, 76.

9. Ibid., 76. See also Karl Deutsch, *Nationalism and Social Communication: An*

Inquiry into the Foundation of Nationality, 2d ed. (Cambridge, Mass.: The MIT Press, 1966), 87–106.

10. J. Bowyer Bell, *Transnational Terror*, AEI-Hoover Policy Study 17 (Washington, D.C.: American Enterprise Institute for Public Policy Research, 1975), 74, 89.

11. Redlick, "The Transnational Flow of Information as a Cause of Terrorism," 77.

12. Claire Sterling, "Unraveling the Riddle," in *Terrorism: How the West Can Win*, ed. Benjamin Netanyahu (New York: Farrar, Straus, Giroux, 1986), 103.

13. For a translation and summation of Judge Martella's investigation see Sterling, "Unraveling the Riddle," 103–105. For further information on the Soviet bloc connection with the attempted assassination of Pope John Paul II, see, for example, Robert Pfaltzgraff, Jr., "Implications for American Policy," in *Hydra of Carnage*, eds. Uri Ra'anan, Robert Pfaltzgraff, Jr., Richard Shultz, Ernst Halperin, and Igor Lukes (Lexington, Mass.: Lexington Books, 1986), 294.

14. Sterling, "Unraveling the Riddle," 103–104.

15. Cynthia Enloe, *Ethnic Conflict and Political Development* (Boston: Little, Brown & Co., 1973), 6.

16. Ted Robert Gurr, *Why Men Rebel* (Princeton: Princeton University Press, 1971), 231.

17. Drawn from Karl Deutsch, "External Involvement in Internal War," in *Internal War*, ed. Harry Eckstein (New York: Free Press of Glencoe, 1964), 100–101.

18. Redlick has chosen to refer to the phenomenon of contagion of terrorism as the demonstration effect. See Redlick, "The Transnational Flow of Information as a Cause of Terrorism," 84–90.

19. Ibid., 85.

20. Drawn from ibid., 91.

21. Drawn from Abraham Miller, *Terrorism and Hostage Negotiations* (Boulder: Westview Press, 1980), 99.

22. Ibid., 30.

23. Ibid., 99.

24. Ibid., 99–100.

25. For an informative view of the Lebanon hostages and Middle East politics, see Brian Jenkins, "Hostage takers are staging a good show," *Las Vegas Review-Journal*, 20 August 1991, 5B.

6

The Media's Influence on the Public's Perception of Terrorism and the Question of Media Responsibility

The modern media's transmission to the public of information about political terrorists includes processing and disseminating as well as gathering that information. Students of communications identify several significant problems normally associated with those functions. For example, the problem of distortion normally abounds in the processing and dissemination of any information. This major problem and others are passed from the communicator to the consumer of information. In the case of the media's coverage of political terrorists, the end result could be the formation of erroneous perceptions by the public.

It should be recognized that the modern media, while seemingly a giant impersonal apparatus, is indeed composed of individual persons, each seeking to achieve personal aims, and each susceptible to human failings. The transfer of information by the media to their audience is, in its basic essence, the communicating of information from one human being to another. All the frailties and failings of humanity are involved in this process. As a simplistic example, the recipient is subjected to the interpretation of the information by the communicator, which may or may not be factual, and at best reflects the values and biases of the communicator.

The numerous difficulties involved in the accurate transmission of information have plagued literally every profession, and studies in this area are voluminous. A review of the literature allows one to more directly focus on those communications issues of importance in the media's coverage of terrorism. Prominent among processing and dissemination issues is the media's portrayal of terrorists and their atrocities.

THE IMPORTANCE OF THE MEDIA'S PORTRAYAL OF TERRORISM

In democratic societies with political systems based on plurality, the public's perception of events may determine which policy alternatives are available to the government. To the extent that the images of political terrorism, as portrayed by the media, affect the public's perception, those images are of significant concern to the society as a whole. The importance of this issue has been illuminated by the Task Force on Disorders and Terrorism of the U.S. National Advisory Committee on Criminal Justice Standards and Goals: "Depictions of incidents of extraordinary violence in the mass media are . . . a significant influence on public fears and expectations."[1]

In discussing the importance of the public's perception of terrorists and their atrocities, Miller has centered on the proposition that sensational terrorist acts publicized by the media can make the public so amazed at the terrorists' description of reality that it will question its own assumptions of morality and the political system. For Miller, such a redefinition of values holds the seeds of revolution.[2] If one accepts the hypothesis that the public's perceptions of events can influence policy alternatives, then it follows that disseminating factual, nondistorted information on important domestic and international events is vital to the stability of a society.

INFLUENCING PERCEPTIONS THROUGH LABELING AND TERMINOLOGY

When reviewing the literature on terrorism, one becomes quickly impressed with the semantic problems of labeling and terminology that apply directly to the media's influence on the public's perceptions. Biased images and false perceptions can be created as simply as with a choice of words. Referring to a group involved in political violence as "guerrilla" imparts an image far different than referring to it as "terrorist." *Guerrilla* is the term for irregular armed forces involved in political violence through the conduct of combat operations against military targets, whereas terrorists do not attack the military strength of their political opposition but rather hit symbolic targets that are most often innocents. Similarly, referring to the killing of a person during an act of political violence as an execution imparts a far different image than if it is referred to as a murder. If the news media choose terminology provided by the terrorists, they may inadvertently transmit terrorist arguments sympathetically to the public.

A review of media broadcasts and publications, as well as scholarly texts on the subject of terrorism, shows a remarkably casual interchanging of the terms *atrocity, incident, act, event,* and *attack.*[3] It is perhaps worth noting that the media and scholars writing in England, Italy, West Germany, and Israel—countries where the realities of terrorist violence may have more personal meaning—tend to describe terrorist violence more as atrocities rather than simply as events or acts. British journalist Nicholas Ashford has also observed that the British press normally refer to the IRA as terrorists and the PLO as guerrillas: "But the IRA affects us directly and the PLO does not."[4]

David Williamson has objected to the media's labeling of practically all violent political events perpetrated by individuals or groups as terrorism. He regards this overuse of the term as dangerous:

There may be value to a disciplined avoidance of the term "terrorism" when the events involved are better defined by older terms: extortion, assault, murder, blackmail, maiming. . . . These are concepts of criminal behavior well understood . . . within a reasonably coherent construct of what is and is not acceptable.[5]

Examples of possible media influence on public perception through labeling and terminology can readily be found in the Middle East. In the mass media of the 1970s, the word *Palestinian* seemed to connote terrorism. The dangers connected with such labeling, and the possible resultant perceptions imparted to the public, became clear during the later Israeli invasion of Lebanon. As noted by Thomas Friedman, the *New York Times* bureau chief in Jerusalem, after the massacre of Palestinians at the Shatila and Sabra refugee camps:

The Christian Phalangist militia, and, to a certain extent, some Israelis, had so dehumanized the Palestinians, labeling everything they touched as "terrorist"—terrorist tanks, but also terrorist hospitals, terrorist doctors, and terrorist nurses—that they could no longer distinguish between true terrorists, guerrilla fighters and innocent women and children.[6]

Friedman noted a similar labeling phenomenon in Israel after the arrests of twenty-seven Jewish men who had committed atrocities against Palestinians in the Occupied Territories:

Some Israeli newspapers describe them as "Jewish terrorists," implying condemnation of the crimes they are accused of. But the defendants' supporters . . . refer to them as the "Jewish underground," a term that evokes images of the underground that fought for Israel's independence in the 1930's and 1940's. The state-run Israeli radio has also come to refer to the 27 men as members of "the underground."[7]

In spite of the heinous nature of the violence perpetrated by the twenty-seven terrorists against innocent civilians, favorable descriptive labeling by the Israeli media likely contributed to the Israeli public's perception that, when polled by the newspaper *Ha'aretz*, showed 31.8 percent regarding the terrorist atrocities as justified.[8]

THE LEGITIMIZATION OF POLITICAL TERRORISTS AND TERRORISM

In their study of the functions of the mass media in contemporary society, Paul Lazarsfeld and Robert Merton have observed that publicity from the mass media in and of itself confers status.[9] Through coverage of terrorists and their atrocities, the news media can also bestow status. The result, and clear danger, of that phenomenon is that terrorists committing such heinous crimes as kidnapping and murder can be transformed from common criminals into political figures. Live televised interviews with terrorists can give them the same status as the media accords to respectable politicians. The elevation of terrorists to the platform of legitimate politicians obviously serves to confuse the public about the true means and goals of the terrorists.

British journalist John O'Sullivan has described television as "a leveling and homogenizing medium." He readily admits it is "very difficult to interview terrorists without presenting them not as a species of criminal but as a species of politician."[10] Brian Crozier, former director of the London-based Institute for the Study of Conflict, has also noted that the television media may specifically contribute to the legitimization of terrorism: "It is in the nature of television as a medium that it tends to favor the revolutionary side."[11]

While Crozier's reflection on the nature of television may be generally agreed, it still remains for the human element of the news media to choose what information is disseminated and how it is portrayed. The aggressive trend toward sensationalism in newscasting, which accelerated in the 1960s, has apparently continued unabated. It is possible that while providing an intense spotlight for the high drama of terrorism, the news media tend to ignore the basic facts. This could justify William Perdue's critique of their "inadequate coverage of the sources of political violence, with bias favoring coverage of the high drama that gives twisted expression to those grievances."[12]

In sum, the public's perception of terrorism can likely be influenced by the media's use of terms and labels, with a significant result being the possible acceptance as legitimate politicians of terrorists guilty of heinous crimes. News media selection of legitimizing terms and labels and the presentation of the high drama of terrorism, especially on television, tends to glorify terrorists in roles of legitimate revolutionaries rather than as kidnappers and murderers.

THE DISSEMINATION OF TERRORIST PROPAGANDA

The public's perception of terrorism can be influenced not only by the content of news coverage but also by the context in which it is presented. Analysis and comment have become increasingly prominent in the news media. It is a skillful exercise for which, especially in the United States, network news stars are paid high salaries. Such handling of the news should be expected in societies with free-enterprise economic systems, where journalism is a competitive business and profits must be realized in order to continue operations. Basically, news events normally offer an equal opportunity for presentation to all the networks and other segments of the news media. It is through the flair of presentation that the competing media hope to influence the public's selection of which news program to view or which publication to purchase. Using television as an example, increases or decreases in ratings derive from the public's selection of a certain news program, and with those ratings come profits or losses.

According to H.H.A. Cooper, within the presentation lies the "true power" of the media: "the ability to convey not news, but the true sense of our life and times."[13] The potential for contemporary news analysts and commentators to influence the public's perception of events indeed appears significant: "It is no exaggeration to aver that he who controls the media is most powerfully equipped in the struggle to win the hearts and minds of the people."[14]

An example offered by a Turkish journalist, discussing the murder of Turkish diplomats by Armenian terrorists, serves to illustrate that propaganda victories could be awarded to terrorists through media analysis of news and history: "News that a Turkish Ambassador has been killed is generally coupled with commentary on how the Armenians were murdered by those Turks seventy years ago. Suddenly the murderers become freedom fighters."[15]

Formal Models of Propaganda

When attempting to evaluate the exploitation of the media by terrorists one is well advised to prepare for the task through familiarization with the arts of semantics and propaganda. Assuredly, by simply employing the basic concepts of business management an analyst could attempt to measure the efficacy of a terrorist campaign. However, with the success of contemporary political terrorism likely hinging upon effective exploitation of the media, one should also be familiar with semantics and propaganda, *semantics* being simply "the relationship between words and what those words represent" and *propaganda* being "a systematic attempt by an individual or a group to control the attitudes of others."[16]

The preceding paragraphs have attempted to illuminate and empha-
size the importance of a segment of semantics—the choice of terms and
labels by the media—in influencing the public's perception of terrorism.
The literature also shows that the media may, inadvertently or intentionally, become involved in disseminating propaganda during their coverage of terrorism. The following are some of the more basic works in
the field of propaganda that enable an analyst to more readily identify
situations in which the media may be influencing public perceptions of
terrorism through dissemination of propaganda.

Inherent within any terrorist propaganda analysis model are four basic
elements: (1) the target of the deception (a population), (2) the medium
for delivering the message (the atrocity), (3) the purpose (the influencing
of political behavior), and (4) the truth (the facts that are to be
distorted).[17]

Among the better known of the propaganda analysis models is that
developed by Lasswell to demonstrate the analysis of communications.
He has most simply demonstrated it in two dimensions:[18]

Communications Question	*Field of Research*
Who	Control analysis
Says what	Content analysis
In what channel	Media analysis
To whom	Audience analysis
With what effect	Effect analysis

Elizabeth and Alfred Lee, of the Institute for Propaganda Analysis,
have developed "Tricks of the Trade," which is a listing of seven methods
used in contemporary propaganda:[19]

1. "Bandwagon": conveying to members of the public that everyone else is
   accepting a concept, therefore they should join the crowd.
2. "Name calling": affixing a derogatory label to a concept, thereby encouraging
   its rejection.
3. "Glittering generality": affixing a virtuous label to a concept to encourage its
   acceptance (opposite of name calling).
4. "Testimonial": connecting a popular or a disliked personality to a concept to
   encourage its acceptance or rejection.
5. "Card stacking": selectively accumulating fact or fiction to support or discredit
   a concept.
6. "Transfer": relating a concept to an existing generally accepted or rejected
   program.

7. "Plain folks": portraying the promoters of a concept as ordinary people, therefore their concept is acceptable.

The Lees' list of propagandist tricks provides a connection between semantics and propaganda models. Modern linguists have progressed beyond the earlier assumption that language was a neutral medium for thought expression. Some now advocate that "what we perceive and how we think are restricted by the language we speak."[20]

Samuel Hayakawa's "ladder of abstraction" is also a valuable tool in considering the effect that the media's vocabulary has upon the public's perception of a reported terrorist event. The pen has been alleged to be more powerful than the sword; likewise, Hayakawa postulates that some words are more powerful than others. As one moves up Hayakawa's ladder, concrete words—factual words upon whose meaning people usually agree—are replaced by less specific words with more abstract meanings. This movement away from a shared semantic understanding creates an environment favoring misinterpretations.[21] The phenomenon is clearly demonstrated when terrorist kidnappings and murders are referred to as incidents or events.

In sum, the analysis of a terrorist propaganda campaign includes examination of both the content and the context of media coverage. Through semantics and conscious or unconscious propagandizing during the processing and dissemination of information, the modern news media can help shape public perceptions of terrorists and their violence that may vary in both objectivity and veracity.

THE NEWSWORTHINESS OF TERRORISM

While performing the basic communication function of gathering information, it is within the general category of disinformation, or omission, that the power of the free press in a democratic society can be most clearly demonstrated. Using the label "newsworthy," media executives can exercise ultimate authority, with no appeal, on what information will be broadcast or published for public consumption and what information will be ignored.

The literature generally agrees that the media's determination of what is newsworthy in terms of terrorism coverage is governed by: (1) the media's evaluation of the relative importance and significance of a specific event as compared to other current events, (2) the specific event's sensational appeal, and (3) the particular media's policy toward covering such events.[22]

Technological advances in communications have also proved to be a powerful force in determining what information is newsworthy. The format of "news" has progressed rapidly in the last half-century from printed word and radio broadcasts, to anchormen reading summaries of the day's events on television, to video coverage of news events as they occur. The term *newsworthy* seems to have been broadened to the extent that video coverage has become a requirement.

As early as 1963, Reuven Frank, NBC's producer of the "Huntley-Brinkley Report," noted that the "highest power of television journalism is not in the transmission of information, but in transmission of experience...joy, sorrow, shock, fear.... This was the stuff of news."[23] Perhaps as recognized by Robert Friedlander, terrorists actually design their atrocities for television: "Terrorism is quintessentially a coup de théâtre, which requires an impressionable audience for its dramatic impact."[24]

The omnipotence and omnipresence of television has brought calls for the need to assume more responsibility for its use. As related by television newscaster Daniel Schorr: "Television has come...to replace government as an authority figure. It confers prestige and identity. It must learn the responsibility that goes with its influence. That means not encouraging terrorists by giving them the rewards of massive notoriety."[25]

The literature on political terrorism illuminates what might be termed a state of naiveté in terms of the power of television to exacerbate violence in general. As stated by television critic Harry Waters, "A better question is whether commercial television—after 25 years of scientific data linking video violence with antisocial behavior—will ever accept the fact that it can be a deadly potent carrier."[26]

In sum, through semantic labeling, the casual employment of terms, and involvement with propagandizing for various ends, the media can create public perceptions of terrorists and their atrocities that vary in both objectivity and veracity. Further, a democratic society's free press possesses absolute power in determining what is sufficiently newsworthy to be disseminated to the public. The medium of television is apparently ideally suited for exploitation by political terrorists. By nature, television news seeks sensational drama, with its related influence on the public's perception of an event. The news media's television coverage of terrorism is especially vulnerable to legitimatizing terrorists as politicians, whereas in reality they are kidnappers and murderers.

TERRORIST STRATEGIES FOR ACHIEVING PUBLICITY

As a weaker form of political violence than total or limited war, terrorism normally involves a relatively longer period of struggle for the achievement of objectives. Strategies for a prolonged campaign of terrorism focus on psychological warfare and its vital element of publicity. In his *Manual for the Urban Guerrilla*, Brazilian Carlos Marighella delineated terrorist strategies for utilizing the media: "Inevitably all armed actions strive as propaganda vehicles that are fed into the mass communications system . . . kidnappings, sabotage, terrorism, and the war of nerves, are cases in point."[27]

History has shown that terrorist strategies and tactics have been modified over time as the benefits offered by technological advances in the media have been recognized and exploited. An early leader of the Algerian resistance, Abane Ramdane, while advocating the urbanization of the FLN campaign of violence, observed that "killing ten French people in the desert went unnoticed while the killing of one French person on a busy street in Algiers would receive coverage in the international media."[28]

After the Israeli defeat of the Arab armies in 1967, PFLP leader George Habash urged the Palestinians to adopt terrorism as a more effective weapon. He noted, "to kill a Jew far from the battleground has more effect than killing 100 of them in battle; it attracts more attention. And when we set fire to a store in London, those few flames are worth the burning down of two kibbutzim. Because we force people to ask what is going on."[29]

There are several instances where political opposition movements, which were relatively unknown but had been in existence for several years, gained international recognition with the commission of a single act of violence with sufficient severity to attract the Western media. The cause of the Croatian separatists, little known to the American public, received extensive coverage by the U.S. media with their September 1976 hijacking of a TWA flight. They carried no real weapons and had no chance of being given sanctuary; their only goals and demands were for the media's attention.[30]

In 1977, three days of continuous media coverage of three simultaneous barricade and hostage atrocities achieved worldwide recognition for previously unknown Hanafi Muslim terrorists. Their leader, Hamass Abdul Khaali, surrendered to Washington, D.C., police with the admission that he never anticipated his demands would be met by the authorities. His obvious primary aim was publicity.[31]

TERRORIST TACTICS FOR EXPLOITING THE MEDIA

The challenge for terrorists in planning a campaign is to design their atrocities to maximize publicity benefits toward achievement of their specific political objectives. Four factors are identified in the communications literature as "media-selection criteria"[32] that terrorists have apparently often considered while planning atrocities: (1) timing attacks as responses to political developments or to coincide with historically significant dates, (2) choosing physical targets with ready access for the news media, (3) affecting a large enough population and inflicting a sufficient number of casualties to ensure coverage, and (4) victimizing elite persons or targeting elite governments.[33]

Examples of precise planning by terrorists for the exploitation of the media are readily available. European terrorist groups have seemingly perfected the tactic. A West German television editor described the coverage of the 2nd June Movement's kidnapping of West Berlin mayoral candidate Peter Lorenz:

For 72 hours we just lost control of the medium. It was theirs, not ours. . . . We shifted shows in order to meet their time-table. Our cameras had to be in position to record each of the released prisoners as they boarded the plane to freedom, and our news coverage had to include prepared statements at their dictate. . . . It must be the first recorded case of how to hijack a national T.V. network![34]

During his Christmas 1975 kidnapping of the OPEC oil ministers in Vienna, Carlos waited in the OPEC headquarters building with his hostages until the television cameras arrived to record their exit. As per the well-known quip: "Don't shoot, we aren't on prime time yet!"

Terrorists operating in differing scenarios assuredly have varying publicity objectives. However, from a review of recorded atrocities one can distinguish common publicity goals for the majority of terrorist groups, especially those with longer histories of operation. Alexander has summarized that, "relying on immediate and extensive coverage of television, radio, and the press for the maximum amount of propagandizing and publicizing, terrorists . . . enhance the effectiveness of their violence by creating an emotional state of extreme fear in target groups."[35]

O'Sullivan has also identified the benefits terrorists can expect to derive from their exploitation of the media. The media "help the terrorist spread an atmosphere of fear and anxiety . . . provide him with an opportunity to argue his case to the wider public . . . bestow an undeserved legitimacy on him."[36]

There is nothing unique about organized political terrorists' exploitation of the media. Even the most demented perpetrators of violence demonstrate an understanding of the phenomenon. In Indianapolis in 1977, a disgruntled customer affixed a gun to the throat of a mortgage firm manager and forced him in front of the television cameras shouting, "Get those goddamn cameras on! I'm a goddamn national hero!" When the U.S. Secret Service began its interrogation of John Hinckley after he shot President Reagan, he immediately asked, "Is it on TV?" Hinckley later told psychiatrists that he had planned the assassination before news cameras to gain maximum media attention.[37]

As per Schlagheck's listing, the media fulfill the terrorist's desires for many things including: (1) the attention of large audiences to publicize grievances and demands, with the opportunity to recruit members from that audience while increasing popular support, and (2) the opportunity to show the inability of the government to protect its citizens, since it appears weak if it negotiates with terrorists and repressive if it chooses harsh measures.[38]

Concern about terrorist exploitation of the Western media is not confined to government or academic circles. A 1986 Gallup poll in the United States showed that 51 percent of the respondents felt the press gave terrorists too much coverage, 60 percent felt that press coverage increased the chances of future terrorist acts, and 52 percent agreed that terrorist manipulation of the press is a major factor in unsatisfactory press coverage of terrorist events.[39]

THE QUESTION OF MEDIA RESPONSIBILITY

With wide recognition of the terrorists' ability to exploit the media, there are frequent calls for the free press to demonstrate more responsibility. However, there seems to be little agreement as to what constitutes media responsibility. Some call for restraints on the media's coverage of terrorism. Others call for what they term media responsibility during the reporting of terrorism, but few offer a precise description of what that responsibility involves or how it should be exercised.

There are apparently at least two boundaries that attach to media responsibility: (1) refraining from assisting terrorists and (2) informing the public. Between those two boundaries are lively discussions of what the media should and should not do in covering terrorists and their atrocities. For example, Cooper has related the issue of responsibility to the media's depiction of terrorism: "The media certainly does not create the terrorist, but like a skillful make-up artist, can assuredly make of him either a Saint or a Frankenstein's monster. . . . If the media indeed contributes to the terrorist problem, it is not too much to hope that it can also contribute to its solution."[40]

The issue of media responsibility in the coverage of political terrorism can be viewed from three functional categories: (1) refraining from inspiring terrorists, (2) avoiding participation in terrorist atrocities, and (3) avoiding tactical errors while covering atrocities.

The phenomenon of contagion, which is often referenced in the literature, falls within the first category of inspiring terrorists. There are many views of how contagion functions, but the primary thrust is that terrorists, or potential terrorists, are influenced by the media's coverage of other terrorists and they attempt to imitate or emulate them. Those who would doubt the contagion phenomenon should consider journalist Daniel Schorr's notation concerning the attempted assassination of President Reagan by John Hinckley: "As television again and again, remorselessly, hypnotically, played the videotape of the shooting, the

Secret Service recorded an astonishing number of further threats against
the President."[41]

The actual participation of the media in terrorist activities can take
various forms depending upon the motivation of the particular journalist. Edward Epstein has identified one motivational aspect that can
lead to what has been labeled "source dependency": "The problem of
journalism in America proceeds from a simple but inescapable bind:
journalists are rarely, if ever, in a position to establish the truth about
an issue for themselves, and they are therefore almost entirely dependent
on self-interested 'sources' for the version of reality that they report."[42]

For example, in 1969 the Black Panthers alleged that the FBI and the
police were involved in a genocide campaign against their organization.
The media accepted that allegation without challenge, and published
the Black Panthers' claim that twenty-eight of their members had been
killed by law enforcement officials. The extent to which this unverified,
and later proven false, claim was accepted by the public was later demonstrated by respected black leader, Dr. Ralph Abernathy, when he also
accused the United States of genocide.[43] In reality, the number of Black
Panthers killed by police was only two, far less than the ten policemen
that had been killed by the Panthers.[44] While that true fact was known
to reporters who worked closely with the Black Panthers, none of them
rejected the Panthers' allegation as false, likely for fear of losing their
special access to information on Panther activities.

The above form of participation could perhaps be termed "willful
ignorance." The U.S. news media are not unfamiliar with the employment of this tactic to gain special access to materials. During the Vietnam
conflict, members of the press recorded and broadcast for the North
Vietnamese staged Christmas celebrations for U.S. prisoners of war. To
gain access to those "events," members of the news media had to ignore
the North Vietnamese preparation of the U.S. prisoners, which included
beatings and other more severe forms of physical and mental torture,
to ensure that the POWs would "perform" properly at the ceremonies.
This same style of willful ignorance was demonstrated by the media
when they covered the visits of Jane Fonda and Ramsey Clark to North
Vietnam, in preparation for which at least one POW was severely
injured.[45]

The phenomenon of source dependency, and the resultant exploitation of journalists by terrorists, is worldwide. A reporter and photog-
rapher for a leading West German magazine once accompanied Baader-
Meinhof terrorists during the actual perpetration of an atrocity in Hamburg. In England, the public-subsidized BBC, along with Independent
Television (ITV), broadcast a televised interview with a leader of the
IRA in which he announced the intensification of an IRA bombing
campaign. A week later the IRA bombed two pubs in Birmingham,

causing the deaths of twenty-one persons. Cooper likened that involvement by BBC and ITV to the World War II broadcasts by "Lord Haw Haw," William Joyce, who announced the departures of the German bombers for their attacks against British cities.[46] Perhaps not too dissimilar from the BBC's involvement was the publication by the *New York Times* of a lengthy article on the Vietnam conflict by Bernardine Dohrn of the Weathermen while she was on the FBI's most-wanted list.[47]

The third category of media responsibility involves the commission of tactical errors by members of the media during ongoing terrorist atrocities. For example, during a 1974 hostage-barricade situation in Washington, D.C., police were able to monitor the terrorists and their hostages through a two-way mirror. This gave the police the distinct advantages of complete knowledge of what was going on and the capability of employing snipers to protect the hostages if necessary. Unfortunately, members of the media became aware of that situation and broadcast it on the radio. The terrorists heard the broadcast and immediately covered the mirror.[48]

As another example, during the 1977 Hanafi hostage-barricade situation in Washington, D.C., a reporter standing by the side of the building observed a basket being lowered from the fifth floor of the eight-story building. It had previously been reported that all hostages were being held on the eighth floor. The reporter deduced that someone must yet be free and hiding from the terrorists. He immediately broadcast that information on radio. Fortunately, the Hanafis missed the report. Hanafi hostage and *Washington Post* columnist Charles Fenyvesi cites this example as illustrating that "terrorism is a war situation . . . a reporter must take sides and must determine whether he is interested in preserving life and helping hostages, or whether he is interested in getting the scoop."[49]

Later during the Hanafi hostage-barricade situation, members of the media observed the police moving containers into the building. The media broadcast that the police were preparing for an assault. The terrorists heard the broadcast and the lives of the hostages hung in the balance before negotiators could finally convince the Hanafis that the containers were only the food they had demanded.[50]

The category of media tactical errors can be divided into two segments, depending on whether the errors are made at the scene of a terrorist atrocity or in a noncontact situation. The noncontact aspect includes situations wherein the media's dissemination of sensitive information serves the terrorists and possibly endangers the lives of others, whether hostages, potential victims, or law enforcement personnel.

As an example, in a 12 May 1985 story, the *Washington Post* reported that President Reagan had approved a covert program designed to prevent terrorism by preempting terrorist strikes on U.S. targets in the

Middle East through the training and supporting of counterterror groups in the area.[51] One such counterterror group consisting mostly of Lebanese, without U.S. authorization, attempted to kill the Hizballah leader Mohammed Hussein Fadlallah with a car bomb. Fadlallah escaped injury but more than 80 bystanders were killed and 200 injured in the Beirut suburb. While the unauthorized actions of that group were clearly regrettable, it is also clear that the story by the *Washington Post* concerning covert U.S. programs to deal with terrorism in Lebanon put the lives of several U.S. hostages and operatives in grave danger, and could have provided the motivation for other terrorist atrocities that closely followed the attempt on Fadlallah.[52] The vilification of U.S. covert efforts, and the inevitable result, was later deplored by columnist Joseph Kraft: "The intelligence community comes back into the headlines, and into the public pillory. American agents abroad do become subject to retaliation. A major asset of foreign policy is thus weakened, if not rendered inoperative. The loss incurred almost always dwarfs the wrong that was to be righted."[53]

While reviewing the results of the *Washington Post*'s revelations of Reagan's covert initiative, Livingstone and Arnold observed that, "If one examines the popular media, it is easy to get the impression that the real threat comes from the governments grappling with the complex threat posed by terrorism rather than from the terrorists."[54]

In sum, the question of media responsibility involves inspiring terrorists to commit atrocities and encouraging violence-prone individuals to become terrorists. It also involves media association with terrorists as sources of information. Further, tactical errors by the media can endanger the lives of hostages, potential victims, and others. To more fully comprehend how such situations can develop, consider Miller's description of the media's motivation in the coverage of terrorism:

Terrorist episodes, especially hostage situations, are made of the stuff that sells copy. They are dramatic and violent, and life hangs in the balance. The pendulum of decision making swings back and forth: demand, counterdemand, give and take. There is the human interest element, the anxiety-ridden relatives waiting for fate to make its move. Whose loved ones will survive and whose will perish? In such situations there is pressure for a scoop, for some new angle, for an exclusive interview with the perpetrators. The journalistic rewards are great, and these sometimes take precedence over common sense and concern for the life and welfare of the victims.[55]

THE MYTH OF A SYMBIOTIC RELATIONSHIP

The media's performance during such crises as the November 1979 seizure of the American embassy in Tehran or the June 1985 hijacking of TWA Flight 847 has prompted numerous academicians, journalists, and government officials to declare that a state of symbiosis exists between the media and terrorists. There are numerous descriptions of this reportedly mutually beneficial relationship. As observed by Miller: "Terrorism is dependent on publicity. . . . Terrorists need public attention, newspeople need news."[56]

For a state of symbiosis to exist between dissimilar organisms both must derive advantages. This mutually advantageous association distinguishes symbiosis from parasitism. To evaluate the relationship between the media and terrorists, their environments and organic functions must be considered.

A free press operating in the marketplace of a liberal democratic society must make a profit to survive. This profitability factor applies on an individual basis to the numerous firms comprising the media of a democracy and is of overriding importance to each of them in the short term. Terrorist atrocities, an attractive source of sensational coverage, sell the news and provide these crucial short-term profits. However, the long-term principal concern of the media as a whole is the survival of their host society. Without the personal freedoms guaranteed by liberal democratic laws, none of the individual firms could operate and the free press would cease to exist.

Political terrorists targeting the governments and citizens of liberal democratic societies seek the destruction of those societies. As explained in previous chapters, media coverage can be a powerful force in creating the environment of fear critical to terrorist achievement of that goal. Individual firms of a free press gain the advantage of profitability and economic survival by sensationalizing terrorist atrocities, and their coverage also contributes to terrorist success. Unfortunately, continued terrorist success, enhanced by media coverage, leads to the ultimate goal of the political terrorist—the destruction of the target society. In the short term, both the terrorists and individual media firms gain advantages, but in the long run, when the terrorists gain their ultimate political goal, the free press, as part of the host society, is destroyed as well. The short-term symbiotic relationship has run its course and the true long-term parasitic nature is revealed.

Almost without exception, the literature's numerous illustrations of the alleged symbiotic relationship are limited to the near term. None extend their investigation into the long term. Such an investigation of the demise of democracy in Uruguay demonstrates that, when nurtured by the media, a terrorist campaign can indeed result in the destruction of the host democratic society and its free press along with it. The originators of the Uruguayan Tupamaros terrorist campaign were intellectuals with a demonstrated appreciation for the value of publicity. They skillfully exploited the Uruguayan and international media. The press initially viewed the Tupamaros sympathetically and contributed to an environment within which the Tupamaros could expand their operations while becoming more effective. As the Tupamaros intensified their violent opposition to the duly-elected government, media coverage of their atrocities contributed to the creation of an atmosphere of fear. Government authorities responded with counterterror policies that increasingly repressed individual rights. Loss of individual freedoms brought a loss of popular support for the government and, in the chaos of fear and repression, a military coup succeeded. The formerly democratic government was ousted by an authoritarian military regime under which democracy and the free press both disappeared. The Tupamaros had achieved an ultimate terrorist goal of destroying the target society. Unfortunately for the Tupamaros, the military regime later demonstrated that political terrorists opposed to a powerful authoritarian government will not long survive.[57]

Miller has also warned of the eventual demise of a democratic society's media when intensive coverage of atrocities provides continued support to terrorists. Choices must be made "between the media's right to disseminate information and a society's right to exist."[58] The often-declared symbiotic relationship between the media and terrorists, when viewed in its entirety, is a myth. The correct label for that relationship is parasitic, not symbiotic.

NOTES

1. National Advisory Committee on Criminal Justice Standards and Goals, *Disorders and Terrorism: Report of the Task Force on Disorders and Terrorism* (Washington, D.C.: Law Enforcement Assistance Administration, 1976); quoted in Abraham Miller, "Terrorism, the Media, and Law Enforcement: An Introduction and Overview," in *Terrorism, the Media, and the Law*, ed. Abraham Miller (Dobbs Ferry, N.Y.: Transnational Publishers, 1982), 4.

2. Miller, "Terrorism, the Media, and Law Enforcement: An Introduction and Overview," 4–5.

3. For example, the murder of 24 schoolchildren by terrorists, and the killing of 20 innocent bystanders by a terrorist car bomb, were labeled "acts" by a professor of political science in Baljit Singh, "An Overview," *Terrorism: Interdisciplinary Perspectives*, eds. Yonah Alexander and Seymour Maxwell Finger (New York: John Jay Press, 1977), 10. Further, the terrorist murder of those 24 schoolchildren and the Entebbe hijacking were referred to as "situations" by an award-winning U.S. political scientist in Abraham Miller, *Terrorism and Hostage Negotiations* (Boulder: Westview Press, 1980), 32.

4. Nicholas Ashford, quoted in *Terrorism and the Media in the 1980's*, eds. Sarah Midgley and Virginia Rice (Washington, D.C.: The Media Institute, 1984), 57.

5. David Williamson, "Terrorism—What Should We Do." in *Terrorism, The Reference Shelf*, ed. Steven Anzovin, vol. 58, no. 3 (New York: H. W. Wilson, 1986), 173.

6. Thomas Friedman, "The Power of the Fanatics," *New York Times Magazine*, 7 October 1984, 68–69.

7. Ibid., 54.

8. Poll cited in ibid.

9. Paul Lazarsfeld and Robert Merton, "Mass Communication, Popular Taste, and Organized Social Action," *The Processes and Effects of Mass Communication*, eds. Wilbur Schramm and Donald Roberts, 2d ed. (Urbana: University of Illinois Press, 1971), 560.

10. John O'Sullivan, "Terrorism and the Media: A Discussion," in *Terrorism, The Reference Shelf*, ed. Steven Anzovin, vol. 58, no. 3 (New York: H. W. Wilson, 1986), 100.

11. Brian Crozier, in U.S. Congress, Senate Subcommittee to Investigate the Administration of the Security Act and Other Internal Security Laws of the Commission on the Judiciary, *Hearings on Terroristic Activity: International Terrorism* (Washington, D.C.: GPO, 1975), 189; quoted in H.H.A. Cooper, "Terrorism and the Media," in *Terrorism: Interdisciplinary Perspectives*, eds. Yonah Alexander and Seymour Maxwell Finger (New York: John Jay Press, 1977), 146.

12. William Perdue, *Terrorism and the State* (New York: Praeger, 1989), 48.

13. Cooper, "Terrorism and the Media," 148.

14. Ibid., 149.

15. Ali Birand, quoted in *Terrorism and the Media in the 1980's*, eds. Sarah Midgley and Virginia Rice (Washington, D.C.: The Media Institute, 1984), 45–46.

16. John Wolf, *Antiterrorist Initiatives* (New York: Plenum Press, 1989), 41.

17. Drawn from ibid.

18. Harold Lasswell, "The Structure and Function of Communication in Society," in *The Communication of Ideas*, ed. Lyman Bryson (New York: Cooper Square, 1964), 37.

19. Alfred Lee and Elizabeth Lee, "The Tricks of the Trade," in *The Fine Art of Propaganda: A Study of Father Coughlin's Speeches*, eds. Alfred Lee and Elizabeth Lee (New York: Harcourt, Brace, 1939), 23–24.

20. Wolf, *Antiterrorist Initiatives*, 43.

21. Samuel Hayakawa, *Language in Thought and Action* (New York: Harcourt, Brace, Jovanovich, 1972), 152–53.

22. Drawn from Bernard Johnpoll, "Terrorism and the Mass Media in the United States," in *Terrorism: Interdisciplinary Perspectives*, eds. Yonah Alexander and Seymour Maxwell Finger (New York: John Jay Press, 1977), 158–59.

23. Reuven Frank, in Frederic Hill, "Media Diplomacy," *Washington Journalism Review* (May 1981): 27; quoted in Neil Livingstone, "Terrorism and the Media Revolution," in *Fighting Back: Winning the War against Terrorism*, eds. Neil Livingstone and Terrell Arnold (Lexington, Mass.: D. C. Heath, 1986), 218.

24. Robert Friedlander, "Coping with Terrorism," in *Terrorism: Theory and Practice*, eds. Yonah Alexander, David Carlton, and Paul Wilkinson (Boulder: Westview Press, 1979), 236.

25. Daniel Schorr, "The Encouragement of Violence," in *Terrorism: How the West Can Win*, ed. Benjamin Netanyahu (New York: Farrar, Straus, Giroux, 1986), 116.

26. Harry Waters, "Gomorrah Revisited," *Newsweek* 87, no. 14 (5 April 1976): 61.

27. Carlos Marighella, *Manual of the Urban Guerrilla*, trans. Gene Hanrahan (Chapel Hill, N.C.: Documentary Publications, 1985), 84–85. For a similar discussion see Jerry Rubin, *Do It!* (New York: Simon and Schuster, 1970).

28. Roland Gaucher, *Les Terrorists* (Paris: Editions Albin Michel, 1965), 262; cited in Miller, *Terrorism and Hostage Negotiations*, 83.

29. George Habash, quoted in Oriana Fallaci, "A Leader of the Fedayeen: 'We Want a War Like the Vietnam War' ", in *Life* 68, no. 22 (22 June 1970): 33.

30. Miller, *Terrorism and Hostage Negotiations*, 82–83.

31. Abraham Miller, "Negotiations for Hostages: Implications from the Police Experience," in *Terrorism: An International Journal* 1, no. 2 (1978).

32. Hillel Nossek, "The Impact of Mass Media on Terrorists, Supporters, and the Public at Large," in *On Terrorism and Combating Terrorism*, ed. Ariel Merari (Frederick, Md.: University Publications of America, 1985), 87.

33. Drawn from ibid., 87–88.

34. Melvin Lasky, "Ulrike Meinhof and the Baader-Meinhof Gang," *Encounter* 44, no. 6 (June 1975): 15–16.

35. Yonah Alexander, "Terrorism and the Media: Some Considerations," in *Terrorism: Theory and Practice*, eds. Yonah Alexander, David Carlton, and Paul Wilkinson (Boulder: Westview Press, 1979), 160.

36. John O'Sullivan, "Deny Them Publicity," in *Terrorism: How the West Can Win*, ed. Benjamin Netanyahu (New York: Farrar, Straus, Giroux, 1986), 120–21.

37. Drawn from Schorr, "The Encouragement of Violence," 115.

38. Donna Schlagheck, *International Terrorism: An Introduction to the Concepts and Actors* (Lexington, Mass.: Lexington Books, 1988), 70.

39. Poll reported in "The People and the Press," *Times Mirror* (Los Angeles), 20 October 1986, 11–12; cited in Schlagheck, *International Terrorism*, 70.

40. Cooper, "Terrorism and the Media," 154.

41. Schorr, "The Encouragement of Violence," 115.

42. Edward Epstein, *Between Fact and Fiction: The Problem of Journalism* (New York: Vintage Books, 1975), 3.

43. Ibid., 33–35.

44. Eugene Methvin, *The Rise of Radicalism: The Social Psychology of Messianic Extremism* (New Rochelle, N.Y.: Arlington House, 1973), 511.

45. For example, the hardships suffered by captured U.S. naval aviator Lieutenant Commander Al Stafford.

46. Cooper, "Terrorism and the Media," 147.

47. Ibid.

48. As reported in Abraham Miller, "Terrorism, the Media, and the Law: A Discussion of the Issues," in *Terrorism, the Media, and the Law*, ed. Abraham Miller (Dobbs Ferry, N.Y.: Transnational Publishers, 1982), 30.

49. Charles Fenyvesi, quoted in *Terrorism and the Media in the 1980's*, eds. Sarah Midgley and Virginia Rice (Washington, D.C.: The Media Institute, 1984), 13.

50. Miller, *Terrorism and Hostage Negotiations*, 87.

51. Bob Woodward and Charles Babcock, "Antiterrorism Plan Rescinded after Unauthorized Bombing," *Washington Post*, 12 May 1985, A1, A26.

52. Drawn from Neil Livingstone and Terrell Arnold, "Democracy under Attack," in *Fighting Back: Winning the War against Terrorism*, eds. Neil Livingstone and Terrell Arnold (Lexington, Mass.: D. C. Heath, 1986), 6.

53. Joseph Kraft, "The CIA in Trouble," *Washington Post*, 16 May 1985, A23.

54. Livingstone and Arnold, "Democracy under Attack," 7.

55. Miller, *Terrorism and Hostage Negotiations*, 86.

56. Abraham Miller, "Foreword," in *Terrorism, the Media, and the Law*, ed. Abraham Miller (Dobbs Ferry, N.Y.: Transnational Publishers, 1982), v, vi.

57. For further details on the Tupamaros, see, for example, Arturo Prozecanski, *Uruguay's Tupamaros: The Urban Guerrilla* (New York: Praeger Publishers, 1973).

58. Miller, "Foreword," vi.

7

Recent Analyses and Current Limitations on the Quantitative Examination of Political Terrorism

Prior to attempting to quantify the relationship between media coverage and terrorist success, one is well advised to consider previous efforts. The following examination of some of those efforts begins with a review of general approaches to the study of terrorism, and proceeds to a brief discussion of quantitative analyses in the current literature. Concentration is on the difficulties encountered in the accumulation of data bases and the operationalization of key concepts.

APPROACHES TO THE STUDY AND ANALYSIS OF TERRORISM

When considering an approach to the study of terrorism, it is useful to compare studies of terrorism with studies of political violence in general. The various approaches used show considerable similarity, with investigations of cause and effect dominating. However, with the strong emergence of international terrorism, there has been a trend toward studying terrorism from the aspect of developing antiterrorism policies for democratic societies. For example, Russell, Banker, and Miller have identified three approaches that could lead to the construction of a knowledge base for the analysis of alternative antiterrorism policies: (1) traditional analytical, (2) speculative, and (3) crisis management.[1] The traditional analytical approach evaluates known terrorist capabilities and forecasts their possible intentions by utilizing accumulated data. The speculative approach evaluates possible terrorist targets and projects future terrorist motivations and capabilities. The crisis management approach investigates those areas of political terrorism wherein information must be accumulated and disseminated to decision makers.

It seems that a considerable base of knowledge, constructed along the lines recognized by Russell, Banker, and Miller, can well serve the needs of a democratic society confronted by the threat of political terrorism. Unfortunately, the literature shows a clear deficiency in the pragmatic analytical approach, with a concentration on the speculative. The lack of acceptable data bases has obviously limited both the analytical and crisis management approaches.

In a 1973 review of major publications directed toward the analysis of terrorism, Bell noted three schools of analysis: (1) focus on a specific campaign, (2) explanation of the phenomenon and preparation of responses, and (3) application of quantitative and other analytical tools.[2]

The study of terrorism has followed a pattern not dissimilar to that found in the political science discipline. The concentration on a specific terrorist campaign approaches the historical-traditional methodology that was prevalent before the 1960s and was predominantly descriptive in nature. Attempts to explain the phenomenon correspond with the behavioral movement of the mid–1960s, which was "concerned with what man does politically and the meanings he attaches to his behavior."[3] The application of quantitative techniques in the investigation of political terrorism corresponds with the employment of similar techniques in the general field of political science that gained prominence during the behavioral revolution and remains important in the postbehavioral era, where the emphasis is on future orientation, relevance, and action.[4]

It seems that a synthesis of all three study approaches can prove valuable to the analysis of political terrorism. Historical observations can constitute an important factor in the formation of data bases, which are currently comparatively sparse. The employment of behavioral techniques can contribute to the construction of a general paradigm, through which both the accumulation of knowledge and the development of a general theory of political terrorism might be accelerated. With the development of a general theory, broadening of the knowledge base, and accumulation of data bases, more precise quantitative measurements of the phenomenon of political terrorism might become more abundant.

THE LIMITATION OF THE MYTH OF RANDOMNESS

The sparsity of quantitative analyses of political terrorism that currently exists can be attributed in part to what Mickolus has referred to as "the myth of terrorist randomness":

Political terrorism can be characterized as a plethora of random attacks by groups who are not subject to the norms of human behavior in a law-abiding society.

Their great strength is their unpredictability, and the totally indiscriminate nature of their actions. Whereas the methods of societal science have proven useful in a number of areas, the activities of terrorists follow no patterns which can be systematically analyzed. In addition to eluding police authorities, terrorists have successfully eluded rigorous investigation by talented academic researchers.[5]

A review of the literature shows that the randomness of political terrorism that Mickolus has described (and labeled a myth) has unfortunately been accepted as a fact by some political scientists. In the face of what some have considered to be an unpredictable phenomenon, scholars have avoided the derivation of a paradigm through which to investigate contemporary international terrorism. As earlier cited, the lack of a universal definition of terrorism has also constrained the emergence of quantitative techniques to examine political terrorism. The lack of a generally accepted definition, and of a paradigm, have obviously contributed to the paucity of a cumulative knowledge base for the study of political terrorism.

Political scientists are not solely responsible for this situation. Governments have tended to classify details of terrorist activities, making them unavailable for general academic review. The media have tended to dramatize and sensationalize terrorist atrocities to the exclusion of factual information. Both actions are seemingly justified: the government's need to safeguard information dealing with national security and the media's need to make a profit. Unfortunately, the result has been a compilation of information on terrorist atrocities and activities that is often incomplete and lacking in meaningful detail. Without a full and complete historical knowledge base, the study of terrorism will remain a mosaic of opinions.

QUANTITATIVE INVESTIGATIONS OF TERRORISTS AND THEIR ATROCITIES

There are, however, some sources of data that are being developed in an effort to make the study of terrorism more scientifically sound. While contributing to the falsifying of the hypothesis that terrorist attacks are necessarily random, Mickolus's *International Terrorism: Attributes of Terrorist Events (ITERATE)* project at Yale is one such attempt to document observations of terrorist phenomena. Utilizing the Rand chronology of 539 terrorist atrocities from 1968–1974,[6] Mickolus's data set employs 107 descriptors of the atrocities to form a central data pool. The characteristics of terrorist atrocities that can be summarized from this pool include the type of attack and its location, the identity and nationality of the perpetrators and victims, the targets of terrorist demands and the nature of those demands, and the results of the attack.[7]

If Mickolus's ITERATE can be constructed so as to lend itself to continual updating of the data base, and if the input is reliable and complete, then indeed such an effort can support his contention that ITERATE serves as a source of research in "summarizing trends, comparing terrorist campaigns cross-nationally and over time, and evaluating policy prescriptions for crisis management and incident negotiation support."[8]

At the Rand Corporation, Brian Jenkins and his associates have published widely recognized basic research on terrorism, with chronologies of international terrorist atrocities, bibliographies, and systematic typologies of groups and atrocities, that could be useful in further scientific studies.[9] Also at Rand, Anderson and Gillogly, in conjunction with Jenkins's studies, have focused on the creation of a computerized artificial intelligence model that could possibly serve in the analysis of terrorist atrocities. Comparing data from a current atrocity to a base of previous data, the model would derive conclusions about the perpetrator's probable behavior during the atrocity.[10]

Not all of the limited attempts at the quantitative analysis of terrorism have been restricted to the observation of trends. In a study at Ketron Corporation, Ric Blacksten has employed game theory, decision trees, and payoff matrices to analyze kidnappings and hijackings. He derived utility values for the terrorists from the various alternatives available to them, and also computed utility values for the government decision makers from the policy options that were open to them.[11]

In a paper for the Conference on International Terrorism at the U.S. State Department in March 1976, Gurr statistically surveyed atrocities and campaigns of domestic terrorism in eighty-seven countries from 1961 to 1970.[12] His research concentrated on the motivation of terrorists.

Utilizing content analysis, Ernest Evans surveyed the debates of the Legal Committee of the U.N. General Assembly during its review of the 1972 U.S.–sponsored convention on international terrorism. He isolated four basic orientations of the delegations that provided insight into the defeat of the U.S. effort.[13]

William Avery has examined the relationship between terrorist political violence and the international transfer of conventional armaments.[14] Accumulating data on acts of violence from Taylor and Hudson,[15] and Banks,[16] and conventional arms-transfer data from U.S. Arms Control and Disarmament Agency estimates, Avery used product-moment correlation (Pearson's r) to test the degree of bivariate association, by geographical region, between violence variables and arms imports over a five-year period. His procedure allowed for a "time lag" to account for response times between terrorist acts and arms deliveries.[17] His bivariate analysis findings showed that arms transfers to African states, after a time lag of one to three years, are strongly influenced by all of the violence variables he employed. For Asia, all violence variables with the exception of riots showed a significant relationship to arms transfers, with the relationship strongest after a four-year lag. For Europe and the Middle East, deaths by political violence showed the strongest relationship to arms transfers, with a two-year time lag involved for the Middle East. Transfer of arms to Latin America was apparently related only to riots, and then after a three-year time lag.[18]

Aggregating the violence variables across nations, Avery employed multiple regression analysis to show that armed attacks had the greatest impact on arms imports. Only two other violence variables—riots and guerrilla warfare—made significant contributions to the explanation of arms transfers. Avery noted that difficulties involved in operationalizing terrorism included the determination of which acts of political violence are, in fact, terroristic in nature. The data collections that he used did not specifically distinguish between terrorist acts and other acts of political violence. The political violence variables that he determined as more closely related with terrorism were armed attack, deaths from political violence, assassination, guerrilla warfare, and riots.[19] Avery's definition of terrorism is apparently considerably more general than that developed earlier in this analysis.

Steve Wright employed a multivariate time series analysis to study the Northern Ireland conflict from 1969 to 1976. In preparation for his analysis, he noted that approaches to the study of substate violence invariably include "a range of inherent assumptions that exclude from consideration certain forms of information produced by the conflict."[20] Noting that it was perhaps impossible for any researcher of political violence to avoid the accusation of bias when simple and objective criteria for making an interpretation of the source of the violence rarely exist, Wright cautioned that one must "assume that the mode of analysis chosen to clarify the dynamics of a conflict will limit in many ways the forms of explanation and understanding that emerge from it."[21]

Through survey research, Gregory Winn investigated the factors underlying student rejection of German society. His quantitative analysis was directed toward exploring some of the causes of terrorism in the Federal Republic of Germany by focusing on the degree and form of alienation experienced by German university students.[22]

In other quantitative analytical efforts in the study of terrorism, Lawrence Hamilton explored the dynamics of insurgent violence,[23] John Gleason demonstrated the use of the Poisson model in examining the occurrence of terrorist atrocities in the Third World,[24] and Edward Heyman and Mickolus explored new analytical techniques for understanding how and why terrorism diffuses in the international system.[25]

Through a review of the foregoing quantitative efforts, one can distinguish the common problem of the lack of a universal concept for political terrorism. The data used to measure terrorism frequently involved forms of political violence that do not conform to a rigorous definition of terroristic violence. That basic difficulty can lead to employment of data bases that yield variables lacking construct validity and thereby weaken the analysis.

JURISDICTIONAL AND ESTIMATION BIAS IN DATA BASES

Two significant problems confront the analyst who undertakes a quantitative assessment of political terrorism: (1) the lack of an agreed-upon definition, and (2) the deleterious effects of that lack of agreement upon the accumulation of usable data.

Data bases accumulated for quantitative analysis of terrorism apparently vary according to jurisdiction. For example, in the United States, FBI statistics are concerned only with domestic terrorism while the Defense Department and other federal agencies must, by law, exclude domestic political violence. The data accumulated by specialized agencies also naturally reflect their specific functions. Without some process of standardization, the cross-functional utilization of such data would cause analytical disruptions and inaccuracies.

Data bases for terrorism are also beset with problems of estimation. For example, Risk International records only those atrocities it deems significant. For psychological and political reasons, governments may intentionally underestimate the level of terrorist activity in their countries. Estimation problems are also obviously involved in the assessment of whether atrocities were committed by terrorists with political motives, criminals with personal motives, or psychopaths. Further, when single-source data (e.g., U.S. newspapers) or specific-genre data (e.g., state documents) are used to assemble a data base for terrorist incidents, there can exist significant estimation bias in the recorded description of the events.

Jurisdictional biases could readily be recognized and compensation is perhaps possible. However, estimation bias stems from the lack of a universal definition of terrorism and standardization of such data would likely prove insurmountable. As demonstrated in the previously cited quantitative analysis by Avery, the estimation bias of what acts of political violence to consider as terroristic can dominate the composition of a data base.

Recognizing the biases in reporting terrorist statistics that come from jurisdictions or estimations, Jenkins has cautioned against using such data to measure levels of terrorism. Rather, he regards those statistics as useful indicators in determining where to proceed with an investigation of terrorism.[26] Rather than attempt to quantify terrorism directly,

Jenkins would evaluate the factors involved in the occurrence of terrorism. His factors include: (1) the mobility and weaponry available to terrorists, (2) the technological vulnerabilities of modern societies, (3) the effectiveness of government countermeasures, (4) the sponsorship and support of some nations for political terrorism, and (5) the publicity provided by the media.[27]

IDENTIFYING THE VARIABLES FOR A QUANTITATIVE ANALYSIS OF TERRORISM

While problems of jurisdiction and estimation may severely limit the usefulness of the end product, some efforts to compile data have proved important in identifying the variables involved in the description, explanation, and prediction of terrorism. When building his data set for ITERATE, Mickolus tested his variables against the Rand Corporation's chronology of international terrorist atrocities occurring between 1968 and 1974. These included terrorist, victim, and target characteristics; casualties and damage; demand and negotiation characteristics; and victim and terrorist fate.[28]

Mickolus's variables share two very important characteristics: (1) they are for the most part empirically observable and measurable, and (2) they are objective by nature and not easily disturbed by jurisdictional or estimation biases. These variables are, however, not all immune to temporal limitations that could lessen their validity and usefulness. This seems to apply when measuring responses to such general demands by terrorists as a change in foreign policy. It indeed seems difficult to measure any concessions to a demand in the general area of political change, since the rhetoric of the target government may differ sharply with its demonstrated policy. Such attempted measures could involve a period of several years and could pose significant problems in constructing a data base. Further, governments might choose to make secret arrangements concerning terrorist demands that never become known, hence even the most carefully constructed data base might lack credibility.

SUMMARY

The literature shows a paucity of quantitative analyses of political terrorism. The lack of a universal definition for terrorism, which would separate its characteristics from those of other forms of political violence, has worked against attempts for both the formulation of a paradigm through which to investigate empirically the phenomenon of political terrorism and the accumulation of a data base free of estimation bias. Existing data bases also occasionally demonstrate jurisdictional bias, which limits the quantitative analysis of terrorism, although that limitation is not so severe as that imposed by estimation bias.

While the aforementioned problems pose difficulties, they need not prevent the development of quantitative analyses of terrorism. The challenge is to follow the generally accepted rules of quantitative analysis while making special provisions for those problems. The analyst must (1) clearly state the definition of political terrorism employed in the analysis, and apply that definition consistently throughout the analysis; and (2) use cross-references and considerable care in deriving a data base to provide the highest level of accuracy obtainable, while clearly stating the limitations of the data and keeping the analysis within those limitations.

NOTES

1. Charles Russell, Leon Banker, and Bowman Miller, "Out-Inventing the Terrorist," in *Terrorism: Theory and Practice*, eds. Yonah Alexander, David Carlton, and Paul Wilkinson (Boulder: Westview Press, 1979), 3–4.

2. For further consideration of J. Bowyer Bell's interpretation of approaches to the study of terrorism, see for example, J. Bowyer Bell, "Guerrilla Analysis: Present Directions," *Military Affairs* 37, no. 4 (December 1973): 155–57.

3. Heinz Eulau, *The Behavior Persuasion in Politics* (New York: Random House, 1963), 5.

4. For a comparative demonstration of approaches to the study of politics see, for example, Ronald Chilcote, *Theories of Comparative Politics: The Search for a Paradigm* (Boulder: Westview Press, 1981), 57.

5. Edward Mickolus, "Statistical Approaches to the Study of Terrorism," in *Terrorism: Interdisciplinary Perspectives*, eds. Yonah Alexander and Seymour Maxwell Finger (New York: John Jay Press, 1977), 209.

6. Brian Jenkins and Janera Johnson, *International Terrorism: A Chronology, 1968–1974* (Santa Monica: Rand Corporation, R–1597-DOS/ARPA, March 1975); cited in Edward Mickolus and Edward Heyman, "Iterate: Monitoring Transnational Terrorism," in *Behavioral and Quantitative Perspectives on Terrorism*, eds. Yonah Alexander and John Gleason (New York: Pergamon Press, 1981), 161.

7. Mickolus, "Statistical Approaches to the Study of Terrorism," 211.

8. Ibid.

9. See, for example, Jenkins and Johnson, *International Terrorism: A Chronology, 1968–1974*.

10. Anderson and Gillogly, *Rand Intelligent Terminal Agent (R.I.T.A.): Design Philosophy*.

11. Ric Blacksten, "Appendix: Hostage Games," in Ric Blacksten and Richard Engler, *Ketron Concept Paper: Hostage Studies* (Arlington, Va.: Ketron, 8 January 1974); cited in Mickolus, "Statistical Approaches to the Study of Terrorism," 254.

12. Ted Robert Gurr, "Some Characteristics of Contemporary Political Ter-

rorism," paper delivered to the Conference on International Terrorism sponsored by the U.S. Department of State, Washington, D.C., March 25–26, 1976; cited in Neil Livingstone and Terrell Arnold, "The Rise of State-Sponsored Terrorism," in *Fighting Back: Winning the War against Terrorism*, eds. Neil Livingstone and Terrell Arnold (Lexington, Mass.: D. C. Heath, 1986), 12.

13. Ernest Evans, "American Policy Response to International Terrorism," paper delivered to the Conference on Terrorism in the Contemporary World, at Glassboro State College, New Jersey, April 26–28, 1976; cited in Marius Livingston, ed., *International Terrorism in the Contemporary World* (Westport, Conn.: Greenwood Press, 1978), 376–85.

14. William Avery, "Terrorism, Violence, and the International Transfer of Conventional Armaments," in *Behavioral and Quantitative Perspectives on Terrorism*, eds. Yonah Alexander and John Gleason (New York: Pergamon Press, 1981), 329–39.

15. Charles Taylor and Michael Hudson, *World Handbook of Political and Social Indicators* II (New Haven, Conn.: Yale University Press, 1972).

16. Arthur Banks, *Cross-Polity Time-Series Data* (Cambridge, Mass.: MIT Press, 1971).

17. William Avery, "Terrorism, Violence, and the International Transfer of Conventional Armaments," 333.

18. Ibid., 334.

19. Ibid., 331.

20. Steve Wright, "A Multivariate Time Series Analysis of the Northern Irish Conflict 1969–76," in *Behavioral and Quantitative Perspectives on Terrorism*, eds. Yonah Alexander and John Gleason (New York: Pergamon Press, 1981), 283.

21. Ibid.

22. Gregory Winn, "Terrorism, Alienation, and German Society," in *Behavioral and Quantitative Perspectives on Terrorism*, eds. Yonah Alexander and John Gleason (New York: Pergamon Press, 1981), 256–82.

23. Lawrence Hamilton, "Dynamics of Insurgent Violence: Preliminary Findings," in *Behavioral and Quantitative Perspectives on Terrorism*, eds. Yonah Alexander and John Gleason (New York: Pergamon Press, 1981), 229–41.

24. John Gleason, "Third World Terrorism: Perspectives for Quantitative Research," in *Behavioral and Quantitative Perspectives on Terrorism*, eds. Yonah Alexander and John Gleason (New York: Pergamon Press, 1981), 242–55.

25. Edward Heyman and Edward Mickolus, "Imitation by Terrorists: Quantitative Approaches to the Study of Diffusion Patterns in Transnational Terrorism," in *Behavioral and Quantitative Perspectives on Terrorism*, eds. Yonah Alexander and John Gleason (New York: Pergamon Press, 1981), 175–228.

26. Brian Jenkins, "Terrorism Prone Countries and Conditions," in *On Terrorism and Combating Terrorism*, ed. Ariel Merari (Frederick, Md.: University Publications of America, 1985), 33.

27. Brian Jenkins, "Statements about Terrorism," in *Annals of American Academy of Political and Social Science* 463 (September 1982): 14.

28. Edward Mickolus and Edward Heyman, "Iterate: Monitoring Transnational Terrorism," in *Behavioral and Quantitative Perspectives on Terrorism*, eds. Yonah Alexander and John Gleason (New York: Pergamon Press, 1981), 154.

8

A Quantitative Analysis of the Relationship Between the Media and Terrorism

This chapter presents an empirical analysis of the relationship between the amount of coverage given by Western news media to international terrorists and their atrocities and the success achieved by the terrorists in obtaining concessions.

THE METHODOLOGY EMPLOYED

To accomplish the purpose of this analysis, the following methodology was pursued:

1. A definition was derived for international political terrorism and the analysis proceeded within that framework.
2. The operationalization of the concept of terrorist atrocities began with the selection of a category of atrocities to be analyzed.
3. Temporal limits were established for the consideration of the selected category of atrocities.
4. The operationalization of the concept of terrorist atrocities continued with the identification of pertinent variables and the accumulation of applicable empirical data, at the required level of detail, thereby providing the necessary information on the selected category of atrocities within the temporal limits.
5. Media sources were selected to provide a cross section of the Western news media's coverage of the atrocities that formed the data base.
6. The concept of news media coverage was operationalized by identifying the pertinent variables involved in the reporting of terrorist atrocities by the

selected media source. By employing direct quantitative observation of those variables, with a limited amount of content analysis, the media sources' coverage of the terrorist atrocities was adequately measured.

7. Bivariate analytical methods, employed to investigate the relationship between the media coverage and the success of the terrorists in obtaining their demands, included comparative tabulations, contingency tables, regression, and Probit analysis.

The Definition of Terrorism

The definition of political terrorism derived earlier was applied throughout the analysis: The perpetration of a unique form of violence against symbolic targets to maximize publicity for the attainment of political goals. The issues of a unique form of violence, symbolic targets, and political goals were previously discussed. Bassiouni's guidance for considering the international aspect of political terrorism, as those incidents that are not limited to the internal affairs of individual states, was also consistently applied throughout the analysis.[1]

The Selection of a Category of Terrorist Atrocities

A scientific approach to any large problem frequently involves its separation into smaller segments for analysis. That approach was pursued to develop this quantitative analysis of the value of media coverage to terrorists. Robert Kupperman and Darrell Trent offer a starting point for such an analytical effort with their morphology of terrorism, which provides the structure for a comparison of different terrorist groups and atrocities in local and global environments.[2] Of particular interest is their typology of terrorist atrocities: kidnapping; barricade and hostage; bombing; armed assault or ambush; hijacking; incendiary attack or arson; assassination or murder; and chemical, bacterial, or radiological pollution. This categorizing of terrorist atrocities, with further examination and application, allows the analysis of the value of media coverage in empirical rather than intangible terms.

The task was to select that category from which the most precise empirical measurements could be obtained. The categories of kidnapping, barricade and hostage, and hijacking almost always involve tangible demands. Ransom, political asylum, safe conduct, and the release of prisoners are examples. The atrocity categories of bombing, armed assault or ambush, incendiary attack or arson, assassination or murder, and chemical, bacteriological, or radiological pollution are all events that generally have publicity as a primary, and sometimes the only, terrorist goal. Since the quality and quantity of publicity required to fulfill terrorist strategic publicity goals is difficult—or perhaps impossible—to empirically determine, those categories of atrocities would be invalid for quantitative analytical purposes. For example, it might be empirically impossible to measure the contribution media publicity made to a terrorist bombing campaign such as the Corsican separatists waged against France. The demands made by those terrorists were usually very general, and the French government's response was equally difficult to ascertain. Such a category of atrocities could not furnish the necessary empirical data required to make a meaningful analysis.

As a minimum, the selected category has to allow empirical determination of terrorist demands and the target government's granting or denial of those demands. The media coverage given to a specific atrocity has to be measurable, which means that the atrocity has to be within temporal limits. A beginning and an end to the atrocity has to be clearly established, during which time frame the commission of the atrocity with coverage by the media, the making of terrorist demands, and the granting or denial of those demands by the target government all has to occur. Bombing campaigns and murders do not fulfill these specifications, nor do kidnappings where the victims might be held for several years. As demonstrated in Lebanon, terrorist kidnappers operating in a benign environment have demonstrated a minimum degree of motivation to enforce deadlines for the meeting of their demands. Indeed, the longer the kidnapping atrocity can be extended, the greater the terrorist access to the media. Kidnapping, rigorously defined, involves the movement of the victims to a location that is relatively safe for the terrorists. Since the terrorists themselves are in no danger, their tangible demands such as ransom are normally secondary to their intangible objective of publicity. Therefore, without temporal constraints and with continuing publicity a primary goal, the measurement of concessions to terrorist kidnapping demands, becomes too vague for quantification.

Fortunately, what is perhaps the most dominant of all terrorist atrocities adequately fulfills all the specifications for quantification. When a terrorist atrocity involves the seizing of hostages and the establishing of a barricade by the terrorists, wherein they hold the hostages and make demands upon the target government, that category of atrocity is perfectly suited to empirical investigation and analysis. "Hostage-taking" or "barricade and hostage" atrocities—performed in buildings or on hijacked airplanes or trains—are frequently the focus of study. Netanyahu describes barricade and hostage as the classic terrorist act because it reveals the basic characteristics of terrorism: "It is an unmistakably deliberate assault on the people who are seized, precisely because they are noncombatants. . . . It affords a stage for dramatization and distortion. The prolonged siege is one of the most effective ways in which terrorists propagate their message."[3]

While the full attention of the terrorists, their symbolic victims, their target population, and the media is normally held during any terrorist atrocity, hostage-taking also ensures the full attention of the target government. As noted by a participant at an international seminar on terrorism, "The government must try to solve problems under duress, with the whole whole watching, and the possibility of the governed feeling that the government is impotent or Draconian in its counterresponse."[4]

Governments are almost always in a no-win situation. If they concede to the terrorists' demands, they appear weak and set the stage for further attacks. If they stand firm and the hostages are killed, then they have failed in a primary obligation associated with democratic governments—to protect the lives of their citizens. As examples of disputes that have arisen over government handling of hostage events, psychologist Ariel Merari of Tel Aviv University's Center for Strategic Studies has cited the Ma'alot incident in Israel, where the storming of a kibbutz nursery by the military resulted in the death or injury of twenty-four children, the death of one soldier and the wounding of eleven more, as well as killing of the five Palestinian terrorists; the procrastination of the Italian government over the kidnapping of Aldo Moro by the Red Brigades, until his body was discovered in a car trunk; and the West German government's firm stance during the Schleyer kidnapping event, where GSG–9's successful storming of the Lufthansa airliner at Mogadishu was offset by the discovery of Schleyer's body after his torture and murder by the Red Army Faction.[5]

With the target government in such a precarious position, one can be assured of the full attention of the Western media. To the benefit of this analysis, this ensures that the terrorist demands become known, since those demands are normally passed to the media. This exposure tends to lessen the chances of inaccurate data that could influence the analysis if the terrorists and/or the government attempted secret negotiations.

For the terrorists, with the exception of suicide bombings, barricade and hostage atrocities are by far the most deadly and complex operations. The barricaded terrorists are constantly exposed to the possibility of armed intervention by the target or host government. To assure success, a great deal of intelligence collection and analysis of targets must be undertaken, with considerable outside assistance required. In spite of the high degree of danger and difficulty, terrorists continue to stage hostage-taking atrocities. Perhaps their motivation is as noted by Ariel Merari, "no other type of terrorist activity is as successful in achieving the terrorists' objectives."[6] The memoirs of Black September leader Abu Ayad indicated that one of the goals of the 1972 Munich Olympic Games massacre was "to exploit the unusual concentration of mass-communications media in Munich in order to give our struggle international publicity."[7]

Examples abound of the media's attention to barricade and hostage events. All three major U.S. networks interrupted normal broadcasting to report the seizure of three buildings in Washington, D.C., by a dozen previously unknown Hanafi Muslim terrorists. Merari has attempted to estimate the monetary value of that intensive coverage to that small group of terrorists by comparing the air time they were given to the cost of advertising during the first showing of the reissued movie *Gone with the Wind* during that same year. So estimated, the Hanafi Muslims would have had to pay more than a billion dollars for the prime air time they were awarded free by the networks.[8]

Hostage events have also proved quite effective in creating conflict between nations when adroitly managed by terrorists—for example, the 1979 kidnapping of the West German ambassador, Count Karl von Spreti, by the Revolutionary Armed Forces (FAR) in Guatemala. The FAR demands included the release of twenty-five jailed comrades and $700,000 ransom. West German officials pleaded with Guatemalan officials to release the prisoners and offered to pay the ransom, but Guatemala refused. When the ambassador was murdered by the FAR, West Germany levied diplomatic sanctions against Guatemala.[9]

In sum, the terrorist atrocity category of hostage-taking, as demonstrated in barricade and hostage events that include hijackings, is perfectly suited for the analysis. It is among the principal atrocities committed by terrorists. It offers a challenge to governments that ensures their full attention. That challenge to governments, as well as the sensationalism that usually accompanies such an event, ensures the attention of the media. With barricade and hostage atrocities essentially taking place "in a fish bowl" for public consumption, the potential for more complete analytical data exceeds that of the other categories of atrocities committed by political terrorists.

Specifying the Temporal Limits

In selecting the time frame for analysis, a span of four years was considered as sufficient to ensure a portrayal of all pertinent variables. While it was deemed desirable to base the analysis on recent information, it was also necessary to allow a sufficient period of time for lengthy legal proceedings, which were sometimes initiated against the terrorists, to run their course. The authenticity of the data base was also at issue in the selection of a time period, from the viewpoint of which era in recent history was the most fully documented in regard to terrorists and their atrocities. The four-year period from 1 January 1978 to 31 December 1981 was selected as fulfilling most of the important considerations.

That period of time proved most fruitful in terms of the accumulation of data for barricade and hostage atrocities. The example of fifty-two

American hostages held for 444 days by Iran, from 4 November 1979 to 20 January 1981, with literally hundreds of hours of international television coverage, proved irresistible to terrorists. During 1980, forty-two embassies and numerous other diplomatic offices were seized, and hundreds of diplomatic personnel, including twenty-two ambassadors, were held hostage and fifty-three people were killed. Indeed, Richard Clutterbuck has referred to 1980 as "the year of the hostages."[10] Notably, the extensive media coverage of the seizure of the U.S. embassy in Tehran is not included in the data because no barricade was involved. Attacks on embassies continued into 1981, with the seizure of twenty-five more, along with three ambassadors and ninety-nine other hostages. Hijackings were also abundant during the four-year period of 1978–1981. In 1981 alone there were twenty hijackings involving a total of 948 passengers taken hostage. In sum, the selected time period yielded an excellent data base for the analysis. It was both ample and representative of the barricade and hostage category of atrocity.

Operationalizing the Concept of Terrorist Atrocities

Appendix 1 is a data base covering all the barricade and hostage atrocities committed by terrorists from 1 January 1978 to 31 December 1981 that meet the above definition of international political terrorism. The original framework of the data base was drawn from publications by the Institute for the Study of Conflict in London. Between 1971 and 1982, the institute published annual summaries of acts of political violence occurring in 129 countries. Along with a chronological listing of events, its country surveys described internal developments and provided detailed assessments of politically subversive or insurgent threats to stability. During the four-year period of 1978–1981, the institute recorded over 6,000 acts of political violence.[11]

The beginning data were supplemented by data from numerous other sources, including Western intelligence agencies, the foreign services of Western governments, and U.N. sources in Vienna, Austria. Later comparison with media accounts was a cross-check on the completeness and accuracy of the data. In those few cases where differences were noted, further investigation usually revealed which was more factual.

The operationalization of the concept of terrorist atrocity was accomplished by separating the selected category of violence into its various components. The useful variables that emerged were:

1. Date and location
2. Number, nationality, organizational affiliation, and fate of perpetrators
3. Number, nationality, status, and fate of victims

4. Nature, national association, and disposition of physical target
5. Nature and satisfaction of demands
6. Target of demands
7. Duration and verbal description of the event
8. Nations granting or facilitating safe haven

All of the variables proved empirically observable. While not all were required for the analysis, all were included in the data base to provide a full disclosure of the atrocity and for possible later expansion of the analysis. For this analysis, the most important dependent variable was the granting of the terrorist demands or, as labeled in the analysis, "concessions" or "no concessions."

It could be argued that governments, proclaiming no-negotiations policies toward terrorism, might have made secret concessions to terrorists. Certainly if they had the analysis would be disturbed. However, with the selection of the barricade and hostage category of atrocity, the probability of such concessions occurring or remaining undetected is greatly diminished by the focus of the media. The observations of concessions or no concessions in the data bank did not terminate with the temporal limits, but have been followed through to the current time. Thus for the first atrocity in the data base, which occurred on 18 February 1978, there has been no apparent change in the concessions or no-concessions categories of the dependent variable for twelve years. In democratic societies, with the demonstrated aggressive diligence of the free press in observing the government's policies toward terrorism, it is doubtful that secret negotiations involving benefits to the terrorists could remain secret for so long a period. From an analytical viewpoint, with the credible population size and the very low probability of appreciable error in the observation of the dependent variable, it is highly unlikely that secret government negotiations produced any effect.

Media Source Selection

While the television media were considered perhaps the most desirable from the viewpoint of audience size, limited financial resources prevented their utilization in this analysis. Television remains a media source to be examined with a methodology similar to that undertaken in this analysis. Limited financial resources directed the selection of the second choice, with the second largest distribution—newspapers. Here again, language limitations restricted the choice to German or English press. Selected as representative of the Western press were newspapers from the United States, the United Kingdom, and the Federal Republic of Germany; an examination of French, Italian, and Spanish newspapers would likely have been highly desirable. Newspapers from the United States, the United Kingdom, and the Federal Republic of Germany were considered on the basis of their demonstrated interest in international affairs, their international reputation, and their domestic reputation. Selected were the *New York Times*, the *London Times*, and *Die Welt* (Hamburg), which represented more than four hundred years of experience in news reporting.

Operationalizing the Concept of Media Coverage

All issues of the *New York Times*, *London Times*, and *Die Welt* were reviewed, and the applicable data recorded, for the four-year time span from 1 January 1978 to 31 December 1981. This lengthy task was accomplished with the assistance and cooperation of the Austrian National Library and the America House Library, both located in Vienna. For those few days when an issue was not available—for example, during the labor strike that occurred at the *London Times*—an issue of the *International Herald Tribune* (Zurich edition) was substituted to provide continuity. A comparison of six months of the *International Herald Tribune* with all three other newspapers had shown the similarity of their coverage of terrorism.

The media coverage was operationalized by depiction and measurement of the functional decisions involved in the selected source's reporting of terrorist atrocities. The categories of the independent variable that emerged were:

1. The number of articles published was considered a measurement of the amount of coverage.
2. The number of photographs included with the article was considered a measurement of the intensity of the coverage.
3. The number of columns in the article, rounded to the nearest tenth of a column, was observed as a measurement of the extent of the coverage.
4. The page number in the newspaper on which the article appeared was interpreted as the priority accorded the coverage.
5. Content of the coverage was analyzed to determine whether or not the affiliation of the terrorists committing the atrocity, and their demands, were specifically identified in the article.

This description of the coverage was completed for all the atrocities listed in the data base, and is included in Appendix 1 with the applicable event.

While the amount of coverage given to the terrorists and their atrocities by the media was likely adequately measured by the number of articles and the column space provided, as is normally considered sufficient in the literature for similar undertakings, the number of photographs was considered an important indication of the intensity of the coverage. At the onset of the analysis, the page number of the article and the identification of the terrorists and the listing of their demands were also considered as measurements of the intensity of the coverage.

Quantification of the Dependent Variable

With the purpose of the analysis to determine the success of terrorists in obtaining concessions, an attempt was made to quantify that dependent variable on an interval scale. When first considered, the granting of demands appeared to be readily quantifiable. The number of demands made by the terrorists could be compared to the number of demands granted by the target government and a percentage measurement of success assigned. However, upon closer investigation of the atrocity events and the demands involved, it became abundantly clear that there was a marked lack of equality among demands. For example, a demand for a $50,000 ransom was not equivalent to a demand for safe passage, since a concession for safe passage is ultimately more valuable to an individual terrorist than a monetary concession.

Consideration was given to the weighting of demands, in a continued attempt to derive an interval scale of measurement for the dependent variable. This effort was also unproductive, since it became obvious that the assignment of weights to various demands involved assumptions as to what was perceived as more important to individual terrorists in each particular event. These assumptions would necessarily have been largely subjective, and would have introduced significant bias into the analysis.

Therefore, to avoid the introduction of bias and possible inaccuracies, the derivation of an interval scale for the dependent variable was abandoned, and with it the use of some of the more powerful analytical tools for estimating bivariate relationships. To maintain a high degree of integrity in the analysis, a nominal scale of concessions or no-concessions was utilized. Even this simplistic scale was not always without its problems. First, terrorists were sometimes granted the concession of refueling a hijacked airliner but with no further concessions. This posed the question of whether the refueling itself should qualify as a concession. To resolve the matter, when refueling concessions led to safe passage those events were recorded as concessions. However, when the terrorists were granted refueling but denied all other concessions and not given safe passage, then the event was recorded as no-concessions. A second test of the nominal scale involved an occasional specific demand for publicity. Since a demand for publicity was automatically granted by coverage in the Western press, the achievement of publicity was not regarded as a concession and the event was classified based on its other merits. Of the forty-nine atrocity events in the data base, twenty-three were classified as concessions granted, and twenty-six as no-concessions granted.

Quantification of the Independent Variable

Most of the data for the categories of the independent variable of media coverage were directly quantifiable on an interval scale: the number of articles published, the number of photos accompanying the article, and the columns of space given to the article. These categories were investigated in their pure numerical form, and were also observed as mean values. Medians were also computed to provide a simplistic observation of the distribution of the data. The independent-variable categories of articles, photos, and columns showed a high degree of reliability in measuring the effect of media coverage upon the granting of concessions. Since news articles are composed of columns and photos, and represent the totality of physical coverage by the newspaper media, their content validity was considered credible. When regression calculations revealed the consistency between those three categories in predicting the granting or denying of concessions, their construct validity was further verified.

INVALID PREDICTORS

The Article Page Number

The page-number category proved highly unreliable in predicting the success of terrorists in obtaining concessions and was not useful in the analysis. This category was observed through calculation of the mean page number on which the articles concerning an atrocity were published. The category had been selected to show the priority of media coverage, with front-page publicity obviously most highly sought. However, the page-number category did not appear to measure the same phenomenon as the article, column, and photo categories. Unlike those categories, the mean page number of articles published on the atrocities in which terrorists were granted concessions did not vary significantly from those in which the terrorists were denied concessions. As can be observed in Table 10 in Appendix 2, the twenty-three events in which the terrorists received concessions had a mean page number of 4.8 compared to the 4.3 for the twenty-six events in which the terrorists received no concessions.

A further investigation of the data base was conducted to determine if the mean page number was more directly associated with the "newness" of an atrocity event. It seemed logical that front-page coverage would normally be associated with the breaking of a story, and if the atrocity event continued for a lengthy period of time, the articles would likely move farther back in the newspaper. This phenomenon would certainly not be restricted to coverage of terrorism, but would seem to be based on financially sound editorial policies.

The analysis to determine the degree of association between the duration of the atrocity event and the mean page number of articles was accomplished with an analysis of pairs methodology. A 4 x 4 table was constructed by dividing both the dependent variable of the mean page number and the independent variable of the duration of the atrocity event in days into four ordinal rankings (see Table 21 in Appendix 2). Since the mathematics of the pairs analysis yielded a large number of ties on both the dependent and the independent variables, Somer's d and Tau_b were employed to measure the association.

The association between the duration of the atrocity and the mean page number of the newspaper media's coverage was found to be positive but not strong. In the employment of pairs analysis, a perfect positive association of +1.0 is possible, as is a perfect negative association of −1.0. The Tau_b value computed for the association was +0.16, and the Somer's d computation yielded +0.18. A further direct mathematical observation of the data showed that 115 of the 391 articles observed appeared on page one, 31 on page two, and 24 on page three, with the median value being page four.

Obviously other factors were involved in determinations of the page number on which to publish the coverage of terrorist atrocities. A logical explanation is that, on occasion, the coverage of a particular phase of a terrorist atrocity was less newsworthy than other simultaneous events that pushed it farther back in the newspaper. Further, the structure of some newspaper editions apparently dictates that international events not carried on the front page are published on a particular page in a later section. This procedure is likely accomplished to facilitate readability by repeat consumers. This editorial policy was observed on numerous occasions in the accumulation of the data base and likely contributed to the invalidation of mean page number as a reliable indicator for the analysis.

The Publication of Terrorist Affiliations and Demands

The categories of the independent variable that involved identification of the affiliation of the terrorists and the specifications of their demands also proved unreliable and invalid as predictors of terrorist success in obtaining concessions. In the early phases of data accumulation it became obvious that, when the information was available, the media included the affiliation of the terrorists and identified their demands in almost every article. Failure to identify the terrorists or their demands was normally limited to those few articles published during the early stages of an atrocity, when apparently only sketchy information was available. Articles published after the full development of an atrocity invariably included the affiliation of the terrorists and their demands.

Interestingly, the literature that discusses restraints on the media's coverage of terrorism frequently includes the recommendation to limit publicity by withholding identification of the terrorists' affiliation and not illuminating their demands. The data in Appendix 1 clearly show how significant a change that would be, with the demonstrated editorial policy apparently calling for ascertaining and reporting the terrorist affiliation and demands. As shown in Table 10 in Appendix 2, the affiliation of the terrorists was reported in 88 percent of all observed atrocity events, while demands were reported 81 percent of the time. There was no appreciable difference in those percentages across the dependent variable categories of concessions or no-concessions.

ARTICLES, PHOTOS, AND COLUMNS AS VALID PREDICTORS

Tabulation of the article, photo, and column space categories of the independent variable revealed a remarkable association between the media's coverage of atrocities and the terrorists' success in obtaining concessions over the forty-nine events included in the data base. As shown in Table 1, the twenty-three events which included concessions to the terrorists received three times as many articles, almost twice as many photos, and more than twice as much column space as the twenty-six events with no concessions. (The summarized data for the individual events can be viewed in Tables 16, 17, 18, and 19 in Appendix 2.)

A smaller N for the dependent category of concessions indicated that a comparison of means for the independent variable categories with the

Table 1
Relationship Between Media Coverage and Terrorist Success

Terrorist Success	Media Coverage		
	Articles	Photos	Columns
Concessions granted (N=23)	75%	65%	70%
No concessions granted (N=26)	25	35	30
	100%	100%	100%
	(391)	(110)	(204.7)

Table 2
Relationship Between Mean Values for Media Coverage
and Terrorist Success

Terrorist Success	Media Coverage (Mean values)		
	Articles	Photos	Columns
Concessions granted (N=23)	12.8	3.1	6.2
No concessions granted (N=26)	3.7	1.5	2.4

dichotomous dependent variable would indicate an even stronger association. As per Table 2, this was indeed true. The mean value for articles published was 3.5 times greater, the mean value for photos used was 2.0 times greater, and the mean value of columns printed was 2.6 times greater for the events in which terrorists were granted concessions.

An investigation of the median values of the independent variable categories indicated that the data were consistent. The median values of articles and photos were twice as high, and the median value of columns more than twice as high, for those events in which concessions were granted. The median values are shown in Table 10 of Appendix 2.

With the dependent variable observed on a nominal scale, the more powerful analytical tool of regression could not be accurately employed. While social scientists have sometimes attempted regression with a dichotomous dependent variable, Morris Fiorina has noted the significant problems that arise:[12]

1. Values of y can only be 0 or 1. However, x values more than x_1 would predict a value of y larger than 1, and x values less than x_0 would predict a value of y smaller than 0, both of which would be impossible.

2. A basic assumption of regression is the random distribution of errors around each value of the independent variable. With a dichotomous dependent variable, all the errors associated with values above x_1 are negative, and all errors below x_0 are positive. This results in inaccurate prediction.

3. If even higher values of x were combined with y, which is precisely the case with media coverage and terrorist success, a regression line would tend to flatten out, indicating a lessening of the relationship when in fact it would be strengthening.

To verify the construct validity of the categories of the independent variable, a regression analysis was performed evaluating the categories

Table 3
Relationship Between Categories of Media Coverage
(Pearson correlation coefficients)

	Articles	Photos	Columns
Articles	–	.8765	.9189
Photos	–	–	.9776

against each other. As could be expected, Table 3 shows a very high degree of correlation. The coefficient values do not vary enough to cast any doubt on whether they all measure the same thing.

In an effort to more definitively view the statistical significance of the predictive capability of the independent variable categories, a Probit analysis was undertaken. Probit is designed for ordinal dependent variables of five or fewer categories. When employed with a dichotomous dependent variable, it yields an S-shaped sigmoid curve that could conform to the data more closely than a linear regression. While a Probit analysis yields coefficients, they are calculated in an entirely different manner than in linear regression. Probit is based on the interpretation that for every unit change in x, there is a measurable change in the Z score of y.[13] The coefficients of Probit are labeled maximum likelihood estimates (MLE). They are more useful in offering a comparison between the differing effects of the independent variable categories upon the dependent variable than for establishing a specific level of correlation between the independent variable and the dependent variable. As indicated by the earlier linear regression, the differences between the independent variable categories of articles, photos, and columns in predicting the dependent variable are not remarkable. The positive association of media coverage (in terms of articles, photos, and columns) with terrorist success (in terms of concessions) is already demonstrated by tabulation and comparison of empirical data and means. Probit analysis was performed because it also allows for the determination of a level of statistical significance. It yields a standard error associated with each MLE. When the MLE is divided by its standard error, it yields a t value that can be used to determine statistical significance.

The Probit computations yielded MLE/se, or t, values for the category of articles at 2.376, columns at 1.547, and photos at 1.367. These values show that the number and length of articles published by the media covering an atrocity, plus the number of photos, help to explain whether or not concessions are granted to terrorists. The statistical significance of the number of articles is a high 95 percent. The number of photos and the column space are only slightly less significant at 90 percent.

CHALLENGES TO THE ANALYSIS

The analysis would not be valid without a thorough investigation of additional variables that could possibly account for whether concessions are granted. In the literature on media coverage of terrorism it is sometimes suggested that terrorists attempting to gain or hold the attention of the media might increase the violence of their atrocities. From this concept, one can hypothesize that media coverage is associated positively with the level of violence.

It seems readily apparent that violence attracts the Western media as they compete for news stories with wide public appeal. As terrorists offer progressively more brutal acts to compete for media attention, concessions may result from the level of violence and not from the level of publicity. At issue is whether terrorists can force target governments to concede to their demands by employing higher levels of violence while attracting more media coverage.

If violence is operationalized by the observation of hostage casualties, one could hypothesize that hostage casualties is a variable accounting for media coverage and/or granting of concessions to terrorists. An examination must therefore be undertaken to determine whether hostage casualties as a control variable is antecedent to both media coverage and terrorist success in obtaining concessions, or whether it is perhaps an intervening control variable with media coverage inspiring hostage casualties that result in concessions.

An elaboration model technique was utilized to determine the effect of an increase in violence, as operationalized by hostage casualties, upon media coverage and terrorist success in obtaining concessions.[14]

To test the hypothesis that inflicting hostage casualties increased the likelihood of the granting of concessions to terrorists, the occurrence of individual events that included concessions was compared to the occurrence of hostage casualties. As shown in Table 14 in Appendix 2, of the twenty-three events that included concessions, only three involved hostage casualties. It seems from this early observation that a negative relationship exists between increased violence and the granting of concessions in the barricade and hostage category of atrocities.

As demonstrated in Table 4, when the variable of hostage casualties is held constant, only three of the thirteen events in which hostage casualties occurred involved granting concessions. Consistent with previous results of this analysis, Table 4 confirms a continued strong positive association between the level of media coverage and the success of terrorists in obtaining concessions. Those casualty events that included

Table 4
Relationship Between Media Coverage and Terrorist Success:
Controlling for Hostage Casualties

Terrorist Success	Media Coverage		
	Articles	Photos	Columns
Concessions granted (N=3)	72%	59%	64%
No concessions granted (N=10)	28	41	36
	100%	100%	100%
	(179)	(79)	(128.1)

concessions to the terrorists received 2.6 times as many articles, 1.4 times as many photos, and 1.8 times as much column space as casualty events in which the terrorists were denied concessions.

While this degree of association between media coverage and terrorist success is slightly less than shown in Table 1, it is still abundantly clear that a strong association remains between media coverage and terrorists obtaining concessions after controlling for hostage casualties.

With the small N of the concessions category, an investigation of the means, as well as the raw data, of the media coverage would be in order. Based on calculations utilizing the mean values of media coverage, details in Table 12 of Appendix 2 reveal a continued strong positive association of media coverage to terrorist success, when controlling for hostage casualties. Within hostage casualty events, the media coverage given to those events in which the terrorists were granted concessions included 8.6 times as many articles, 4.9 times as many photos, and 6.0 times as much column space. Comparison of the median values yielded similar results. Based on this simple tabular comparison of accumulated data, one can state that, after controlling for increased violence as measured by hostage casualties, media coverage continued to demonstrate a strong positive association with terrorists' success in obtaining concessions.

To establish the statistical significance of this observation, a Probit analysis was performed comparing the most statistically significant of the media-coverage variables, articles published, and hostage casualties against the dependent variable of terrorist success for all forty-nine events. Both articles published and hostage casualties were statistically significant at the 95 percent level. However, hostage casualties demonstrated a negative relationship to concessions with a -1.8338 MLE as compared to a $+0.18132$ MLE positive relationship for articles published. Based on this finding, one can state that a negative relationship exists between the increase of violence in the form of hostage casualties and the granting of concessions to terrorists in international barricade and hostage atrocities with a significance level of 95 percent.

A Probit investigation of the thirteen casualty events with the independent variable category of articles published yielded a t value of 1.5699. This indicated that, within the category of casualty events, media coverage continued to be a predictor of terrorist success in obtaining concessions at a significance level of 87 percent.

The relationship between hostage casualties and media coverage was also investigated with a regression analysis. Hostage casualties demonstrated a positive, but weak, correlation with media coverage, yielding Pearson correlation coefficients of .2453 with articles published, .4643 with photos displayed, and .4320 on column space, with statistical significance at 90 percent or higher.

While this demonstrated weak relationship casts doubt on the construct validity between the variables of media coverage and hostage casualties in the measurement of concessions to terrorists, it is imprudent to postulate that the media would not be strongly attracted to terrorist atrocities that yielded the level of sensationalism normally associated with brutalization of hostages. Table 11 in Appendix 2 shows the tabulation and comparison of empirical data on media coverage associated with hostage casualties. With N = 13 for hostage casualties events and N = 36 for no hostage casualties events, an investigation of the independent variable means is in order. That comparison yielded the expected results of 2.3 times as many articles, 6.8 times as many photos, and 4.7 times as much column space given to the casualty events as to the noncasualty events. However, one must recall that Table 4 shows a negative association between hostage casualties and terrorist success in obtaining concessions. Further, Table 4 demonstrates that, controlling for hostage casualties, the strong positive association between media coverage and granting concessions to terrorists continues.

An examination of the data pertaining to hostage casualties assists in clarifying the negative association between hostage casualties and concessions. Table 5 shows that, of the fifty-eight casualties suffered by the hostages in international barricade and hostage events over the four-year period 1978–1981, 68.9 percent were incurred during the rescue phase of the atrocity. Since rescue attempts were normally associated with the denial of concessions to terrorists, the reason for the negative association of casualties and concessions becomes obvious.

With only 12.1 percent of the hostage casualties incurred during the captivity phase, it appears that terrorists, with some notable exceptions, did not normally choose to increase the violence of their atrocity, even to attract the media.

The notable excepetions to the observed terrorist tactic of avoiding

Table 5
Relationship of the Phase of Atrocity to Hostage Casualties

	Hostage Casualties (Percentage)		
Phase	Killed	Injured	Combined
Take-over	0.0	19.4	12.1
Captivity	22.7	5.6	12.1
Escape	4.6	8.3	6.9
Rescue	72.7	66.7	68.9
	100.0	100.0	100.0
	(N=22)	(N=36)	(N=58)

hostage casualties are revealed in further investigation of the event data in Tables 16, 17, 18, and 19 in Appendix 2. There were 2,787 hostages and 595 terrorists involved in the forty-nine events in the data base. This yields a "normal" hostage-to-terrorist ratio of 4.7:1. As demonstrated in Table 6, in those five events where terrorists inflicted casualties on the hostages during the captivity phase of the atrocity, the hostage-to-terrorist ratio was 19.5:1. Discussions with various sources have indicated that inflicting hostage casualties during captivity can be partly attributed to a terrorist tactic for controlling a large group of hostages—for example, during the hijacking of an airliner. The tactic calls for creating an intense level of fear to ensure submission of the group by the random killing or injuring of a hostage.

While the tactic of inflicting casualties might provide a means of hostage control, it did not increase the probability of gaining concessions.

Table 6
Media Coverage versus Terrorist Success and the Ratio of Hostages to Terrorists for Events with Hostage Casualties During Captivity

	Events	Media Coverage (Means)			Hostages/Terrorists
		Article	Photo	Column	
Concessions	1	30.0	11.0	23.1	147/3
No Concessions	4	6.0	5.3	7.4	223/16
					370/19

As shown in Table 6, only one of the five events where terrorists inflicted hostage casualties during captivity yielded concessions.

The value of media coverage for obtaining concessions is also demonstrated in this small sample, where the mean value of articles published was 5.0 times larger, the mean value of photos displayed was 2.1 times larger, and the mean value of column space provided was 3.1 times larger for the events that included concessions. Owing to sample size, the evidence could certainly not be deemed statistically significant. However, one must recall that the sample in this case is the universe for all international barricade and hostage atrocities that occurred in a four-year period.

MEDIA COVERAGE LINGERS ON BRUTAL VIOLENCE

While hostage casualties have been shown to be negatively associated with terrorist success in obtaining concessions during barricade and hostage events, the media coverage data in Appendix 1 shows that the attention of the Western media to terrorist atrocities that included brutalization of hostages did not end with the termination of the event. Table 7 demonstrates that, following termination of terrorist atrocities, the media focused more strongly on those events in which hostages had been killed or injured. Over twice as many articles were published, with the column space three times as long, and three times as many photos were included. Terrorist recognition was provided by identification in over 90 percent of the articles.

It appears to be an empirical fact that, for the four-year period 1978–1981, international terrorists perpetrating barricade and hostage atrocities in which hostage casualties were inflicted received significantly more publicity than did their counterparts who did not harm their captives. This realization is clearly perceived by terrorists. For example, in March

Table 7
Media Coverage After Event Termination

	Casualties	No Casualties
Mean Articles per Event	3.9	1.5
Mean Columns per Event	2.4	0.8
Mean Photos per Event	1.6	0.5
Article ID of Terrorist	92.2%	90.1%

1981, terrorists from Pakistan's Al Zulfikar group hijacked a Pakistani airliner to Afghanistan. For three days they adhered to what seemed to be the standard operating procedure for terrorist hijackings. They released twenty-seven women and children and attempted to publicize their demands through the Afghan government. The Soviet-controlled state to which they had taken the airliner and hostages was a sanctuary, with the headquarters of their terrorist organization in Kabul. During the first three days they received little attention from the international media. On the fourth day, they murdered a Pakistani diplomat and threw his body out on the Kabul airport runway before directing their hijacked airliner to Syria. With that act they gained the attention of the Western media. During the next ten days in Syria, they had continual access to the media. Together with live television coverage, they were accorded forty articles spanning twenty-three columns, with eleven photographs, and appeared fourteen times on the front pages of the *New York Times*, *London Times*, and *Die Welt*. The atrocity finally terminated with full granting of terrorist demands by the Pakistani government and the release of fifty-four imprisoned members of the Al Zulfikar group who were flown to Syria. The Syrian government then flew twenty-five of those former prisoners, and the three terrorists, back to their headquarters in Kabul.

THE NATURE OF DEMANDS GRANTED

The hypothesis of a positive association between increased coverage by the media and the granting of terrorist demands has held true in phase one of this analysis, where the variable of hostage casualties was allowed to fluctuate; it also held true in phase two, where it was held constant. What remains is to further empirically investigate whether media coverage can in fact lead to the granting of concessions to terrorists by target governments. This issue has been discussed at length earlier. It seems reasonable to postulate that media information influences public attitudes and beliefs, which in turn influence government policies and procedures in democratic societies. However, for media coverage to be credited with terrorist success in obtaining concessions, it must first be determined whether the terrorist demands considered in the analysis are indeed political in nature, and therefore within the jurisdiction of the target governments. Table 8 summarizes the nature of the demands in the data base (Appendix 1).

When one considers the vested authority of national law enforcement agencies regarding terrorist atrocities, it is difficult to postulate granting any demands without the approval of target and/or host governments. However, the data for terrorist demands in Table 8 have been grouped

Table 8
Barricade and Hostage Atrocities:
Nature of Terrorist Demands

Demand	Number of Occurrences
Political	
Safe passage	29
Release of prisoners	28
Political asylum	10
Establish or break	
diplomatic relations	3
Terminate state of siege	3
Arrest and punishment of	
counterterror groups	2
Investigation of human	
rights violations	2
Repatriation of exiles	1
Denounce treaties	1
Conference with authorities	1
Regional autonomy	1
Expulsion of Jewish diplomats	
and military	1
Subtotal	$\overline{82}$
Political and Private	
Airliner and/or refueling	38
Press conference or publishing	
of manifestoes	7
Ransom	7
Reopening of factory	1
Subtotal	$\overline{53}$
Total	$\overline{135}$

into two categories: political, which requires only government action to grant concessions, and political and private, which involves government approval in conjunction with actions by the private sector.

As demonstrated, 61 percent of the known 135 demands included in the 1978–1981 data base were strictly political in nature. However, the demand category of an airliner and/or refueling could be placed in either the political or private sector, in that the airports from which these services are available are normally government owned or controlled. If that category is moved to the political sector, then 85 percent of the terrorist demands could be classified as strictly political in nature.

THE MEANING OF TERRORIST SUCCESS

With the demonstrated positive association between media coverage and terrorist success in obtaining concessions, one could perhaps question the value of those concessions to the terrorists. When the media's transmission of the violence of their atrocities satisfies the terrorists' strategic objectives by creating an atmosphere of fear in the target population, the value of that media transmission is intangible and can be approximated but not empirically measured. However, in this limited quantitative analysis, whereby media coverage has been shown to be related to the granting of concessions to terrorists, the value of specific concessions to particular terrorists can be at least partly quantified.

An examination of the data in Table 8 shows that 94 of the 135 demands made by the terrorists involved their personal safety and security. If the concept of terrorist personal safety and security is operationalized by quantitatively evaluating the fate of the terrorists, then one can determine the empirical value of terrorist success in about 70 percent of the forty-nine atrocities in the data base. A review of the individual atrocity data in Tables 16, 17, 18, and 19 in Appendix 2 yields the results of terrorist success shown in Table 9.

With two-thirds of the terrorists being granted concessions, their overall efforts could be regarded as successful. An interesting approach, and one used by some more prominent terrorist leaders of the last two decades, is to regard each atrocity as a battle in a war. When an army wins two-thirds of its battles, by military standards it is regarded as successful. In this scenario, even though the "war" is of undetermined duration and the "battles" certainly are not all of equivalent value, a two-thirds success rate by the terrorists could be regarded as highly significant.

The 9.1 percent terrorist casualty rate is significantly higher than the 2.1 percent rate suffered by the hostages, although the raw data are quite similar with fifty-eight hostage casualties vs. fifty-four terrorist casualties. However, a barricade and hostage atrocity—or for that matter, any terrorist atrocity qualifying under the definition of international political terrorism in this analysis—is not a confrontation between terrorists and victims. Rather, the terrorists are confronting the power—military and political—of their target governments. If one again uses the scenario ascribed to by some terrorist leaders, with each atrocity a battle, then a 9.1 percent casualty rate during a 267-day face-to-face battle against overwhelming odds would be readily accepted by any schooled military commander. (Table 10 in Appendix 2 shows the 267 days involved in the forty-nine atrocities.)

With two-thirds of the terrorists either granted safe passage or escaping, as compared to one-fourth arrested and about one-twelfth killed, one could comment that, although terrorist leaders rank barricade and

Table 9
Relationship of Terrorist Risk to Success During Barricade
and Hostage Atrocities

	Number of Terrorists (N=595)	Percentage of Total
Success Rate		
Granted concessions	397	66.7
Denied concessions	198	33.3
Total	595	100.0
Casualty Rate		
Killed	42	7.1
Injured	12	2.0
Total	54	9.1
Safety and Security Rate		
Granted safe passage	370	62.2
Arrested	153	25.7
Killed	42	7.1
Escaped	30	5.0
Total	595	100.0

hostage as one of their most dangerous missions, the survival rate is comparatively favorable and is not dissimilar from that experienced by some U.S. Navy aircraft carrier air wings during the Vietnam conflict.[15]

When the results of this analysis are compared to a study prepared by the Rand Corporation covering sixty-three major terrorist barricade and hostage events between 1968 and 1974,[16] it seems that terrorism is becoming more productive, with little increase in the risk to the perpetrators. The 1968–1974 Rand study found that 29 percent of the terrorists achieved concessions, while the 1978–1981 data in this analysis show a success rate of 67 percent. The Rand study also showed that 79 percent of the terrorists escaped punishment or death, while the 1978–1981 data show a somewhat higher risk, with 67 percent going free.

In sum, over a fourteen-year period (1968–1981), it appears that terrorists perpetrating barricade and hostage atrocities became more than twice as successful in obtaining concessions. It would be interesting to compare the technological advances and expansion of the news media during this same period. By 1981, terrorists seizing hostages and establishing barricades were being granted about two-thirds of their demands, and two-thirds of them were avoiding punishment or death.

CONCLUSIONS

Through the measurement of media coverage accorded barricade and hostage atrocities perpetrated by international terrorists from 1978 to 1981, quantitative analysis shows that a significant positive relationship exists between the level of media coverage and the concessions of target governments to terrorists' tangible demands. Depending on the category of coverage, atrocities wherein terrorists were granted concessions received between two and three times as much media coverage as was accorded those events that terminated with no concessions.

The independent variable categories of articles published, photos included, and column space provided proved to be reliable predictors of terrorist success in obtaining concessions. While a dichotomous dependent variable of concessions or no-concessions prevented the employment of the more powerful analytical tool of linear regression, Probit analysis of the data substantiated that the categories of the independent variable were statistically significant at levels between 90 to 95 percent.

An elaboration technique was employed to control for hostage casualties as an antecedent or intervening variable that could perhaps cause a spurious relationship between media coverage and terrorist success. However, with hostage casualties held constant, both overall and in the captivity phase of the atrocity, media coverage continued to show a strong positive association with terrorist success in obtaining concessions. Hostage casualties proved to have a negative association with the granting of concessions. Data investigation revealed that most of the hostage casualties had occurred during rescue attempts. Linear regression showed weak but positive Pearson correlation coefficients between hostage casualties and media coverage.

The relationship between hostage casualties and ratios of hostages to terrorists was examined. It appears that hostage casualties are more likely to occur when the ratio of hostages to terrorists approaches 20:1 and less likely at ratios of about 5:1.

An investigation of continued media coverage after the termination of the event revealed that terrorists who had inflicted hostage casualties could expect to receive about two to three times as much continued coverage as those who had not brutalized their captives.

An analysis of the nature of terrorist demands indicated that about 85 percent were political to the extent that governments would be the major or sole authority for deciding whether or not to grant concessions. About 15 percent of the demands required both government and private-sector approval to grant concessions.

When a small group of terrorists confronts the resources of a national government in a barricade-and-hostage situation, the results achieved by the terrorists must be considered highly successful. Two-thirds of the terrorists were granted concessions, and two-thirds went free and were unharmed.

NOTES

1. M. Cherif Bassiouni, ed., *International Terrorism and Political Crimes* (Springfield, Ill.: Charles C. Thomas, 1975), 5.

2. Robert Kupperman and Darrell Trent, *Terrorism: Threat, Reality, Response* (Stanford, Calif.: Hoover Institute Press, 1979), 123.

3. Benjamin Netanyahu, "Terrorism: How the West Can Win," in *Terrorism: How the West Can Win*, ed. Benjamin Netanyahu (New York: Farrar, Straus, Giroux, 1986), 206.

4. Quoted in Ariel Merari, "Government Policy in Incidents Involving Hostages," in *On Terrorism and Combating Terrorism*, ed. Ariel Merari (Frederick, Md.: University Publications of America, 1985), 173.

5. Ibid., 164.

6. Ibid., 163.

7. Abu Ayad, *Le'lo Moledet* (Without a Homeland) (Jerusalem: Mifras, 1978), 158; quoted in ibid., 164.

8. Merari, "Government Policy in Incidents Involving Hostages," 164.

9. Ibid., 164–65.

10. Richard Clutterbuck, "The Year of the Hostage," in *Annual of Power and Conflict: 1980–81* (London: Institute for the Study of Conflict, 1981), 1.

11. See the chronologies of events listed in the 1978–1981 issues of the *Annual of Power and Conflict* published by the Institute for the Study of Conflict in London.

12. Drawn from Morris Fiorina, *Retrospective Voting in American National Elections* (New Haven: Yale University Press, 1981), Appendix A; cited in Susan Welch and John Comer, *Quantitative Methods for Public Administration: Techniques and Applications*, 2d ed. (Chicago: The Dorsey Press, 1988), 306.

13. See, for example, Welch and Comer, *Quantitative Methods for Public Administration*, 307.

14. For a detailed explanation of elaboration techniques see Welch and Comer, *Quantitative Methods for Public Administration*, 168–74.

15. For example, the losses suffered by Carrier Air Wing Sixteen aboard the USS Oriskany in Vietnam combat deployments in 1966–1968.

16. As reviewed in Paul Wilkinson, "Terrorist Movements," in *Terrorism: Theory and Practice*, eds. Yonah Alexander, David Carlton, and Paul Wilkinson (Boulder: Westview Press, 1979), 115; and David Milbank, *International and Transnational Terrorism: Diagnosis and Prognosis* (Washington, D.C.: Central Intelligence Agency, PR 76 10030, April 1976).

9

A Comparison of National Experiences with Political Terrorism and the Media

Numerous proposals have been made for the media to consider in attempting to prevent exploitation by terrorists. Most proposals share the common assumption that representatives of the media will assume greater responsibility for their actions. That assumption is somewhat reminiscent of the Hutchins Commission's 1947 optimism: "Self-correction is better than outside correction, so long as self-correction holds out a reasonable and realistic hope,"[1] which could be loosely translated that the media should be left to control themselves so long as they control themselves.

AVOIDING AND MINIMIZING EXPLOITATION

The proposals to prevent exploitation can be categorized as (1) recommendations for preventive action to be taken before an atrocity occurs, and (2) damage-minimization policies to be followed during and after an atrocity. Livingstone's specific recommendations exemplify the preventive category:

If the media would announce guidelines restricting the use of material produced by terrorists . . . the incentive for terrorists to produce videotapes could be eliminated. . . . If the media make public statements on record of their positions and their efforts to control terrorism, it will be far more difficult for them to explode later in an orgy of media coverage following a major terrorist incident.[2]

The damage-minimization category was illustrated by recommendations from psychologist Preston Horstman at a conference of the Radio-Television Directors Association. They included (1) withholding identification of the terrorists, (2) denying terrorists live coverage, (3) avoiding the publication of terrorist communiqués, and (4) portraying the terrorists and their atrocity as despicable.[3]

Also within the damage-minimization category, Bassiouni suggests that the media establish a pool for coverage of a terrorist atrocity. Such a procedure could lessen the competition and aggressive search for scoops that usually lead to media magnification of the violence. The media pool concept was employed by coalition forces during the Persian Gulf conflict, and perhaps lessons learned by both the authorities and the media during that sensitive period will strengthen Bassiouni's proposal. He has further recommended the creation of a media council to supervise and coordinate voluntary restraints on media activities as terrorist atrocities are occurring.[4] Charles Fenyvesi also envisioned the formation of a media council to declare news media emergencies and prevent the endangerment of lives, with media employers holding their individual members responsible for conforming to the council's rulings.[5]

The response by media executives to such damage-minimization proposals has not been overly enthusiastic. Some have suggested that no special policies are required. As observed by the president of NBC News, "We hire sensible people ... tell them to be careful ... and it works out okay. Every once in a while, it doesn't."[6] Those remarks were made in 1977, two years before the media's extensive coverage of the seizure of the American embassy in Tehran. During that 444-day episode, a decision by NBC prompted the resignation of one of its journalists, Fred Rowan. NBC had agreed to televising a five-minute harangue by an Iranian spokeswoman in exchange for an interview with a hostage. Rowan accused his employers of "irresponsible journalism,"[7] trying unsuccessfully to get NBC to air a two-minute interview with a State Department spokesman on the same telecast.

A CROSS-NATIONAL COMPARATIVE ANALYSIS STUDY APPROACH

A cross-national comparison of four major Western democracies seriously threatened by political terrorism during the last three decades affords an opportunity to observe the problems with terrorist manipulation of the media and some attempted solutions. The democratic governments of Italy, the Federal Republic of Germany, and the United Kingdom have experienced strong internal threats and have been accommodated by a cooperative media. The experience of the United States is unique, in that an internal threat has been minimal while the external threat from international terrorists has been significant. Further, the U.S. media have chosen an adversarial role in relation to the government.

A comparative analysis should preview the societal environment in which the various national media have functioned in order to understand and evaluate their actions. At issue would be (1) the historical experiences of the state in terms of the nature of the threat from political terrorism, (2) the countermeasure policies to terrorism that have evolved within the state, (3) the role of the media, and (4) the relationship that has emerged among the government, the press, and the public with regard to the media's coverage of terrorism.

As an introduction to the comparison of cases, a brief review of responses by various regimes and societies to political terrorism might prove beneficial. From the historical perspective, Wilkinson has assembled five categories: (1) submission, (2) soft-line approach, (3) tough-line approach, (4) counterterror and ruthless repression, and (5) counterterror against foreign-based terrorists.[8] The example of Lebanon has shown that when a government faced with intensifying terrorist attacks is submissive and fails to take necessary measures for internal defense, the people take the law into their own hands with a vicious cycle of terror and counterterror that leads to civil war. Jenkins's survey at Rand has shown the results of soft-line approaches, with 79 percent of the terrorists worldwide evading punishment for their crimes. The iron-fist policies of the Israeli Likud coalition toward the Palestinians have demonstrated the harsh measures of the tough-line approach. The death squads in Argentina exemplify a counterterror approach, while the tsar in Russia is the classic example of ruthless repression. Lastly, Israel has employed counterterror against foreign-based terrorists with attacks outside its borders, with limited tactical success and high political costs.

Along with a consideration of the historical experiences of a state and the current threats of political terrorism against it, identification of countermeasure policies employed by the state establishes the framework through which the actions of the media can be evaluated. Observation of the resulting relationship among the press, the public, and the government contributes to an understanding of the appropriateness of the media's coverage.

EMERGENCE OF THE MODERN TERRORIST THREAT IN WESTERN EUROPE

The dramatic increase in terrorism across Western Europe in the 1960s has been attributed to many factors, including (1) a contagion effect from protests in the United States against the Vietnam conflict, (2) empathy with emerging guerrilla movements in Latin America, and

(3) the internationalizing of Palestinian terrorism. As related earlier, the expansion of terrorism in the West was nurtured by the Soviets, directly and through surrogates. The Palestinians funneled substantial Soviet support to various terrorist organizations across the continent and were ably assisted by the efforts of Qadhafi and Castro.

With Western Europe plagued by a sharp increase in the intensity and severity of terrorist attacks during the 1970s, public opinion polls there showed a steady progression of support favoring the statement, "Our present society must be valiantly defended against all subversive force"; likewise, there was decreasing support for the statement: "Our society must be gradually improved by reform."[9] By 1977, the polls also indicated that the public favored capital punishment for terrorists, with military reprisals where possible and even assassination of terrorist leaders.

The rapidity with which an adroitly managed campaign of political terror can challenge a staunch democracy was demonstrated after the 1977 kidnapping and murder of West German industrialist Hanns-Martin Schleyer by RAF terrorists. A public opinion poll taken by Emnid-Institute disclosed that 61 percent of the Germans surveyed felt helpless against terrorism.[10]

THE EVOLUTION OF THE TERRORIST THREAT IN THE UNITED KINGDOM

The major terrorist challenge to the United Kingdom comes from the Provisional Irish Republican Army (PIRA), which was created in 1969 when nationalists advocating violence broke away from Marxist leadership in the official Irish Republican Army (IRA). The IRA had formed as a terror organization in 1922 at the end of Ireland's civil war. While the official IRA continued with some 200 members in 1982, it has apparently not engaged in terrorism since 1972.

In the late 1960s, the Northern Ireland Civil Rights Association (NICRA) staged peaceful demonstrations in an effort to call attention to what it perceived as discrimination against Catholics in Northern Ireland. Violence broke out when the organization was opposed by militant Protestants, and in August 1968, further public demonstrations by the NICRA were banned. When continued NICRA demonstrations violated the ban, Royal Ulster Constables used violent methods to disperse marchers. When a January 1969 Catholic civil rights march from Belfast to Londonderry was attacked by Protestants, the Royal Ulster Constabulary did not offer protection. With charges that the police were favoring the Protestants during the upsurge of violence that followed, the Provisional wing broke away from the official IRA with a pledge to protect the Catholics.

By 1982, active terrorist membership in the PIRA numbered about 300. The group had also formed a political wing called the Provisional Sinn Fein (PSF). In 1974, the Irish Republican Socialist Party also split away from the official IRA and formed its own terrorist wing, the Irish National Liberation Army (INLA). By 1982, the INLA had some fifty active terrorists.[11]

The Catholic terrorist organizations were countered by Protestant terrorist groups like the Reverend Ian Paisley's Ulster Protestant Volunteers, the Ulster Defense Association, the Ulster Freedom Fighters, and the Ulster Volunteer Force. When British troops were deployed by the U.K. government to quell the violence, they also became targets of the terrorism that engulfed Northern Ireland.

Violence erupted on a large scale in 1972, with the PIRA bombing of a British Army officers' mess in Aldershot. The death toll from political violence had increased sharply from 13 in 1969 to a peak of 467 killed and nearly 5,000 injured in 1972. Between 1970 and 1984, an average of 160 people were killed each year.[12]

The PIRA and INLA have links with the international terrorist network. Originally anti-Moscow, the PIRA became leftist in the 1970s. It committed itself to "demolish the Quisling Regime in the Free State of Ireland and the colonial regime in the Northern war zone."[13] The Soviets evidently preferred to deal with the PIRA through their Libyan and PLO surrogates. In the early 1970s, the PIRA developed close ties with the Palestinian Black September hard-core terrorists.[14] In May 1972, George Habash and Wadi Haddad brought the PIRA into the inner circle of the international terrorist network at the Baddawi summit meeting in Lebanon. In July 1972, Habash's PFLP signed a formal "Declaration of Support" for the IRA.[15] PIRA terrorists had been trained in Palestinian terrorist camps in Jordan as early as 1969.[16] In 1971, arms from Czechoslovakia intended for the PIRA were intercepted in Amsterdam.[17] Soviet RPG–7 rocket launchers were supplied to the IRA in 1972.[18] Libya has been an important supporter of the PIRA with funds, arms, and volunteers. In March 1973, the S.S. *Caudia*, captained by PIRA commander Joe Cahill, was stopped by the Irish Navy. It carried five tons of Soviet-bloc arms from Qadhafi for the PIRA.[19] In the late 1970s, Qadhafi was contributing $5 million per year to the PIRA.[20] The North American Irish National Aid Committee, which normally contributes about $100,000 per year, collected $250,000 for the PIRA during the first half of 1981 when Bobby Sands, elected Member of Parliament and PIRA activist, died in prison from a hunger strike.

With significant external support, the PIRA has shown no signs of agreeing to a cease-fire or settlement. When the Fitzgerald Plan was proposed in 1979, it responded with the murder of Lord Mountbatten.[21] Both the PIRA and INLA terrorist organizations now operate with secure cellular structures. Their international capability was adequately demonstrated by a March 1987 attack on a British Army on the Rhine officers' club in West Germany. Red Army Faction German terrorists supplied the stolen car for the bomb, Iranian terrorists supplied the explosives, and the PIRA parked it outside the club during a Friday night party. Thirty-eight people were injured, mostly West German guests.

The United Kingdom's Legislative Response to Terrorism

Antiterrorism laws in the form of the Civil Authorities (Special Powers) Act have existed in the United Kingdom since 1922. That act, in effect all all levels of authority, enables the Minister of Home Affairs, or Royal Ulster Constabulary officers, to "take all such steps and issue all such orders as may be necessary for preserving the peace and maintaining order."[22] The special powers authorized include internment without public trial, detention of any person for forty-eight hours for questioning, search and seizure of property without warrant, search and arrest of persons without warrant, censorship of printed material, and dispersion of public assemblies. While those 1922 provisions had been infrequently employed since the violence that accompanied the partitioning of the island subsided, Northern Ireland's prime minister asked Parliament to resume the internment of suspected terrorists in 1971.[23] During the first six months after his request was granted, 2,357 persons were arrested and 598 interned.[24] Parliament continued with further legislation to broaden the 1922 statute, including the Northern Ireland (Emergency Provisions) Acts of 1973, 1975, and 1978 and the Prevention of Terrorism (Temporary Provisions) Acts of 1974 and 1976. As demonstrated by these excerpts from the Emergency Provisions Act of 1973, the powers granted were broad, extensive, and potentially controversial:[25]

1. There may be trials without jury for certain offenses (Part I, No. 2, Chapter 53).
2. Constables may arrest without warrant persons suspected of terrorism (Part II, No. 10, Chapter 53).
3. Members of Her Majesty's forces may arrest without warrant persons suspected of committing, or intending to commit, any offense (Part II, No. 12, Chapter 53).
4. The unauthorized collecting, recording, or publishing of information about the police or Her Majesty's forces that could be useful to terrorists is unlawful (Part III, No. 20, Chapter 53).
5. Illegal organizations include the Irish Republican Army, Sinn Fein, and the Ulster Volunteer Force (Schedule 2).

With over 15,000 British soldiers deployed in Northern Ireland in 1974, the PIRA increased its terrorist activities in England. Westminster and the Tower of London were bombed in the summer, and in the fall, 21 persons were killed and 180 injured in the bombing of two pubs in Birmingham. Parliament responded with the Prevention of Terrorism Acts of 1974 and 1976, which (1) outlawed the PIRA and banned public displays of support for it, (2) extended the previous Northern Ireland emergency powers throughout the United Kingdom, and (3) allowed for the deportation of suspected terrorists. The November 1974 Act was passed without debate.

In 1975, the Special Powers Act of 1922 was modified to allow imprisonment without trial through the authority of the Northern Ireland government. Trial by jury was also suspended with the institution of the "Diplock Courts," named after the judge who recommended the procedure. In 1979, police detained 857 persons under the Provisions of Terrorism Act, as compared with 622 the previous year. From 29 November 1974 to 31 December 1979, about 4,600 people were detained.[26]

The outpouring of legislation in the United Kingdom against a significant terrorist threat can best be evaluated as per Miller's observation that elected legislators "keep an ear to the ground listening to the political footsteps of the public." Further, when the electorate is threatened by the extremes of terrorist violence, "legislatures can seldom be expected to uphold a libertarian view of the law."[27]

To some extent, Ireland has supported the United Kingdom's policies against terrorism in Northern Ireland. The Republic of Ireland's anti-terrorism laws date from 1920. Its legislation likely poses greater restrictions on civil liberties than that of any other Western democracy. The 1939 Offenses Against the State Act was amended in 1972 to establish special criminal courts for terrorist threats to the state, with three judges and no jury. Further, an individual alleged to be a member of the outlawed PIRA has to prove his or her disassociation. A statement by a senior police officer is considered sufficient proof to establish an accused as a member of the PIRA.[28] The Irish Criminal Law Jurisdiction Act of 1975 covers crimes committed outside the republic. A similar law passed in the United Kingdom is perhaps a modest beginning of increased legal cooperation with Ireland. While the Republic of Ireland does not allow extradition for political offenses, the Irish Constitution, Article 29.3, does state, "Ireland accepts the generally recognized principles of international law as its rule of conduct in its relations with other States."

The U.K. Media and Legislative Restraints

In those countries where terrorist atrocities occur on a frequent basis, strong public attention is apparently given to terrorist exploitation of the media. Such has been the situation in the United Kingdom since 1972. Cooperation between the government and the media has been attempted, but the results have apparently been less than completely satisfactory. A number of provisions from the Prevention of Terrorism Acts of 1974 and 1976 could be applied to the media's coverage of terrorism. However, such was not the case until the election of the Thatcher government in May 1979. Thatcher's Conservative government often threatened the news media with the application of antiterrorist legislation and, on occasion, exerted that authority.

On 30 March 1979, the INLA registered one of its most significant interruptions of the British domestic political scene with the car-bomb murder of opposition spokesman Airey Neave inside the House of Commons's underground parking lot. When BBC later broadcast an interview with a disguised INLA terrorist who claimed a connection with the murder, Thatcher directed the attorney general to investigate a possible BBC violation of the 1974 Prevention of Terrorism Act. After viewing the broadcast, she was strongly critical of the BBC: "I am appalled.... It reflects gravely on the judgment of the BBC."[29]

Public opinion in the United Kingdom was apparently supportive of Thatcher's criticism. The Lord Mayor of London said: "What a pity it is when an institution like the BBC puts someone who claims to have assisted in the murder of Airey Neave on the box and gives him a platform."[30]

The Bishop of Chester made a poignant plea for more responsibility on the part of the British news media: "What is the limit of responsibility. ... If I am aware of the identity of a person who has committed a serious crime, am I not required as a citizen to inform the appropriate authorities? If I pay money to a self-confessed traitor and murderer in order to gain a supposedly valuable news-story, am I not myself a traitor and guilty of 'aiding and comforting' the enemy?"[31] BBC's ethics were also criticized by Lord Chalfont: "The excuse that it was a 'newsworthy event,' and therefore in some way excluded from the normal canons of human behaviour, is symptomatic of the state of moral and intellectual confusion which the organs of public communication consistently display on the subject of terrorism."[32]

In the face of this sharp criticism, the BBC attempted to justify its actions. Director-General Ian Trethowan presented the BBC view: "We believe that the public has the common sense and stability to judge very accurately the character of the people they are seeing.... We do not believe that a BBC interview with the INLA will worsen by one iota that central problem of Northern Ireland: the inability of two communities to reach rational settlement of their problems."[33] However, the BBC was forced to retreat later when Mrs. Thatcher challenged the broadcast of a "Panorama" television program that was to include scenes taped at a

PIRA roadblock in Northern Ireland. The broadcast was canceled and two BBC editors were reprimanded.[34]

These confrontations between the Conservative government and the media occurred in spite of two previous agreements between law enforcement officials and the news media. After a freelance radio reporter was involved in the 1975 kidnap and murder of a girl in England, a conference had been held between senior law enforcement officials and national and international media executives. While the conference was in session, another kidnapping occurred. During this event, the media agreed to a voluntary news blackout and the girl was eventually released unharmed. While the arrangement was at best a "gentlemen's agreement," the Home Office incorporated it into its campaign against terrorism. Britain's fifty-one chief constables were advised in August 1976 that terrorist activities could produce situations wherein it might become necessary to request the media not to publish certain information until the situation could be rectified.[35]

A second agreement was reached in March 1979 between the BBC and the New Scotland Yard. After a BBC broadcast portraying corruption in the law enforcement system, the Metropolitan Police had sought a formal contract with the BBC for the right to review in advance BBC broadcasts that concerned them. After nine months of high-level negotiations, a written agreement was reached to govern BBC broadcasts of information that the Metropolitan Police considered sensitive or affecting national security or similar concerns.[36]

It has been suggested that perhaps the BBC has avoided more stringent government controls in its reporting of terrorism by accepting "mediated intervention, in which spokesmen in the sphere of politics have defined the permissible limits, and these conceptual orientations have been picked up and reproduced within the media."[37] Wilkinson objected to the Home Secretary's pressure on the BBC Board of Governors that resulted in the banning of a documentary called, "At the Edge of the Union." While the program would have included an interview with an alleged PIRA terrorist leader, Martin McGuinness, Wilkinson believed the program contained a strong message on the futility and horror of extremist violence. His principal objection was the ban by Mrs. Thatcher and Mr. Brittan without first reviewing the program's content: "I too want to prevent, so far as possible, the hijacking and manipulation of the media by the terrorists. But the proper way to do this in a democracy is to encourage the mass media to develop and enforce their own voluntary guidelines and self-restraint in terrorism coverage.... Any introduction of censorship, in whatever guise, plays into the hands of enemies of democracy."[38]

The BBC has established guidelines similar to those published by CBS in the United States. In addition, there is a formal procedure established to ensure adherence to those guidelines. At state-owned BBC radio and television, stories concerning terrorism are checked through several levels of management to ensure compliance. Such a procedure is not new in the United Kingdom. During World War II, "D-notices" (defense notices) were provided by the government to editors to prevent publication of stories harmful to national security. Following this tradition, independent television firms and newspapers as well as the BBC have cooperated with Scotland Yard in limiting the disclosure of information concerning investigations of terrorist attacks. Such cooperation by media management has brought occasional criticism from journalists. BBC reporters staged a worldwide twenty-four-hour strike in 1985 against their board of governors' decision to ban the documentary, "At the Edge of the Union." Other programs banned by the BBC board included "24 Hours" in 1971, "The Scottish Connection" in 1976, and "The City on the Border" and "A Bridge of Sorts" in 1978.

Not unlike the U.S. media, British journalists are extremely competitive. They have produced a contested study that concludes that attempted government control of the news media has resulted in public mistrust with regard to coverage of domestic terrorism and has prevented the public from fully understanding the violence in Northern Ireland.[39] However, unlike the U.S. media, members of the British press must frequently walk streets in their own country that are littered with the aftermath of terrorist atrocities. Perhaps this contact with the stark reality of terrorism constrains somewhat their objections to close cooperation with the government in matters of national security and their coverage of terrorism. Media objections have been limited, and there has been no outcry from a British public, endangered by terrorist attacks, about denying terrorists publicity by restraining the press.

Balancing Democratic Principles and Terrorist Countermeasures in the U.K.

The British public, subjected to terrorist atrocities for more than twenty years, have accepted seemingly controversial antiterrorist legislation as necessary for the preservation of law and order. American professor Barton Ingraham has observed: "What is surprising—if not shocking—to the foreign observer in the light of English history in the preceding century is the alacrity with which the English surrendered practically the totality of their cherished liberties to the discretion of Government officials during an emergency."[40] Ingraham's statement apparently disregards the democratic process of representative legislation by which the English citizens "surrendered" their liberties.

It would seem that American journalism professor Walter Jaehnig has more correctly summarized the United Kingdom's experience as demonstrating that, when a society has been exposed to a long and vicious campaign of political terrorism, "The state will place its highest priority upon protecting itself, despite its expressed concerns about both the professional responsibility of the news media and the protection of civil liberties."[41]

It is important to note the special characteristics of the emergency legislation enacted by the British government during a time of serious terrorist threats to its citizens. In his review of the antiterrorism legislation enacted by Parliament, Crozier noted, "It is very important to make it clear that any emergency legislation that is introduced, including detention without trial, is temporary in nature and will be revoked as soon as possible."[42] Crozier further noted four provisions that were important to the acceptance and success of the United Kingdom's emergency legislation:

(1) draft laws must be easy to understand; (2) the purpose of the emergency legislation is to control an insurgent group that has demonstrated its absolute disdain for the law; (3) all "war measures" must be closely monitored and reviewed periodically; and (4) all laws must be effective and applied equally to all.[43]

Perhaps an overriding factor in the relatively amiable relationship among the British public, press, and government has been a phenomenon recognized by Miller: "Even when legislation exists to restrict the media, democratic social and political norms can prevent the laws' implementation."[44]

Summation of the Comparative Factors for the United Kingdom

The nature of the threat. The conflict in Northern Ireland has defied resolution. PIRA and INLA terrorists, with external support, have threatened U.K. targets both internally and abroad. To the extent that the interest of communist sources in creating difficulties for the United Kingdom can be perceived as having declined, it could be noted that the total capacity of those political terrorist organizations could also have declined. Unfortunately, this decline could possibly be offset in the future by external support from sources opposed to British Middle East foreign policy and U.K. participation in the Persian Gulf conflict. The extremism generated by the deep religious cleavage in Northern Ireland indicates a continuing threat of terrorist violence to the domestic tranquility of the United Kingdom.

Countermeasures to terrorism. Since the onset of violence in Northern Ireland, the government of the United Kingdom has focused on legislative processes to develop and formalize countermeasures. The policies that have emerged are generally moderate, and while some legislative edicts have provided for the restraint of some personal liberties and democratic procedures, one must note that those edicts were imposed through normal democratic legislative processes. With the continuation of PIRA and INLA terrorist attacks into the 1990s, it is apparent that earlier legislated countermeasures have not effectively suppressed terrorism, although declining trends in fatality rates do indicate improvement since the mid–1970s. The U.K. experience demonstrates that the nature of the threat is perhaps the dominant factor in evaluating the challenge of political terrorism to a democracy.

The role of the media. The actions of the BBC in challenging the Thatcher government have demonstrated that a public-subsidized press is not necessarily a government-controlled press. The government appears to have exerted pressure and prevailed in those confrontations only when they have been supported by public outcry. Cooperative agreements reached among the public-subsidized media, the independent media, and the government have been openly publicized and have apparently not drawn significant objection from the media or the public. Compared to the U.S. press, the British subsidized and independent media both appear to be relatively cooperative with government administrations. Previous wartime experience has been credited with the adoption of this cooperative role. When directly challenged by the Conservative government's enforcing of antiterrorist legislation to prevent certain BBC broadcasts, some members of the British press did display their independence by a one-day strike. That demonstration was relatively limited and apparently occurred only once in the two decades following the onset of terrorist violence in Northern Ireland.

The relationship among government, press, and public. The extensive body of antiterrorism legislation that exists in the United Kingdom is a demonstration of public support for the countermeasure policies that have emerged. That legislation has included restraints on the media in the coverage of terrorism, to the extent that it can literally prohibit publication of information on the outlawed PIRA or INLA. However, during the first fifteen years that current antiterrorism legislation has been in effect, the executive branch has only occasionally chosen to invoke its authority by restraining the media in the broadcast of a few specific programs. Only on one occasion did that result in a meaningful protest from the media.

In sum, after more than twenty years of combating a significant domestic terrorist threat supported by external interests, the United Kingdom has adequately demonstrated that countermeasures against terrorism, including restraints on the media's sensationalizing of terrorists and their atrocities, can be applied, and will be accepted by the public, when those countermeasures are developed and implemented through normal democratic legislative processes. The United Kingdom's emergency legislation, including that which restrains the press, has withstood the test of time. Democracy has continued to thrive in the United Kingdom, as has its "bridled" media.

THE EMERGENCE OF CONTEMPORARY TERRORISM IN WEST GERMANY

Modern political terrorism in the Federal Republic of Germany originated with the general dissatisfaction of the Socialist Student Organization with the constitutional left in the early 1960s. The grand coalition of the Social Democratic Party (SPD) with the Christian Democratic Union (CDU) and Christian Social Union (CSU) offered a fundamental challenge to radical student groups. Ulrike Meinhof, as editor of the radical publication *Konkret*, expressed frustration with what was considered a lack of movement toward ambitious reforms: "All Leftists have run over to the Right to boil the common pot and cook in it; there is nothing but one anger, one hatred, one lament...and the exclusion, the hereticising, the bedevilment of what remains has sired a kind of Left. A 'New Left' as it calls itself, so as to doubly signal its appearance."[45]

The new left, with its formal designation as the Extra-Parliamentary Opposition (APO), disintegrated in 1968 and some of its members opted for terrorism as a strategy to pursue political goals. Horst Mahler, an original member of the Baader-Meinhof Gang and a founder of the Red Army Faction, expressed frustration with the failure of the APO to gain acceptance in the West German formal political system:

It can only be termed deeply frustrating to recognize the necessity of a revolution with growing clarity and yet be unable to know who and where the revolutionary class, in other words the beneficiaries of this upheaval itself, actually are.... How easily can such a state of affairs lead to a mood of desperation! From this point, via a completely abstract identification with the liberation struggles in the Third World, the further course led to out-and-out adventurous concepts.[46]

The Baader-Meinhof Gang committed its first terrorist atrocity in 1968 with the firebombing of a Frankfurt shopping center. It stated that to attack was to "prevent the voice of the Extra-Parliamentary Opposition from not being able to find a hearing."[47]

From its inception Baader-Meinhof, which later evolved into the Red Army Faction, considered itself Marxist-Leninist and a part of the "worldwide revolutionary movement." Since 1977, it has concentrated its efforts against the "world's two main imperialistic powers," the United States and West Germany.[48] Specific targets have been U.S. military personnel and facilities, NATO activities, and West German elites.

While Mahler and Meinhof directly linked their atrocities to a political ideology, the motivation of Andreas Baader and some of their other colleagues was more directly related to a cult of violence.[49] Radicals dedicated to revolution, they resorted to "systematically and repeatedly breaking the law," so that the masses would be "weaned from obedience."[50] After being trained by Dr. George Habash's PFLP in 1970 in Lebanon and Jordan, they adopted the name of *Rote Armee Fraktion* (Red Army Faction, or RAF) and robbed numerous banks to finance their operations. They stole 11.6 million Deutsche Marks between 1970 and 1978. They armed themselves by stealing weapons from NATO facilities.

The RAF made six serious bomb attacks in May 1972 across West Germany, at Frankfurt, Munich, Augsburg, Hamburg, Karlsruhe, and Heidelberg. Following tips from the frightened German public, authorities arrested six key members of the group—Baader, Meinhof, Meins, Raspe, Ensslin, and Müller. Within a year, the group had regained its strength with strongholds in Frankfurt, Hamburg, and Amsterdam, and had set as is primary goal the freeing of its imprisoned leaders. However, the group was again penetrated and demolished by German and Netherlands authorities in February 1974. It rebuilt for a third time in 1975 and switched to more violent tactics with the murder of officials and diplomats.

In April 1975, RAF terrorists seized the West German embassy in Stockholm and murdered the military and commercial attachés. Their principal demand was for the release of their jailed colleagues. However, security forces overpowered the attackers and they were also imprisoned.

In November 1976, the arrest of two lawyers, Siegfried Haag and Roland Mayer, at an autobahn checkpoint produced evidence that the RAF had again reformed. Despite the imprisonment of its leader, Haag, the RAF was strong enough to commit several atrocities in 1977, including the murder of Attorney General Siegfried Buback and his guards, the murder of banker Jurgen Ponto, and the kidnapping and murder of Hanns-Martin Schleyer after his guards had been killed.

The operational history of the RAF is unique in that its imprisoned leaders were able to continue to direct the activities of the organization through lawyer contacts. The lawyers, who linked those in prison with their operating colleagues, also recruited other young lawyers. By 1979, one of the three main groups of the organization was composed entirely of lawyers. Into the 1980s, the RAF was concentrated in Hamburg, Baden-Württemberg, Hessen, and Berlin. It numbered about 150 members, about 25 of whom were active terrorists. More than half of the operatives were women.[51]

The 2nd June Movement lacked the clear political goals and consistency of the RAF, but its tactics were apparently more effective. In 1975, 2nd June kidnapped Christian Democrat leader Peter Lorenz in Berlin and succeeded in exchanging him for the release of five of their imprisoned colleagues, who were given safe conduct to South Yemen. Authorities were successful in suppressing 2nd June activities after the Lorenz kidnapping, but four female members of the group escaped from a West Berlin prison in 1976. In 1978, four members of 2nd June were arrested in Bulgaria and extradited to West Germany.[52]

The Revolutionary Cells (RZ) have received less publicity than the RAF and 2nd June. However, they were responsible for twenty bombings and incendiary attacks between 1973 and 1979, in which several people were killed. Unlike the RAF and 2nd June, the RZ does not operate entirely underground. The majority of its members are unknown to authorities. The RZ organization consists of small groups of three to five members who consider themselves "off-hours" terrorists. They lead normal lives participating in left-wing politics and make "anti-imperialist" and "anti-Zionist" terrorist strikes at U.S. and Israeli targets mainly in West Germany. They have developed links to the PIRA as well as to Palestinian terrorist groups.

Three main terrorist groups were operating in West Germany during the 1980s—the left extremist Red Army Faction, the Revolutionary Cells, and the neo-Nazi Hepp-Hexel organization. Although a right extremist group, the neo-Nazi Hepp-Hexel organization professes an anti-imperialist ideology. Founded in 1982, its atrocities are mainly aimed at U.S. military personnel and facilities. It views the United States as occupying West Germany, with the West German government an alien regime imposed upon the Germans. Having undergone training by the PLO in Lebanon, its members also are concerned with attacking Israeli targets.

Considerable support for German terrorist groups has come from the Soviet bloc and from the Palestinians. Crozier has cited Moscow's support for Baader-Meinhof and specifically for Klaus Rainer Rohl and his wife, Ulrike Meinhof: "The Baader-Meinhof Gang was secretly subsidized by the East Germans, whose Ministry of State Security is under the control of the KGB." Rohl and Meinhof were both "secret members of the Communist party from 1956 to 1964, and Rohl received about $250,000 (some sources say $400,000) in subsidies through East Berlin and Prague."[53]

The Baader-Meinhof Gang, and later the RAF, received continual support from the East German secret police in the form of training, arms and ammunition, money, and false papers and identity cards.[54] After a 1975 car accident in Belgium, police found documents revealing the existence of a KGB center in Vienna, working to "enliven" terrorist formations in West Germany, Italy, Belgium, the Netherlands, and France. Alexander Benyaminov, head of the Soviet delegation to the U.N. International Atomic Energy Agency, was reportedly in charge.[55]

All the hard-core members of the RAF were trained by Palestinians in the South Yemen camps.[56] German terrorists took part in Palestinian atrocities, such as the kidnapping of the OPEC oil ministers by the Carlos organization in 1975. In return, the Palestinians gave operational support to German terrorists, such as the diversionary hijacking to Mogadishu of a Lufthansa airliner during the RAF's kidnapping and murder of German industrialist Hanns-Martin Schleyer.[57]

Speaking at an international seminar on terrorism in Tel Aviv in 1979, the director of the West Germany Department for Defense of the Constitution, Hans-Josef Horchem, noted that, between January 1970 and April 1979, thirty-one people had been murdered by terrorists in Germany, including three diplomats, four justice officials, and nine policemen. Ninety-seven had been injured in terrorist bombings and shootings, and 163 were taken hostage. Terrorists had committed ten cases of arson, twenty-five bombings, and thirty bank robberies with losses estimated at DM 5.4 million.[58]

The Prompt Response to Terrorism by West Germany

Unlike the United Kingdom, terrorism in West Germany in the 1960s and 1970s was not anchored in historic nationalism or religious conflict. The new-left ideology and terrorism of Baader-Meinhof began in the 1960s with no government countermeasures in existence. The initial concentration of atrocities was against political figures and institutions and against prosperous industrialists. This selection of targets perhaps proved somewhat derogatory to the terrorists' success, in that the endangerment of the elite likely created a sense of urgency in the development of countermeasures. There were, however, sufficient atrocities committed against random targets to create an atmosphere of fear in the general public.

For the first twenty years after the formation of the Federal Republic of Germany, the ruling coalition of the CDU and the CSU had stressed domestic security as its most prominent electoral theme.[59] In May 1968, the West German government drafted emergency legislation to deal with growing student unrest and demonstrations, which were considered a leftist threat. The Bundestag passed the emergency measures by a vote of 384 to 100, with 1 abstention. The first antiterrorism legislation was enacted in December 1971, with stiffer prison sentences for hijackers and kidnappers. For example, a minimum penalty of five years' imprisonment was imposed for the hijacking or attack of an aircraft. If manslaughter occurred during such an event, ten years became the minimum sentence. By the 1976 elections, numerous attacks upon the elite had brought terrorism to the fore as a challenge to domestic security and a critical political issue.

After Interior Minister Hans-Dietrich Genscher's attempt to negotiate with Black September terrorists at the 1972 Olympic Games in Munich failed, conflict developed between Bonn and Munich.[60] The West German government then accelerated the establishment of a countermeasures program that included creation of the antiterrorist unit *Grenzschutzgruppe* 9 (Border Protection Group 9, or GSG–9), composed initially of six units of thirty members each. Thoroughly trained in terrorist tactics, psychology, and differing modes of combat, GSG–9 units were deployed around the Federal Republic.[61] An elaborate computerized intelligence system was also developed to combat terrorists.

Also in 1972, the powers of the Office for the Protection of the Constitution were expanded to allow for the observation of politically motivated anticonstitutional activities. Other countermeasure legislation included the *Radikalenerlass* (Radicals Ordinance) of 1972, which requires that all prospective employees of the FRG civil service indicate if they have ever been affiliated with any extremist organization. By August 1977, about a half million Germans had been checked.[62] The government also moved to increase airport security and established telephone hotlines to encourage the public to participate by informing on terrorists.

Bonn was embarrassed in February 1975 when the government's "Grand-Crisis Committee" conceded to 2nd June Movement demands for the release of five jailed terrorists in exchange for kidnapped CDU West Berlin mayoral candidate Peter Lorenz.[63] In April, Chancellor Schmidt described the Holger Meins Commando attack[64] upon the West German embassy in Stockholm as, "the gravest challenge our constitutional state has faced in its 26 years of history."[65]

The FRG parliament reacted with antiterrorism legislation that included increased prison terms for terrorists. In view of the RAF's demonstrated success in conducting operations through the legal counsels for their imprisoned leaders, legislation was enacted that forbade one attorney to defend several clients accused of terrorism. Additionally, a defense attorney suspected of involvement in a defendant's crime could be excluded from the trial. It was also made possible to conduct a trial with the accused not present, as in the case of a hunger strike by the defendant. Laws also were made to control written communication between a defense lawyer and a client accused of terrorism, to provide separation panels between lawyers and accused terrorists during meetings, and to prevent contact between defense lawyers and accused terrorists when such contact was deemed to be involved with an escape.

In January 1976, the Anti-Constitutional Advocacy Act provided for prosecution of those who publicly advocated or encouraged others to "commit an offense against the stability and security of the Federal Republic."[66] The June 1976 Anti-Terror Law outlawed the formation of terrorist associations and increased the penalties for membership. Laws that permitted detention without trial, as well as fines and imprisonment for publishing terrorist manuals, were also written in 1976. A 1978 law allowed the search of all apartments within an apartment block when residents of one apartment were suspected of involvement with terrorism.

The Evolution of Media Cooperation with the West German Government

Until 1975 Bonn had normally attempted negotiations with terrorists and frequently granted concessions. Horchem indicates that a demonstrated government policy is a decisive factor for terrorists considering the commission of atrocities. He regards Chancellor Schmidt's firm stance during the 1975 seizing of the West German embassy in Stockholm (which followed the government's earlier capitulation to 2nd June Movement terrorists' demands for the release of prisoners in exchange for the life of Peter Lorenz) as a contributing factor to the cessation of terrorist atrocities for the following eighteen months.[67]

Horchem is adamant in his belief that the media can either seriously undermine or credibly support a firm policy by the government. He cites as a positive example the kidnapping of Hanns-Martin Schleyer in 1977, in which the initial terrorist demands included media broadcasts of prisoner releases and a videotape of Schleyer. During the two months of Schleyer's captivity, the RAF provided numerous videotapes and photographs to the media, along with ultimatums and communiqués. However, "the West German press conducted itself with remarkable restraint,"[68] denying the RAF the publicity upon which it had planned. Practically no mention was made in the press of the fact that the RAF was demanding the release of its leaders in exchange for Schleyer's life. Additionally, a disinformation tactic was coordinated between authorities and the press to mislead the terrorists about efforts to release their leaders.

During the sixty-day standoff between the RAF and Bonn, a Palestinian terrorist group attempted to aid the RAF in breaking the silence of the media by hijacking a Lufthansa airliner to Mogadishu, Somalia. Continuing their firm stance, the West Germans dispatched a GSG–9 unit that successfully stormed the airliner and rescued the hostages after the terrorists had murdered the captain. Apparently realizing that the government was not going to capitulate and release their jailed leaders, the RAF terrorists murdered Schleyer. Four of the jailed leaders committed suicide in Stuttgart-Stammheim prison when they learned of the rescue at Mogadishu.[69]

In 1986, close cooperation between the government and the media was again demonstrated when West German security forces captured a

Lebanese terrorist who had participated in the 1985 hijacking of TWA Flight 847 to Beirut. When the international media announced that the United States would seek extradition of the terrorist, other Shiite terrorists promptly kidnapped two West Germans in Beirut and demanded an exchange. The West German government and media then cooperated on a news blackout of the extradition proceedings that denied the Beirut kidnappers vital information and allowed negotiations between the United States and the Federal Republic of Germany to proceed without interruption.

Cooperation between the media and the government in West Germany did not automatically commence with the emergence of terrorism. West German ZDF Television Washington correspondent Dieter Kronzucker has described the evolution of media cooperation with West German authorities. He observed that the 1970 killing in Guatemala of a German ambassador taken hostage by the FAR drew sympathy from the West German press because of the poor social and economic conditions in Guatemala. At that time, Latin American guerrillas were reportedly regarded as romantic revolutionaries by some of the West German press. However, when terrorists began kidnapping prominent Germans in the Federal Republic, the mood changed. After the 2nd June Movement demanded, and received, live coverage by both TV networks of the release of its jailed members in exchange for the life of Peter Lorenz, Kronzucker noted: "This changed a lot of the minds of my fellow colleagues. It was the start of cooperation between the government and many journalists."[70]

A challenge emerged to media cooperation with the government as a result of the Schleyer kidnapping and murder. Pridham has reported that the media's cooperation in restricting coverage initiated a controversy over the principle of informing the public, which was later magnified when government mistakes made during the search for Schleyer came to light, including ignoring a tip that might have saved Schleyer.[71] Nevertheless, Chancellor Schmidt was able to capitalize on the success of the Mogadishu rescue. He was characterized by the press as "After Mogadishu: The Admired German."[72] He used his popularity to increase government antiterrorist measures. This included a concentrated attempt to use the media to apply psychological pressure on the terrorists, and to more fully inform the public about increasing security measures.[73]

Public Support of West Germany's Countermeasures

The German public has been most supportive of its government's antiterrorist policies, which have been complemented by a cooperative media. The people were genuinely frightened by the terrorist atrocities. In the midst of the Schleyer affair, a public opinion poll showed that 67 percent favored a return to the death penalty (banned under FRG Basic Law).[74] In May 1975, an Allensbach poll had shown that 69 percent of the West Germans would accept limitations on their personal freedoms for the sake of combating terrorism; by March 1978, another Allensbach poll showed 90 percent of the population believing that West Germany was threatened by terrorism.[75] By the end of 1978, an Infas poll also showed that 83 percent thought terrorism would increase.[76]

There were, of course, a few voices raised in dissent. The degree of self-censorship practiced by the West German media led noted author Heinrich Böll to comment: "The media have become so careful, that the laws don't actually have to be changed."[77]

The West German government displayed a great deal of political expertise early in the war against terrorism by encouraging participation by the public. Photographs of known terrorists were widely distributed, and hotlines were made available for reporting suspicious activity. The direct participation of a German public in law enforcement can be regarded as part of their political culture. In their 1963 classic, *The Civic Culture*, surveys by Gabriel Almond and Sidney Verba found the Germans more politically informed and considerably prouder of their nation than the citizens of the United States, the United Kingdom, Italy, or Mexico. Motivated by a genuine fear of terrorism, politically aware of the situation, and concerned with protecting their nation, the German people united in their time of national stress. Self-restraint on the part of the news media and the public's cooperation with government anti-terrorist policies, including actual participation in the identification and reporting of terrorists, enabled German authorities to suppress terrorist organizations that held potential for rapid expansion. As reported by Schlagheck:

The antiterrorist emergency laws and other state policies have been very well received by the German public. No election has raised the issue of overreacting to terrorism and thereby imperiling democracy; to the contrary, the German public has supported government efforts to end terrorism and "restore law and order."[78]

Summation of Comparative Factors for West Germany

The nature of the threat. The atrocities committed by terrorist organizations against West German targets commencing in the late 1960s were equally vicious and intense as those committed by the PIRA and the INLA against the United Kingdom. However, the roots of the West German terrorist groups were not anchored in such extremism as that inspired by the religious cleavage in Northern Ireland. The leftist ideology upon which the principal terrorist movements were based did not find support in a prosperous and expanding West German democracy. Consequently, lacking internal support in the face of effective counter-measures, and with external support from communist sources lessening, the political terrorist threat in West Germany was declining or largely suppressed by the late 1980s.

Countermeasures to terrorism. The first terrorist challenges to the post–World War II West German government were external groups, predominantly in Latin America, which enjoyed some early sympathy from the German public and press. Consequently, an early policy of negotiation emerged. When the threat became internal and more intense, negotiation policies were replaced by a more firm stance by the executive branch, which was in turn augmented by legislative actions to provide for more staunch countermeasure policies. By the late 1970s, a balance of effective legislation and firm executive response against terrorism had been achieved.

The role of the media. The West German media during the 1960s to 1980s was a mix of some public-subsidized broadcast media and an increasing number of independent newspapers and other publications. Early in the threat period they demonstrated a vulnerability to terrorist exploitation not unlike the highly competitive U.S. media. However, after the kidnapping of Peter Lorenz in February 1975, during which both Bonn and the television news media were made to look powerless, the West German press evidently chose to pursue a supportive role against political terrorism. The guidelines, media-government agreements, and detailed legislation on media coverage of terrorism that emerged in the United Kingdom were not forthcoming in the Federal Republic, although some portions of the 1976 Anti-Constitutional Advocacy Act could have been enforced to constrain the media's coverage of terrorism if it had been deemed necessary.

The relationship of government, press, and public. The West German public proved highly supportive of increasingly firm antiterrorist legislation and policies. Perhaps a strong postwar motivation for personal security dominated their beliefs and actions. This was certainly reflected in the political platforms of the successful parties. The public evidently readily accepted the self-restraint the media demonstrated in the coverage of terrorism. The West German news media reported on terrorist atrocities as they were occurring, however, as demonstrated during the Schleyer affair, their reporting was relatively carefully designed to avoid exploitation by terrorists and was positively supportive of the efforts of law enforcement agencies in combating terrorism. While terrorist organizations still exist in West Germany, the unification of public, media, and government in opposition has sharply limited their activities and will likely continue to do so in the future, the reunification process of a divided Germany that is likely to enhance the possibility of increased economic and social dissatisfaction and political violence notwith-standing.

TERRORISM AND ITALY'S MULTIPARTY DEMOCRACY

Carlo Pisacane was an Italian socialist who died in an attempt to rally the peasantry of southern Italy against the Bourbons in 1857. In his *Political Testament* he noted the precedence of the propaganda of deeds over the propaganda of ideas: "The propaganda of the idea is a chimera. . . . Ideas result from deeds, not the latter from the former. . . . Conspiracies, plots and attempts are the series of deeds by which Italy proceeds to her goal."[79]

Pisacane's forecast for violent domestic politics in Italy seemed to hold after World War II. Terrorism came from the right as well as the left. The right was initially viewed by the Allies as a stabilizing influence. It was strongly anticommunist and contained the core of bureaucrats, judiciary, and military personnel inherited by the new regime from twenty-one years of fascist dictatorship. Terror from the right emerged with an extreme right-wing party, the Italian Social Movement (MSI). The strategy of its 1968 leader, Giorgio Almirante, was "combining the double-breasted suit with the club."[80] He attempted to ensure the survival of the MSI in Italy's parliament by aligning with the Monarchist Party while simultaneously giving support to neofascist violence.

Furlong has attributed the beginning of what he terms the first phase of post–1968 Italian violence to the right wing. A 12 December 1969 bombing of the National Agricultural Bank at the Piazza Fontana in Milan killed seventeen persons. Anarchists Pietro Valpreda and Giuseppe Pinelli were arrested. Pinelli died shortly thereafter when he fell from a window at Milanese police headquarters.[81] It took nine years to process the case, during which time Valpreda was acquitted and two neofascists were convicted in absentia, in the midst of accusations of security forces involvement in right-wing terrorism. After an abortive coup d'état in December 1970, right-wing extremists continued with bomb attacks against political targets through the end of 1973.[82]

Terror from the left gained prominence with the initiation of Red Brigades violence in Milan in August 1970.[83] Leaders Renato Curcio and Margherita Cagol emerged from a group called the Sinistra Proletaria. Their early 1970s attacks were more symbolic than spectacular, with the destruction of automobiles of known neofascists and industrialists. Occasionally they would conduct a heavily publicized kidnapping, with a "proletarian trial" followed by the release of the victim. It has been estimated that more than 12,000 terrorist acts occurred in Italy between 1969 and 1980.[84]

In Furlong's second phase of Italian terrorism (1974–1979), violence increased dramatically, from 422 terrorist attacks in 1974, to 628 in 1975, to 1,201 in 1976, to 2,127 in 1977, and 2,395 in 1978.[85] Declaring its strategy to "strike at the heart of the state,"[86] the Red Brigades strove for maximum political impact with such atrocities as the kidnapping of Public Prosecutor Mario Sossi in Genoa in April 1974, the murder of Genoa's Chief Magistrate Francesco Coco in June 1976, and the kidnapping and murder of Aldo Moro, leader of the Christian Democratic Party (DC) in March 1978. The Red Brigades apparently united with other Western European terrorist groups against NATO, with their kidnapping of U.S. Army General Dozier in 1982.

During the terror decade of the 1970s the most important political issue in Italy was the entry of the Communist Party (PCI) into the government. The PCI policy toward the Red Brigades and other similar groups was not to consider them as leftist organizations but rather as perpetrators of violence akin to the neofascists.[87]

Like the Soviet Union, the Red Brigades viewed the Italian Communist Party's merger with the Italian political system as a betrayal of communist ideology. The Red Brigades described its terrorist attacks as a version of a class war in which it was the leader of the proletariat's armed struggle:

The Red Brigades are not the Communist Party of Combat, but an armed vanguard which works inside the metropolitan proletariat for its construction. While we affirm that BR and Party of Combat are not identical, we affirm with equal clarity that the armed vanguard must "act as a Party" from the very beginning.[88]

The Red Brigades received considerable support from the Soviet bloc, most of which was relayed to them through the PLO. Grenades, antitank mines, explosives, machine guns, and Strella missiles were passed through the Palestinians to the Red Brigades, and its leaders were trained in Palestinian camps in Jordan in 1970.[89] Substantial numbers of Italian terrorists were also trained at the Czechoslovakian Karlovy Vary camp.[90] Significant quantities of Soviet-bloc weapons were delivered to the Red Brigades from Prague, by way of Hungary and Austria.[91]

Italy's Political Response to Red Brigades Terror

Furlong notes that it took Italian political parties "at least five years to alert themselves seriously to the problem of terrorism."[92] In describing the Italians' long suffering from terrorism, Furlong explains:

Major failings in the response to terrorism have been the deliberate manipulation of organised political violence to satisfy short-term goals—goals that have been predominantly electoral but that have also been concerned with the formation of alliances within and between parties—and, more broadly, the continued underestimation by politicians and senior civil servants of the capacity of clandestine groups to strike politically significant targets and of their intention to do so. . . . The Italian state has been attempting to "ride the tiger."[93]

The Christian Democratic Party used terrorist attacks to discredit the parties of the left. The PCI was initially pressed into a defensive stature on questions of internal security. The disclosure of information linking government security forces with neofascists, and increased political power from election victories, allowed the PCI to move to a more offensive position on internal security, and the major parties could then finally agree on antiterrorism strategies.

Before 1974, the DC advocated stronger law enforcement measures while the Socialist Party (PSI) and the PCI looked for reform and democratization of the *Carabinieri* (national police). In 1949, DC ministers had refused to demilitarize the police. Their view was that the major function of the police was maintaining public order rather than the pursuit of criminals. Hence, the *Corpo delle Guardie di Public Sicurezza* (local police) were ill equipped to combat the overwhelming intensity of terrorist attacks in the 1970s. The lack of a coordinated response to terrorism in Italy was sarcastically noted by Leonardo Sciascia:

The central error of the Red Brigades consists precisely in believing that they can succeed in striking at the heart of the State. The heart of the Italian State does not exist. Neither, any longer, does its brain. And it is that which paradoxically is its strength or at least its capacity to resist.[94]

Italy's criminal code that existed in 1969 had its roots in the fascist era. Article 270 outlawed organizers and members of subversive associations, while Article 306 penalized those who became involved with armed groups for the purpose of overthrowing the state.[95] With such pervasive powers already in effect, Leonard Weinberg and William Eubank have noted that "it is not surprising that Italian legislators did not react immediately to the onset of terrorism by enacting a wholly new set of emergency measures. . . . The state already had what it needed to fight it."[96]

After bomb attacks in Brescia and Bologna in 1974, the General Inspectorate for Action Against Terrorism and Armed Bands was formed to allow greater coordination of the police and the *Carabinieri*. A special unit to combat the Red Brigades was also created under *Carabinieri* General Carlo Alberto dalla Chiesa.[97] Both of these units were later disbanded and their functions placed under the Defense Information Service (SID) in 1976.[98] As a result of the Aldo Moro kidnapping, a June 1978 administrative decree again formed a special antiterrorist group from various law enforcement agencies, with General dalla Chiesa at the head. His success against Red Brigades terrorists gained for him the support of all major parties and his reappointment in August 1979. He was later assassinated by the Mafia in Sicily.[99]

Legislation accompanied the improvement of antiterrorist law enforcement organization. The Reale Law of May 1975 contained provisions for all forms of violence against the state. More severe sentences for terrorists, restrictions on bail, arrest without formal warrant, and increased law enforcement authority to search were included. Article 1 imposed mandatory confinement for those awaiting trial for terrorist acts. The police were also granted broader authority involving the apprehension of suspected terrorists. When those powers brought forth protests about the endangerment of civil liberties, a national referendum in June 1978 (after the murder of Aldo Moro) substantially sustained the laws.[100] July 1977 amendments to the Reale Act included controls on the use of firearms and explosives. After the murder of Aldo Moro, further amendments allowed interrogation without the presence of defense lawyers and increased penalties for kidnapping. The *Carabinieri* and the local police also formed special antiterrorist assault teams. U.S. General James Dozier was rescued from the Red Brigades by one of those teams known as the *teste di cuoio* (leather heads).[101]

When Red Brigades terrorists reacted to the introduction of the even broader December 1979 Urgent Measures for the Protection of the Democratic Order and Public Security Act by murdering four magistrates, their atrocities likely served to encourage wider public agreement with the imposition of even harsher policies. The draft 1979 emergency measures were passed in 1980 and later upheld by a national referendum in 1981.[102]

While slow to get underway, Italy's legislative actions against terrorism have been rated by some as the toughest in Europe. As per Friedlander's observations, legislation enacted by the Italian parliament in February 1980,

authorizes warrantless searches and wiretaps in a pre-Watergate fashion, permits Italian police to arrest and hold suspects for forty-eight hours without notifying anyone, allows accused terrorist actors to be detained for up to twelve years without trial, encourages the questioning of suspects outside of the presence of a lawyer, and mandates a life sentence for anyone convicted of murdering policemen, judges, attorneys, witnesses, and union officials.[103]

A study of Italian elections from 1968 to 1979 has shown that the political parties "were rewarded when they were perceived in the electorate and elsewhere as opposed to political violence and punished when they were viewed however dimly as somehow linked to terrorism."[104]

The eventual realization by the multiparty leadership that the growing terrorist threat was overwhelming the state's law enforcement capability, dalla Chiesa's leadership in the reorganized law enforcement structure, supportive legislation inspired by the Moro atrocity, and a judicial system that refused to be intimidated by the campaign of terror ultimately resulted in the suppression, but notably not the destruction, of the Red Brigades.

The Enlightenment of the Italian Media

In the splintered Italian multiparty political system, where shifting coalitions have produced power changes at the rate of almost one new government per year, the Italian news media have become political pawns. Attempting to prosper in a democratic free-market environment, segments of the free press have sought to align their interests with political power groups and have been drawn into Italy's political morass.

Il Tempo correspondent Marino de Medici chose these words to describe the Italian news media: "It has been a political propagandist, effectively employed by political parties.... Journalists are politicians. In Italy we are political participants."[105]

In the early days of the Red Brigades violence, the Italian press tended to glamorize their attacks. In this regard, the media were merely reflecting the insincerity of the political parties toward political violence. As the atrocities of the Red Brigades worsened, the Italian news media initially sensationalized the brutality. With the hideous murder of the popular leader Aldo Moro in 1978, the media and the public abruptly realized the extent of the terrorist threat. The press responded to the public outcry within the deglamorization of the Red Brigades. As noted by Weinberg and Eubank, "there was an increasing tendency to depict their acts as ones of senseless bestiality, devoid of serious political content."[106] Italy's successful suppression of their terror quickly followed.

Correspondent de Medici noted that there was an initial sympathy in the Italian press for the Red Brigades, and the Red Brigades capitalized on that sympathy with clever exploitation. However, "when a picture of a judge ... appeared with the entire transcript of his 'interrogation' by the Red Brigades, people finally began to ask.... What did this have to do with the people's right to know?"[107]

Summation of Comparative Factors for Italy

The nature of the threat. Post–World War II violence in Italy originated with neofascist groups and other right extremists with connections to legalized political parties. The emergence of the leftist Red Brigades began a decade of terror for Italy in the 1970s. The Red Brigades had its roots in Italy's universities, which allowed a base for rapid expansion. As it became more violent, it gained external support from Soviet sources critical of the integration of the Italian Communist Party into the Italian political system, and who likely viewed the Red Brigades as an instrument with which to threaten Italy's domestic tranquility and NATO's southern flank. At the height of the violence in 1978, Italy was enduring more than six terrorist attacks a day. Italy's public, press, fragmented political system, law enforcement agencies, and judiciary finally united to overcome the threat, but the Red Brigades has been suppressed, not destroyed. With the decline of external support from communist sources, its capability has been significantly reduced. However, Italy's participation in the coalition forces during the Persian Gulf crisis could result in increased support for the Red Brigades from radical Middle East sources.

Countermeasures to terrorism. A fragmented multiparty system and a disorganized law enforcement system delayed an effective national response to the 1970s terror in Italy. While the 1974 formation of a special antiterrorist law enforcement agency and 1975 antiterrorist legislation marked the beginning of political cooperation to oppose the threat, it was likely the 1978 murder of Aldo Moro served as the catalyst to unite Italy against the Red Brigades. Increasingly harsh legislation followed that now marks Italian antiterrorist laws as among the toughest in Europe.

The role of the media. Immersed in the splintered politics of Italy, the media initially romanticized the Red Brigades and likely conjured a measure of public acceptance of its early, low-level violence. As the violence turned terroristic, the Italian press found itself discredited before the public by the skillful manipulation and exploitation of the Red Brigades. Apparently the shocking murder of Aldo Moro and several judicial figures in the late 1970s motivated members of the Italian media to disentangle themselves from the terrorists and become more supportive of the surging unification movement to suppress the Red Brigades. However, the nature of Italy's splintered multiparty political system appears to have been conducive to an equally splintered news media with tendencies to participate in the political process. The ultimate opposition of the Italian media to the Red Brigades could be only an aberration, and is likely not an indication of future Italian media unity against terrorist exploitation.

The relationship of government, press, and public. Public outrage over the seemingly always more hideous atrocities committed by the Red Brigades was likely a potent motivational force behind the strict antiterrorist legislation finally enacted. While Italian politics demonstrates the difficulties with the formulation and implementation of effective policies in a democratic multiparty system, it also demonstrates that, when threatened to an extreme extent, the system could respond sufficiently to ensure its own survival. It also seems likely that public sentiment was important in influencing the media to limit their exploitation by the Red Brigades and become more sympathetic to the seriously threatened state. The Italy of the 1970s is a disturbing example, and a stern warning, of how dangerous a terrorist campaign can become when it is waged in an environment of an indecisive government, an exploitable media, and a vulnerable public.

COMPARATIVE SUMMATION OF THE UNITED KINGDOM, WEST GERMANY, AND ITALY

The historical experience of the state with terrorism is evidently an important factor in determining counterterror policies and the media's role. When the level of threat is sufficient, countermeasure policies will emerge and restraints on the media will be self-imposed or willingly accepted by both the press and the public.

The case of the United Kingdom emphasizes the importance of the originating source of political violence. When terrorism erupts from cleavages within, especially from deeply held religious convictions and loyalties, the problem of suppression may be overwhelming. The U.K. experience demonstrates a democratic response of immediate and extensive legislation to combat the threat. It also shows that the media can be coopted to contribute to countermeasures even in a volatile and emotional environment. It is important to view the cooperation of the media in the United Kingdom in terms of their personal exposure to the terrorist threat, and the relatively less competitive nature of a combined public-subsidized and private media.

The case of the Federal Republic of Germany indicates that the public can be an important force in the suppression of terrorism. Along with support for countermeasure policies and active participation in the apprehension of terrorists, the West German public's opinion was an important force in encouraging the media to resist exploitation by the terrorists. As evidenced in the Federal Republic in the early 1970s, when terrorist exploitation of the media reaches a level of absurdity, and the citizenry experiences a certain level of threat from terrorists, public pressures on the legislative and executive institutions contribute to restraining the media. As per the United Kingdom, the West German case vividly illustrates that (1) media exploitation can be restrained during a terrorist campaign without damaging the democracy, and (2) where terrorist exploitation of the media is restrained, terrorism declines.

Italy has demonstrated the vulnerability of a multiparty democratic system to terrorist attack. When the initial reaction of fiercely competitive parties is to use the occurrence of political violence to their own electoral advantage, countermeasures are slow to develop. However, Italy's experience has also shown that when the democratic institutions of law enforcement and judiciary stand fast, the nation can endure until the political parties come into line and unite against the terrorist threat. Like the United Kingdom and West Germany, Italy is another example that there is a threshold at which the threatened public will no longer tolerate terrorist exploitation of its media, and changes will be brought about. In the United Kingdom the media were restrained mostly by legislative and executive pressure; in the Federal Republic, they were restrained by themselves and by public opinion; in Italy, media restraint was mostly self-imposed in response to public outcry.

Very importantly, the United Kingdom, the Federal Republic of Germany, and Italy demonstrate that terrorist exploitation of the media can be reduced without destroying democracy, and such restraint on the media is normally accompanied by a decline in terrorism.

NOTES

1. Commission on Freedom of the Press, *A Free and Responsible Press* (Chicago: University of Chicago, 1947), 126–27.

2. Neil Livingstone, "Terrorism and the Media Revolution," in *Fighting Back: Winning the War against Terrorism*, eds. Neil Livingstone and Terrell Arnold (Lexington, Mass.: D. C. Heath, 1986), 225–26.

3. Preston Horstman, remarks in a debate sponsored by the Radio-Television Directors Association, Washington Chapter, Washington, D.C., March 1977; quoted in a report to the National News Council, "Paper on Terrorism," in *Terrorism, the Media, and the Law*, ed. Abraham Miller (Dobbs Ferry, N.Y.: Transnational Publishers, 1982), 138.

4. M. Cherif Bassiouni, seminar remarks in *The Media and Terrorism: A Seminar Sponsored by the Chicago Sun-Times and Chicago Daily News* (Chicago: Field Enterprises, 1977), 9; cited in a report to the National News Council, "Paper on Terrorism," 137–38.

5. Charles Fenyvesi, seminar remarks in *The Media and Terrorism: A Seminar Sponsored by the Chicago Sun-Times and Chicago Daily News* (Chicago: Field Enterprises, 1977), 30; cited in a report to the National News Council, "Paper on Terrorism," 138.

6. Richard Wald, lecture at University of California-Riverside, 21 March 1977; quoted in a report to the National News Council, "Paper on Terrorism," 137.

7. *New York Times*, 14 December 1979, A16.

8. Paul Wilkinson, "Terrorism versus Liberal Democracy: The Problem of Response," *Conflict Studies*, no. 67 (London: Institute for the Study of Conflict, 1976).

9. Survey questions and polls cited in Brian Jenkins, "Statements About Terrorism," in *Terrorism, The Reference Shelf*, ed. Steven Anzovin, vol. 58, no. 3 (New York: H. W. Wilson, 1986), 17.

10. *Die Welt* (Hamburg), 31 October 1977, 2.

11. Staff, Institute for the Study of Conflict, "Western Europe," in *Annual of Power and Conflict 1981–82* (London: Institute for the Study of Conflict, 1982), 185.

12. Royal Ulster Constabulary Press Office, Belfast, cited in Paul Wilkinson, *Terrorism and the Liberal State*, 2d ed. (New York: New York University Press, 1986), 88.

13. *An Phoblacht* (Dublin), 12 April 1977; quoted in Claire Sterling, *The Terror Network: The Secret War of International Terrorism* (New York: Holt, Rinehart and Winston, 1981), 158.

14. John Biggs-Davison, "Moscow's link to Irish troubles," in *Christian Science Monitor*, 14 March 1977, 31.

15. Sterling, *The Terror Network*, 158–59.

16. Document of the U.S. Congress, House Committee on Internal Security, 1 August 1974; cited in Sterling, *The Terror Network*, 155.

17. Maria McGuire, *To Take Arms: A Year in the Provisional IRA* (London: Macmillan, 1973), 37–68.

18. John Barron, *KGB: The Secret Work of Soviet Secret Agents* (New York: Bantam Books, 1974), 347.

19. *Daily Mail* (London), 2 April 1973; cited in Sterling, *The Terror Network*, 160.

20. *Daily Telegraph* (London), 3 September 1979; cited in Sterling, *The Terror Network*, 161.

21. Sterling, *The Terror Network*, 167–68.

22. Roger Hull, *The Irish Triangle: Conflict in Northern Ireland* (Princeton, N.J.: Princeton University Press, 1976), 211.

23. Donna Schlagheck, *International Terrorism: An Introduction to the Concepts and Actors* (Lexington, Mass.: Lexington Books, 1988), 106.

24. John McGuffin, *Internment* (Tralee, Ireland: Anvil Books, 1973), 87; cited in Schlagheck, *International Terrorism*, 106.

25. Drawn from Schlagheck, *International Terrorism*, 107–108.

26. Peter Janke and Richard Sim, "Western Europe's Political Advance," in *Annual of Power and Conflict: 1979–80* (London: Institute for the Study of Conflict, 1980), 69.

27. Abraham Miller, "Terrorism, the Media, and the Law: A Discussion of the Issues," in *Terrorism, the Media, and the Law*, ed. Abraham Miller (Dobbs Ferry, N.Y.: Transnational Publishers, 1982), 44.

28. Republic of Ireland, *Offences Against the State (Amendment) Act 1972*, 3(1)b and 3(2); cited in E. Moxon-Browne, "Terrorism in Northern Ireland: The Case of the Provisional IRA," in *Terrorism: A Challenge to the State*, ed. Juliet Lodge (New York: St. Martin's, 1981), 157.

29. Margaret Thatcher, quoted in Walter Jaehnig, "Terrorism in Britain: On the Limits of Free Expression," in *Terrorism, the Media, and the Law*, ed. Abraham Miller (Dobbs Ferry, N.Y.: Transnational Publishers, 1982), 118.

30. The Lord Mayor of London, quoted in ibid.

31. *Daily Telegraph* (London), 13 July 1979, 1.

32. Alan Chalfont, "There Should Be No Free Publicity for Terrorists," *Financial Weekly* (London), 13 July 1979, 9.

33. *Daily Telegraph* (London), 14 July 1979, 14.

34. Kenneth Gosling, " 'Panorama' editor reprimanded for IRA film," *Times* (London), 21 November 1979, 2.

35. *United Kingdom Home Office Circular*, 128/1976, 18 August 1976, 1; cited in Jaehnig, "Terrorism in Britain: On the Limits of Free Expression," 113.

36. The agreement is Addendum A in Jaehnig, "Terrorism in Britain: On the Limits of Free Expression," 123–24.

37. Philip Schlesinger, *Putting "Reality" Together* (London: Constable, 1978), 205.

38. Wilkinson, *Terrorism and the Liberal State*, 177.

39. Philip Schlesinger, "The BBC and Northern Ireland," in *The British Media and Ireland*, ed. Peter Taylor (London: Constable, 1978); cited in Schlagheck, *International Terrorism*, 75.

40. Barton Ingraham, *Political Crime in Europe: A Comparative Study of France, Germany, and England* (Berkeley: University of California Press, 1979), 295.

41. Jaehnig, "Terrorism in Britain: On the Limits of Free Expression," 121.

42. Brian Crozier, *A Theory of Conflict* (London: Hamish Hamilton, 1974), 150–51; quoted in John Wolf, *Antiterrorist Initiatives* (New York: Plenum Press, 1989), 121.

43. Ibid.

44. Abraham Miller, "Foreward," in *Terrorism, the Media, and the Law*, ed. Abraham Miller (Dobbs Ferry, N.Y.: Transnational Publishers, 1982), vi.

45. Ulrike Meinhof, quoted in Jillian Becker, *Hitler's Children: The Story of the Baader-Meinhof Terrorist Gang* (Philadelphia: J. B. Lippincott, 1977), 141–42.

46. Horst Mahler, quoted in *Die Zeit* (Munich), 9 September 1977.

47. Ulrike Meinhof, quoted in *Aus Politik and Zeitgeschichte*, 20 May 1978, 13; cited in Geoffrey Pridham, "Terrorism and the State in West Germany during the 1970s," in *Terrorism: A Challenge to the State*, ed. Juliet Lodge (New York: St. Martin's, 1981), 19.

48. Quotations from the Chief of the Office for the Protection of the Constitution, Christian Lochte, "Fighting Terrorism in the Federal Republic of Germany," in *Terrorism: How the West Can Win*, ed. Benjamin Netanyahu (New York: Farrar, Straus, Giroux, 1986), 171.

49. Becker, *Hitler's Children*, 74–77.

50. Jillian Becker, "Case Study I: Federal Germany," in *Contemporary Terror, Studies in Sub-State Violence*, eds. David Carlton and Carlo Schärf (New York: St. Martin's, 1981), 132.

51. Drawn from Hans-Josef Horchem, "Political Terrorism—The German Perspective," in *On Terrorism and Combating Terrorism*, ed. Ariel Merari (Frederick, Md.: University Publications of America, 1985), 63–64.

52. Ibid., 64–65.

53. Brian Crozier, "The Direct Support," paper delivered at the Jerusalem Conference on International Terrorism, sponsored by the Jonathan Institute, Jerusalem, 2–5 July 1979; quoted in Ray Cline and Yonah Alexander, *Terrorism: The Soviet Connection* (New York: Crane, Russak, 1984), 58.

54. Don Cook, "A Terrorist's Many Connections," *Washington Post*, 7 September 1975, B5.

55. Brian Crozier, "The Year of Passive Appeasement," in *Annual of Power and Conflict: 1978–79* (London: Institute for the Study of Conflict, 1979), 13.

56. *Rheinplatz* (Ludwigshafen), 24 August 1978.

57. For a further description of the Schleyer kidnapping, see Pridham, "Terrorism and the State in West Germany during the 1970s," 34–36.

58. Horchem, "Political Terrorism—The German Perspective," 63.

59. Geoffrey Pridham, *Christian Democracy in Western Germany* (London: Croom Helm, 1977), 340–41.

60. *Süddeutsche Zeitung* (Munich), 9–10 September 1972; cited by Pridham, "Terrorism and the State in West Germany during the 1970s," 49.

61. For additional information on GSG–9, see Rolf Tophoven, *German Response to Terrorism* (Koblenz: Bernhard & Gräfe Verlag, 1984).

62. John Wolf, *Fear of Fear: A Survey of Terrorist Operations and Controls in Open Societies* (New York: Plenum Press, 1981), 130.

63. *Frankfurter Allgemeine*, 14 March 1975.

64. RAF participants named their attack for a Baader-Meinhof leader who had died from a hunger strike in prison.

65. *Frankfurter Allgemeine*, 26 April 1975; quoted in Pridham, "Terrorism and the State in West Germany during the 1970s," 34.

66. Pridham, "Terrorism and the State in West Germany during the 1970s," 47.

67. Horchem, "Political Terrorism—The German Perspective," 67.

68. Ibid.

69. Drawn from Horchem, "Political Terrorism—The German Perspective," 67–68.

70. Dieter Kronzucker, in *Terrorism and the Media in the 1980's*, eds. Sarah Midgley and Virginia Rice (Washington, D.C.: The Media Institute, 1984), 51–52.

71. Pridham, "Terrorism and the State in West Germany during the 1970s," 37.

72. *Der Spiegel*, 24 October 1977.

73. See, for example, K. H. Krumm, "Problems der Organisation and Koordination bei der Terrorismus—Beikämpfung in der Bundesrepublic," in *Terrorismus: Untersuchungen zur Strategie und Struktur revolutionärer Gewaltpolitik* ed. M. Funke (Bonn: Bundeszentrale für politische Bildung, 1977), 324.

74. *Panorama* (Italy), 27 September 1977; cited in Pridham, "Terrorism and the State in West Germany during the 1970s," 42–43.

75. *Frankfurter Allgemeine*, 10 March 1978; cited in Pridham, "Terrorism and the State in West Germany during the 1970s," 43.

76. *Frankfurter Rundschau*, 30 October 1978; cited in Pridham, "Terrorism and the State in West Germany during the 1970s," 43.

77. Heinrich Böll, quoted in James Hoge, "The Media and Terrorism," in *Terrorism, the Media, and the Law*, ed. Abraham Miller (Dobbs Ferry, N.Y.: Transnational Publishers, 1982), 93.

78. Schlagheck, *International Terrorism*, 97.

79. *The Italian Socialist Movement*, trans. R. Hostetter, vol. 1, origins 1860–1882 (Princeton, N.J.: Van Nostrand, 1958), 23; quoted in Paul Furlong, "Po-

litical Terrorism in Italy," in *Terrorism: A Challenge to the State*, ed. Juliet Lodge (New York: St. Martin's, 1981), 63.

80. Furlong, "Political Terrorism in Italy," 68.

81. Leonard Weinberg and William Eubank, *The Rise and Fall of Italian Terrorism* (Boulder: Westview Press, 1987), 32, 41–42.

82. Furlong, "Political Terrorism in Italy," 70.

83. For a chronological description of Red Brigades' activities see V. Tessandori, *Br, imputazione: banda armata* (Milan: Aldo Garzanti Editore, 1977). For a history of the Red Brigades see Soccorso Rosso, ed., *Brigate Rosse* (Milan: Feltrinelli, 1976).

84. Maurio Galleni, ed., *Rapporto sul terrorismo* (Milan: Rizzoli editore, 1981), 49; cited in Weinberg and Eubank, *The Rise and Fall of Italian Terrorism*, 6.

85. Italian Ministry of Interior source cited in Furlong, "Political Terrorism in Italy," 73. Weinberg and Eubank, *The Rise and Fall of Italian Terrorism*, 123, view the second phase of Italian terrorism as beginning in 1976–77 and ending in 1982–83.

86. Furlong, "Political Terrorism in Italy," 74.

87. See, for example, Weinberg and Eubank, *The Rise and Fall of Italian Terrorism*, 16–18; and F. D'Agostini, "L'uso politico del caso Moro e la crisi d'oggi—intervista con Allesandro Natta," *Rinascita* 36, no. 3 (16 February 1979): 3–5.

88. "Brigate Rosse, Risoluzione della Direzione Strategica, February 1978", *CONTROinformazione* 5, no. 11–12 (July 1978): 93; cited in Furlong, "Political Terrorism in Italy," 66.

89. Sterling, *The Terror Network*, 220–22.

90. *Il Giornale Nuovo* (Milan), 11 January 1980; cited in Sterling, *The Terror Network*, 221.

91. *Il Giornale Nuovo* (Milan), 16 April 1980; cited in Sterling, *The Terror Network*, 221.

92. Furlong, "Political Terrorism in Italy," 77.

93. Ibid., 86.

94. Leonardo Sciascia, quoted by J. Binde, "Entretien avec Leonardo Sciascia," *Le Monde*, 4–5 February 1979, 16.

95. Weinberg and Eubank, *The Rise and Fall of Italian Terrorism*, 121.

96. Ibid., 121–122.

97. Ibid., 123.

98. Ibid., 125.

99. Ibid., 126.

100. Ibid., 124.

101. Ibid., 127.

102. Ibid., 128.

103. Robert Friedlander, *Terror—Violence: Aspects of Social Control* (New York: Oceana Publications, 1983), 183.

104. Weinberg and Eubank, *The Rise and Fall of Italian Terrorism*, 137.

105. Marino de Medici, quoted in *Terrorism and the Media in the 1980's*, eds. Sarah Midgley and Virginia Rice (Washington, D.C.: The Media Institute, 1984), 47, 55.

106. Weinberg and Eubank, *The Rise and Fall of Italian Terrorism*, 138–39.

107. de Medici, quoted in *Terrorism and the Media in the 1980's*, 48.

10

The Threat of Terrorism to Americans and the Adversarial Media

Americans have remained relatively immune to domestic political terrorism. After a weak upsurge during the unrest of the 1960s, the perpetration of political terrorism within the United States has been minor. However, it is important to note that there is a credible threat that could wreak havoc in the United States if perceived political circumstances warrant it. As previously mentioned, Iranian leaders were quoted as saying that "one thousand suicide bombers poised to strike were in the United States."[1] U.S. leadership of coalition forces in the Persian Gulf war could also serve to incite radical factions with long histories and modern experience in the waging of campaigns of terror.

POTENTIAL TERRORISM AT HOME

Livingstone and Arnold have identified more than forty foreign terrorist groups, with links to the international network, that have operatives in the United States.[2] There also exist domestic groups like the violent separatist Armed Forces of Puerto Rican National Liberation (FALN), and the pro–El Salvador leftist Armed Resistance Unit and Guerrilla Resistance Movement that demonstrated their capability by bombing the Washington Navy Yard and the U.S. Capitol building in 1983. Additionally, the Jewish Defense League, the United Jewish Underground, the American Nazi Party, the Ku Klux Klan, the Posse Comitatus, the Aryan Brotherhood, and dozens of other radical groups are well armed, trained in paramilitary tactics, and have the capability to commit terrorist atrocities.[3]

One cannot ignore the deadly possibility that exists for political terrorism to come to America. The technology of chemical and biological weaponry, as well as the ever-present danger of nuclear devices, is readily available to terrorists desiring to threaten or destroy large populations. For example, fifteen years ago persons producing nerve gas for the terrorist market were arrested in Austria.[4] During a raid on a Red Army Faction safe house in Paris in 1980, police discovered a laboratory that had been used to produce botulin toxin. At another RAF safe house in West Germany, several hundred kilograms of organophosphorus compounds were found.

Nuclear weapons are deployed around the globe. While security safeguards are in place, it could be debated how really secure those weapons are from a determined terrorist group backed by the significant resources available at the state-supported level. According to the Report of the International Task Force on Prevention of Nuclear Terrorism: "There have been published reports of one terrorist group in Europe having tried unsuccessfully to obtain information on NATO nuclear-weapon storage facilities, and of another having sought unsuccessfully to enlist the help of a nuclear scientist regarding nuclear weapons they considered stealing."[5]

A retired senior U.S. military officer, previously involved with the control of nuclear weapons, has commented on the security of those weapons:

In theory, nuclear weapons should be consistently secured by the highest quality systems and personnel. One suspects, however, that the military community includes a normal spectrum of good and bad, some ineptitude, and the vagaries of administration characteristic of an excessively large bureaucracy. How well does military security protect against terrorism? The Beirut attacks confirm that it was not designed with terrorism in mind.... Theft of nuclear explosive materials has to be considered a serious threat.[6]

U.S. Arms Control and Disarmament Agency Chief Scientist Robert Kupperman has noted that, "only when it is too late, when the weapon of mass destruction has been detonated, does the threat become clearly credible."[7]

THE INCREASING THREAT TO AMERICANS ABROAD

While Americans at home have remained immune, those abroad have increasingly been targeted by political terrorists.[8] The symbolic attractiveness, and proven media value, of U.S. targets abroad resulted in American citizens and property being victimized in over 50 percent of the international terrorist atrocities committed during the 1970s. Between 1968 and 1975, only Israel was targeted more times than the United States.[9]

It seems that the foreign policy pursued by the U.S. administration over the last decade served to increase the risk to American citizens and property abroad. Throughout the 1980s, the Reagan administration apparently evaluated its foreign policy principally against the standard of anti-Sovietism. Human rights were openly cast aside during the emphasizing of that standard. Those individuals and groups perpetrating violence in foreign countries who were in opposition to pro-Soviet regimes were considered freedom fighters, while those in opposition to anti-Soviet regimes were regarded as terrorists. The authoritarian characteristics of some regimes seemed of little consequence. The excesses of Pinochet in Chile and Marcos in the Philippines were ignored, and the position of the United States as a world leader in human rights was seriously eroded. As expressed by Beres: "Many of the world's peoples now see this country as an affliction, and insurgent groups throughout the world are likely to accelerate their activities against the United States. . . . By supporting invidious regimes in pursuit of anti-Soviet advantage, we spark and sustain a worldwide insurgency against the United States."[10]

Beres sees increased terrorism generated against the United States from two sources: "(1) by insurgents fighting U.S.-backed regimes; and (2) by the successor governments that harbor ill will toward the United States for its prior indifference to human rights."[11]

The successful employment of state-sponsored terrorism against the United States can hardly be denied. Its growing impact on U.S. foreign policy saw the withdrawal of U.S. military presence from Lebanon. Earlier, the Carter administration had been thoroughly discredited by the hostage crisis in Tehran, and the following Reagan and Bush administrations appeared powerless against Iranian-backed kidnappers in the Middle East.

The employment of psychological warfare against the American public by state-sponsored terrorists has become increasingly sophisticated. The long-term kidnapping of Americans in Lebanon by Iranian-backed terrorists is obviously characteristically related to two events that had a penetrating effect on public opinion in the United States during the last thirty years: (1) the POW-MIA issue from the Vietnam conflict, and (2) the seizure of American hostages in Tehran.

U.S. interests abroad are openly threatened on a daily basis. Abu Nidal was quoted by a French journalist as saying, "You will see . . . we are going to mount operations against the Americans, and the billions of dollars their forces have will be insufficient to protect them."[12]

U.S. COUNTERTERROR POLICIES

U.S. administrations of the 1960s and 1970s, particularly within the Department of Justice, tended to view political terrorism as a criminal act to be dealt with by the nation in which the attack might occur. With most terrorist atrocities occurring outside the physical confines of the United States, and not involving the domestic politics of the U.S. government, American politicians and bureaucrats could afford to ignore them. Spared the horror of the bombings and airport massacres that swept through Western Europe, American citizens at home could accept the view that political terrorists were simply criminals to be dealt with by the democracies abroad that hosted their spectacular assaults.

Certainly Americans are not unfamiliar with deadly violence. Based on World Health Organization data, the 1983–1984 homicide rate in the United States was 1,114 percent higher than in the United Kingdom, 844 percent higher than in Greece or the Netherlands, 750 percent higher than in Denmark or Spain, 672 percent higher than in Norway or Sweden, 608 percent higher than in West Germany, and 554 percent higher than in France.[13]

There is, of course, considerable difference between the strategy, tactics, and operational procedures of international political terrorists and the actions of psychopaths or perpetrators of domestic crime for personal gain. While democracies abroad have placed high priority on developing countermeasures to political terrorists, Americans have necessarily been more interested in combating domestic crime. Consequently, the emergence of effective countermeasures to political terrorism from U.S. administrations has lagged considerably behind that of other major democracies. The exception to that observation is perhaps the countering of commercial aircraft hijacking. The high cost to all major nations of the surge in hijackings in the late 1960s and early 1970s gave a sense of urgency for all to participate in instituting effective countermeasures worldwide. History shows that it took the cooperation of East and West to curb the frequency of hijacking atrocities, although the threat of attack on commercial aircraft remains significant.

The Early Evolution of a Deterrence-by-Denial Policy

A process of policy development by evolution began at the end of the 1960s. In 1969, U.S. Ambassador Charles Elbrick was kidnapped by Brazilian terrorists. Secretary of State William Rogers asked the Brazilian government to grant the terrorists' demand for release of political prisoners in exchange for Elbrick. The United States later formally thanked the Brazilian government when the exchange took place and Elbrick was returned alive.[14] When U.S. Agency for International Development adviser Daniel Mitrione was kidnapped by the Uruguayan Tupamaros the following year, the U.S. policy stiffened and the administration refused to bargain with the terrorists. Mitrione's body was found ten days after he was kidnapped.

Modern international terrorism began to pose a significant problem for the United States in the early 1970s, with the hijacking of American airliners and an increasing number of attacks on U.S. diplomats and citizens overseas. Ernest Evans, staff researcher for the Senate Armed Services Committee, labeled the two policies that were developed to counter those terrorist attacks as (1) the policy for the "dual-phase" incident, in which hostages and negotiations were involved; and (2) the policy for the "single-phase" incident, which covered other situations such as bombings and assassinations.[15]

Both of these U.S. policies involved the attempted deterrence of terrorism. Alexander George and Richard Smoke have described deterrence as a process during which an opponent is convinced not to pursue a certain course of action because the risks and costs for that option outweigh the benefits. Deterrence is achieved by increasing the risks and/or the costs, which is termed deterrence by punishment, or by decreasing the benefits, which is termed deterrence by denial.[16]

With the Senate confirmation of Henry Kissinger, the U.S. State Department adopted a strict hard-line policy of deterrence by denial: "If terrorist groups get the impression that they can force a negotiation with the United States and an acquiescence in their demands, then we may save lives in one place at the risk of hundreds of lives everywhere else. ... It is our policy that American Ambassadors and American officials not participate in negotiations on the release of victims of terrorists."[17]

When Ambassador Beverly Carter later acted as an intermediary between the parents of three kidnapped American students and Tanzanian terrorists, she was reprimanded and denied an expected appointment as ambassador to Denmark. This occurred in spite of the fact that the students and their Netherlands companion were released unharmed.[18]

Evans evaluated Kissinger's deterrence-by-denial policy by a comparison of the United States and West Germany in the first half of the 1970s. The Germans had experienced an unfortunate incident in March of 1970 when their ambassador to Guatemala was killed after the Guatemalan government refused to pay a ransom and release several prisoners. Bonn had exerted considerable pressure on the Guatemalans to grant the terrorist demands, and expelled the Guatemalan ambassador from Bonn when the German ambassador was killed.[19] Following that atrocity, the West Germans, for five years, pursued a soft-line policy of negotiations with terrorists—directly opposite to that proclaimed by Kissinger. If Kissinger's denial policy was the correct one to deter terrorism, then the United States should have been victimized less often than West

Germany during those five years. However, Evans's study showed that between 1970 and 1975 there were thirty-four international kidnappings involving demands on the U.S. government or private interests, while there were only eleven such kidnappings involving the West German government or private interests. The effectiveness of the U.S. deterrence-by-denial policy for "dual-phase" incidents could indeed be questioned.

The Shifting Emphasis to Deterrence by Punishment

Evans noted that early U.S. deterrence of "single-phase" terrorist incidents emphasized deterrence by punishment and involved mostly the negotiation of multilateral treaties.[20] Prominent among these were the antihijacking conventions at Tokyo in 1963, the Hague in 1970, and Montreal in 1973; as well as the Convention to Prevent and Punish Acts of Terrorism Taking the Form of Crimes Against Persons and Related Extortion that Are of International Significance, adopted by the OAS General Assembly in February 1971; and the United Nations Convention on the Prevention and Punishment of Crimes Against Diplomatic Agents and Other Internationally Protected Persons, adopted in December 1973. However, in this attempt at deterrence by punishment the United States suffered a resounding defeat at the U.N. General Assembly in 1972. Secretary of State Rogers had introduced a draft convention on international terrorism that would have required extradition or punishment of terrorists. Covered under the draft convention were attacks that (1) took place outside the territory of the perpetrator's state, (2) were perpetrated against foreigners in the state in which the attack took place, (3) did not involve military hostilities, and (4) targeted a state or international organization.[21]

The draft convention was opposed by a coalition of Arab, African, Asian, and communist states because it did not address the "right of national self-determination and wars of national liberation." The United States attempted to shift to a second resolution brought by Western Europe and Latin American nations, but the communist–Third World coalition succeeded in passing its own version that "condemned racist and colonialist regimes as terroristic." The issue was then passed to an ad hoc committee with the obvious intent that it should languish there.

Following Kissinger's lead, U.S. administrations continued to reiterate a hard-line policy through the 1970s and into the 1980s. Speaking two years before the seizure of the American embassy in Tehran, the Carter administration secretary of state, Cyrus Vance, told a U.S. Senate Committee: "We have made clear to all that we will reject terrorist blackmail. We have clearly and repeatedly stated our intentions to reject demands for ransom or for the release of prisoners."[22]

Carter failed to hold the hard-line policy of deterrence by denial against Iran. With the principle objectives of terrorists in hostage events normally being a comparative demonstration of their power and the incapability of the target government, while obtaining maximum publicity, the weakness of a hard-line policy is as illuminated by Merari: "These results, especially publicity, are achieved by the terrorists whether or not the government yields.... Since the most important damage is done ... there is no sense in prolonging the drama and jeopardizing the lives of innocent hostages."[23]

While the Reagan administration proclaimed a deterrence-by-denial policy against terrorism with abundant no-negotiations rhetoric, a more aggressive policy of deterrence by punishment emerged. National Security Decision Directive 138 (NSDD 138) was signed into effect by President Reagan on 3 April 1984. While portions of NSDD 138 remain classified, its principal themes are: (1) international cooperation to oppose terrorism, (2) increase the costs and risks to states employing or supporting terrorism, and (3) increase the emphasis on preventing terrorism. As noted by Defense Department official Noel Koch, NSDD 138 "represents a quantum leap in countering terrorism, from the reactive mode to recognition that pro-active steps are needed."[24]

On 26 April 1984, President Reagan sent to the U.S. Congress four proposals for antiterrorist legislation. These bills included broader laws against kidnapping and stronger laws against aircraft hijacking to conform with international agreements; authorization of $500,000 rewards for information against terrorists; and prison terms and fines for persons providing assistance to groups or nations deemed by the secretary of state to be involved in terrorism.[25] A White House statement cited President Reagan as specifying that the legislation was aimed at countries that support terrorism and use it as a foreign policy tool.[26]

The Shultz Doctrine of an Escalating Response to Terrorism

From NSDD 138 emerged the Shultz Doctrine that, as articulated in October 1984, advocated a U.S. response to terrorism that "should go beyond passive defense to consider means of active prevention, preemption, and retaliation."[27] The Shultz Doctrine was demonstrated in 1986 with the attack on Libya.

President Reagan had accused Libya of armed aggression against the United States after the attacks by the Abu Nidal terrorist organization at the airports in Rome and Vienna on 27 December 1985. Fifteen people were killed in the attacks, including five Americans. In retaliation against Qadhafi, Reagan froze Libyan assets in the United States, ordered all Americans working in Libya to leave the country, and proposed a trade embargo.[28] The effectiveness of Washington's nonviolent retaliation proved limited when America's allies were generally unwilling to support economic sanctions. French Prime Minister Fabius predicted the sanctions would have no effect with the observation, "There's no point beating the air with a sword."[29]

Reagan was perhaps encouraged by public opinion polls to employ more aggressive actions against Qadhafi. A Harris poll after the Vienna and Rome atrocities showed the majority of Americans favoring punitive action. Seventy-two percent advocated the invasion of countries supporting terrorism, and 79 percent would impose a universal death penalty for terrorists.[30]

When terrorists bombed the La Belle disco in West Berlin in March 1986, killing one American, Reagan retaliated with an air strike on Libya. In attempting to justify the attack, the administration relied on an earlier U.S. determination that patterns of attacks could constitute a level of armed attack, justifying the use of force in self-defense. The United States reported to the U.N. Security Council, immediately after the air strike, that it had exercised its right of self-defense under Article 51 to an ongoing pattern of attacks by the Libyan government against U.S. nationals. The United States, the United Kingdom, and France then vetoed a draft Security Council resolution that would have condemned the air strike on Libya as a violation of the United Nations Charter and the norms of international conduct.

If the Reagan administration had intended to inflict a reprisal on Libya under customary international law, then it would have not been acceptable. The force employed in the U.S. reprisal was out of all proportion to the force used in the commission of the alleged offense by Libya. As was later revealed, the attack on the La Belle was actually perpetrated by two Palestinians and a German. In January 1988, the West German police offered a reward of $93,000 for information leading to the arrest of Christina Endrigkeit, whom they identified as the prime suspect in the bombing of the La Belle. She had been linked to the two imprisoned Palestinians.[31]

The Shultz Doctrine for terrorist countermeasures could be labeled a policy of escalation, allowing for progression from deterrence by denial to deterrence by punishment with reprisal. The later phases of this policy matched that demonstrated by the Israelis in their air strike on PLO headquarters in Tunis six months earlier. Like that of the Israelis, there is no evidence to show that the Shultz Doctrine of deterrence by punishment through reprisal, justified as extended self-defense, has yielded significant results in combating terrorism. In retrospect, it seems that Reagan administration countermeasures to international terrorism were not particularly effective. Terrorists killed more Americans during the first five years of the Reagan administration than under any other presidency. With the debatable exception of the air strike against Libya, only one act of retaliation—the arrest of the *Achille Lauro* hijackers after the interception of their Egyptian airliner by U.S. Navy fighter pilots over the Mediterranean Sea—represented any success. Even that success was dampened when Italy freed the terrorists. That demonstrated lack of support by the Italian government exemplifies the frustrations encountered by those following the Shultz Doctrine.

A PROCLAIMED POLICY WITHOUT AN IMPLEMENTING ORGANIZATION

U.S. counterterrorism policy over the last twenty-five years has escalated from (1) soft-line negotiations, to (2) deterrence by denial, to (3) proclaimed deterrence by denial with secret negotiations, to (4) deterrence by punishment with reprisal. However, there has been no effective organization to support this escalation and U.S. counterterror policy has apparently constituted mere rhetoric.

In 1977, President Carter's National Security Council identified the State Department as the lead agency for processing terrorist incidents involving international relations. The powers of the State Department's Office for Combating Terrorism were also expanded to include both domestic and international terrorism. In retrospect, these initiatives were only bureaucratic reshuffling.[32]

Before the November 1979 seizure of the U.S. embassy in Tehran, the Carter administration formed the Federal Emergency Management Agency. Among its assignments was the management of terrorist incidents, however in a crisis the National Security Council would coordinate the counteroperation.[33] This again only added a bureaucratic layer to the counterterrorism organization, at the expense of efficiency in coordination and direction.

At an international seminar on combating terrorism, held in Tel Aviv in 1979, a simulation exercise was conducted for a theoretical situation in which American hostages were being held in Iran by the Khomeini regime.[34] Participants included the director of the U.S. State Department's Office for Combating Terrorism. When the U.S. embassy in Tehran was seized a few months later, it was not readily apparent that any benefits had been gained at the seminar. The demonstrated lack of organization and the official confusion in the Carter administration made it appear that state sponsorship of terrorism and the taking of hostages were new international issues. Although a deterrence-by-denial policy had been expounded by the United States for many years, the Carter administration both negotiated with, and made concessions to, the Iranians.

Eighteen months before the seizure of the U.S. embassy in Tehran,

President Carter had formed the antiterrorist Delta Force. Composed of volunteers from various branches of the U.S. military, its purpose is to conduct surgical strikes against terrorists who attack Americans abroad. In its first major mission, Operation Eagle Claw, on 24 April 1980, Delta Force failed in an attempt to rescue the American hostages in Tehran. Eight members of the unit were killed in the collision of an RH–53 helicopter and a C–130 aircraft at a remote staging base in Iran, after which the mission was canceled and the unit withdrawn. Spectacular and detailed U.S. media exposure of the tragedy brought forth huge celebrations in the streets of Tehran.[35] The failed attempt made Washington look even more powerless, and was an important victory for Khomeini, which he used to strengthen his radical domestic policies.

Investigations into the Operation Eagle Claw tragedy revealed coordination problems among the branches of the military, not unlike those that contributed to the heavy casualties suffered during the *Mayaguez* incident under President Ford.

After the Tehran hostages debacle, which cost the United States considerable prestige abroad, Congress attempted to restructure the antiterrorism organization. In 1980, under the sponsorship of Senator Strom Thurmond, the Senate formed the Subcommittee on Security and Terrorism. Unfortunately, the Reagan administration's early focus on Nicaragua and the *contras* distracted lawmakers from formulating an effective antiterrorism organization, and America was ill-prepared for the intensification of the terrorist campaign that erupted in Lebanon after the 1982 Israeli invasion.

Following the 1983 bombing of the U.S. Marine Corps barracks at the Beirut airport, a commission was established to investigate the atrocity and evaluate U.S. Defense Department counterterror capability. The Long Commission considered its most important finding to be that "terrorism had become tantamount to an act of war; a conflict in which the United States military was ill-equipped to engage."[36] The commission further noted that the definition used by the Department of Defense as a basis for counterterrorism strategies and tactics did not allow planners to even consider state-sponsored terrorism.[37] In response, Secretary of Defense Caspar Weinberger allowed that "our current antiterrorist posture could be improved."[38] During the course of the commission's investigation, the Marine commander of the parent regiment for the Beirut airport barracks observed: "People have this notion that there's this magic package of counterterrorism training that would have prevented that attack. . . . Only about 5 percent of the Marines' training before going to Beirut was keyed to the specific mission. The rest is general training."[39]

Following the Long Commission's recommendation that "the Secretary of Defense direct the development of doctrine, planning, organization, force structure, education, and training necessary to defend against and counter terrorism,"[40] the Department of Defense formed three new antiterrorist organizations. The U.S. Navy commissioned the Antiterrorist Indication and Warning Alert Center on 19 December 1984. The Navy had been sharply criticized by a military review board after the Beirut airport bombing for failing to fully inform the Marine Corps barracks as to the threat against them.[41] The Alert Center is now tasked with collecting, analyzing, and disseminating to field commanders, in useful form, information on domestic and international terrorist threats.

Since 1984, the United States has sponsored an Anti-Terrorism Assistance Program that has provided training for foreign civilian law enforcement agencies. Numerous law enforcement organizations have participated in training for airport security, bomb detection and disposal, and hostage negotiation and rescue. Recently, representatives from Hungary and other Eastern European nations have taken part in this popular program.

As a response to the upsurge of state-sponsored terrorism in the Middle East, there has been increased liaison between the Central Intelligence Agency and its foreign counterparts. Representatives from the United Kingdom, Italy, Israel, Egypt, Turkey, Greece, Colombia, Honduras, Denmark, India, Pakistan, the Netherlands, and France have conducted interagency conferences with the United States on how to improve bilateral cooperation in combating terrorism.[42]

In February 1985, the U.S. State Department formed the Overseas Security Advisory Council to facilitate the exchange of information and recommendations on closer cooperation against terrorism between the public and private sector. The State Department's Threat Analysis Group is also available to firms in the private sector that might become involved in security issues abroad.[43]

Under Director William Casey and Deputy Director Robert Gates, the CIA established a counterterrorism center to allow antiterrorist analysts to interact with field operatives in order to improve operational capabilities. Unfortunately, the publicity of the Iran-*contra* affair dealt a severe, untimely blow to U.S. covert antiterrorist operations. At the onset, one must realize that counterintelligence is at the heart of any attempt to successfully suppress terrorism. Without accurate, timely, and sufficient intelligence, no organizational structure can successfully counter terrorism, especially an international threat. Since the terrorist threat to the United States is principally from abroad, the country must rely on its own covert operations, and the cooperation of the intelligence services of its allies, to accumulate the necessary information upon which to base effective antiterrorism policies, structure organizations, and implement operations.

The openness of American society makes the accumulation of meaningful intelligence about terrorist groups very difficult. The continual leakage and disclosure to the media of sensitive information, as has occurred during congressional investigations of intelligence agencies, has hindered the development of important contacts by U.S. antiterrorist organizations with individuals who have access to terrorist groups. Realizing that their identity may suddenly become known, these individuals are naturally hesitant to work with the CIA or other U.S. agencies.[44] The seriousness of this problem was exemplified by the success of Khomeini's revolution in Iran, which caught America completely offguard. The House of Representatives Permanent Select Committee on Intelligence noted that the CIA had been unable to produce any assessment of the situation from anti-Shah sources for almost three years.[45] The counterterrorism intelligence services of allies are also often hesitant to work with U.S. counterparts because of the poor record of confidentiality established by U.S. intelligence services.

Chaired by George Bush, the Vice President's Task Force on Combating Terrorism emphasized the need for effective intelligence in countering terrorism. A Consolidated Intelligence Center was recommended for the collection and analysis of all available information from other antiterrorist agencies. The task force also made detailed recommendations for an incentive program for persons contributing information about terrorists.[46]

According to CIA antiterrorism chief Charles Allen, his department has doubled its analytical and operational resources since 1984, working actively "to penetrate terrorist networks, mount operations to sow seeds of suspicion among the cadres and among the leaders, and identify new technical capabilities."[47] Unfortunately those efforts are apparently not succeeding. For example, a Cuban intelligence officer who defected through Czechoslovakia in June 1987 reported that about 90 percent of the CIA's covert operations in Cuba were penetrated, and then controlled, for years by Castro's agents: "The Cubans fed bogus intelligence to almost all the agents who weren't actually working for them."[48]

The 1980s saw more failures than successes for U.S. policies and operations against terrorism. On some occasions the United States was embarrassed. For example, in November 1984, Sikh terrorists from India, who were later charged with conspiring to kill Prime Minister Rajiv Gandhi, completed a $350 two-week training course at a private guerrilla warfare school in Alabama. Four Sikh suspects were arrested in New Orleans in May 1985, when an FBI undercover agent learned they had acquired a gun to assassinate an Indian official. After that arrest, two accomplices that had also trained at the Alabama facility, Lal Singh and Ammand Singh, disappeared. They later became suspects in the bombing of the Air India airliner over the Atlantic which killed 329 persons.[49]

Finally, as evidenced by the steady increase in the threat of state-sponsored terrorism against the United States abroad that continued into the 1990s, U.S. counterterrorism policies have failed to resolve two major problems: (1) the vulnerability of U.S. diplomats and citizens abroad, and (2) the difficulty in obtaining the necessary cooperation of allies.

The perpetration of terrorism against U.S. targets in the late 1980s was not an everyday affair (hostages in Lebanon excepted). Hence, U.S. officials could afford to continue to regard terrorism as a nuisance rather than a primary threat. Only when a terrorist atrocity momentarily drew them into a situation where they appeared inept were they forced to react. With such a low priority, realistic antiterrorist contingency plans and the resources to support them obviously received inadequate attention. As noted by Jenkins, "the rhetoric against terrorism exceeds the commitment of resources to combat it."[50]

COMBATING TERRORISM AND AN ADVERSARIAL PRESS

Historically, Washington has been the loser in terrorist dramas. U.S. administrations are usually caught unaware and unprepared. With the news media focused on the government's every word and deed, officials have often appeared incompetent or impotent. Seldom are they able to make meaningful responses to terrorist atrocities. Only occasionally have they been cast in the role of hero. The U.S. media have focused strongly on Washington's immediate reactions during a terrorist crisis, and have tended to disregard long-term programs or the overall record against terrorist aggression. The danger of unbalanced reporting is obviously that the world's public could perceive the U.S. government as unable to deal with terrorism.

The media in the United States regard themselves as the watchdogs of government. There is ample evidence in the daily reporting and analysis of news to demonstrate the adversarial role they have adopted. This contrasts sharply with the West German media's cooperative approach, deviates widely from the partial control of the media by the British government through the BBC, and bears little resemblance to the politically oriented press of Italy. Nossek has made the astute observation that the media "run the United States. . . . They have brought down presidents and therefore feel strong and self-confident."[51]

With exploitation of the media against the target government a key to a successful terrorist campaign, Jaehnig has questioned the appropriateness of the U.S. media's adversarial role in relation to government: "Can the news media assume adversarial roles in relation to public authority when the social order, its tenets and values are endangered? How can the public's right to know be fulfilled when the publication of specific material could cause direct harm to members of the public or support for its enemies?"[52]

Employing Misinformation Techniques Against an Adversarial Press

Faced with an often hostile and, at a minimum, adversarial press, Washington has sometimes resorted to misinformation tactics during an antiterrorist campaign. For example, while the Carter administration was planning Operation Eagle Claw to free the fifty-four hostages at the embassy in Tehran, it consistently communicated a commitment to negotiating the hostages' release without the use of military force. Later, after the U.S. embassy's political attaché in Beirut, William Buckley, was kidnapped and tortured to death by Iranian-backed Shiite terrorists, the Reagan administration secretly negotiated with Iran for the release of American hostages in return for weapons and spare parts to assist the Iranian war effort against Iraq. These secret negotiations took place while the Reagan administration was publicly espousing, through the press, a no-negotiations policy with the terrorists holding hostages in Lebanon.

The Reagan vs. Qadhafi affair is perhaps the most elaborate example of how Washington has sought to offset the disadvantage of an adversarial media by using them in a planned misinformation campaign. In August 1981, two U.S. Navy carrier-based F-14 fighters shot down two Libyan SU–22 fighters over the Gulf of Sidra. Security for President Reagan was increased shortly afterwards. According to Copson, "There was speculation in the press that these arrangements might be related to the threat of a Libyan-sponsored assassination attempt in retaliation for the Gulf of Sirte incident. . . . Press reports indicated that U.S. intelligence officials had received information . . . indicating that a Libyan assassination team . . . might have entered the United States. . . . This assassination team was said to have plans to kill the President."[53]

Qadhafi denied the reports and called on Washington to produce evidence. Continuing the spiral of misinformation, President Reagan's reply was simply, "We have the evidence and he knows it."[54] While Ray Cline, former deputy director of intelligence for the CIA and expert on terrorism, told journalist John Weisman, "There was no evidence," and Jeff Gralnick, executive producer of ABC's "World News Tonight" verified that "No news organization had any finite proof at all,"[55] the spiral continued. The media sensationalized the event with numerous high-drama and colorful reports. Frank Reynolds of ABC reported that Libyan agents were "in this country for the purpose of assassinating the highest officials of the U.S. government."[56] Dan Rather of CBS reported that "a squad of terrorists infiltrated the United States on a mission to kill the President and his top aides."[57] NBC reported the team was composed of three Libyans, three Iranians, three Syrians, one East German, one Palestinian, and one Lebanese. ABC agreed on the Libyans, East German, Palestinian, and Lebanese, but claimed two Iranians and no Syrians. CBS strangely reported no Libyans in the supposedly Qadhafi-sponsored group. Columnist Jack Anderson went even further astray when he reported that two leaders of the Amal (a Shiite political and military organization in Lebanon openly opposed to Qadhafi) were included in the alleged hit team. When the British press focused on Anderson's Amal error, he claimed to have been set up by an unnamed intelligence agency.[58] Phil Jones of CBS reported that the alleged hit team was in Mexico and that "intelligence reports indicate that the teams have been in contact with the Weather Underground terrorist group." He later related that the story was given him by members of the Senate Intelligence Committee who claimed to have been "entrapped" by CIA briefers.[59]

After the Reagan administration's air strike on Libya in April 1986, it attempted to continue the misinformation campaign by leaking plans for additional reprisals as a means to further intimidate Qadhafi. Eventually uncovering this scheme, the U.S. news media retaliated by publishing an exposé of the administration's misinformation tactics.[60]

Bob Woodward of the *Washington Post* exposed the Reagan administration's misinformation program for Libya. He reported that Admiral John Poindexter of the National Security Council had forwarded a memorandum that called for a campaign through the media to make Qadhafi "think that there is a high degree of internal opposition to him within Libya, that his key trusted aids are disloyal, that the U.S. is about to move against him militarily."[61] Bernard Kalb, State Department spokesman who had been assigned to release the false stories, resigned in protest. One could evaluate the U.S. media's adversarial role toward the government as self-defeating when such a noncooperative stance encourages the government to employ misinformation and misdirection campaigns to safeguard national security in the face of a terrorist threat.

O'Sullivan views exaggeration of the antagonism between the media and the government in a democratic society, "with the press bent upon exposure and defending the public's right to know," as being particularly inappropriate when the government is attempting to cope with a campaign of terrorist atrocities; "as if murder were a sort of opinion which the public should respect."[62] As noted by Schlagheck in her comparative discussion of the relationship between the media and democratic governments, "The learning process continues, and the search goes on for a way to deny terrorists—but not the public—the benefits of a free news media."[63]

THE ROLE OF A FREE ENTERPRISE MEDIA, THE CORPORATE PRESS IN AMERICA

It is an economic fact of life that enterprises operating in the free-market economy of a democratic society must earn a profit. Firms that do not show a return on their investment sufficient to pay operating costs quickly disappear. With economy of scale a law in almost every section of the private sector in a free enterprise system, firms that do not show sufficient profit for capital expansion are soon overpowered by those that do. Hence, those firms that survive the competition tend to grow larger and more powerful over time.

Within the United States, the media are not exempt from the forces of the free market. While the public has shown some support for public broadcasting systems, market competition dominates the actions of the media, the "free" press. Over time it has been clear that the market forces and economic laws that control the majority of firms in America's free enterprise system also control the "free" press. Thus, those media firms that have been able to show a profit and expand have grown relatively powerful.

Radio Corporation of America (RCA) formed NBC in 1926 to conduct radio broadcasting operations. By 1985, NBC was the mainstay of RCA's entertainment division, with more than 200 television and 500 radio affiliates. However, NBC's sales of $2.4 billion constituted less than 25 percent of RCA's total business, which in 1985 included insurance, automobile renting, satellite communications, and carpets in addition to electronics.[64] General Electric, a multinational corporation with revenues of about $37 billion, acquired RCA (and NBC) in 1986 for $6.4 billion in cash. In 1990, General Electric's domestic interests included aerospace, aircraft engines, defense systems, steam and gas turbines, and locomotives, as well as electrical equipment for homes and factories. It is one of the world's largest and most diversified corporations. In 1989 its international interests included General Electric of Canada, General Electric Plastics B.V. of the Netherlands, and Yokogawa Medical Systems of Japan, with 79 manufacturing plants in nineteen foreign countries and 182 in the United States.[65] In 1990, NBC sales of $3.64 billion represented only 7 percent of General Electric's $50.1 billion in revenues.[66]

CBS began broadcasting in 1927 under the name United Independent Broadcasters. By 1989, its net sales totaled almost $3 billion, with 212 television affiliates in the United States and subsidiary companies in thirty-six foreign countries, spanning the globe from Finland to South Africa and Panama to Japan.[67]

ABC was a diversified communications and entertainment company when it was acquired in 1986 by Capital Cities Communications for

$3.375 billion. In 1990, the corporation had revenues of $4.96 billion.[68] Capital Cities has acquired eleven other companies involved with the publishing of books and newspapers, and with the distribution of data.[69]

While Cable News Network (CNN), a division of Turner Broadcasting, appeared to be rapidly gaining strength in the news broadcast media, its 1990 revenues of $172 million were only 5 percent of its NBC competitor.

While the three network giants—NBC, CBS, and ABC—dominate the broadcast industry in the United States, concentration and integration have also occurred in the print media. In the early 1980s, more than half the daily newspaper sales in the United States were made by only twenty organizations. Similarly, only eleven organizations made over half the revenue from book sales.[70]

Michael Parenti has illuminated the concentration of control of the media within the United States:

Ten business and financial corporations control the three major television and radio networks (NBC, CBS, ABC), 34 subsidiary television stations, 201 cable TV systems, 62 radio stations, 20 record companies, 59 magazines including *Time* and *Newsweek*, 58 newspapers including the *New York Times*, the *Washington Post*, the *Wall Street Journal* and the *Los Angeles Times*, 41 book publishers, and various motion picture companies like Columbia Pictures and Twentieth Century Fox.[71]

The "Free" Press and Corporate Influence in America

What this overwhelming corporate control of the "free" press in the United States means is economically clear. While the media companies within the parent corporations are expected to show a profit, they are also required to conform to corporate policy; this in almost every case means being supportive of other companies within the corporation. The fate of the "free" press within the American system now approaches the description offered by Gaye Tuchman:

The predominance of private ownership in the broadcast industry does not mean that radio and television are either socially or politically independent of the corporate capitalism that dominates the American economy.... In fact, as in other industries, the ownership pattern of television stations is one of local monopolies, regional concentrations, multiple ownerships, multi-media ownerships and conglomerates. Similarly, one might expect to find shared social and political values.[72]

It would be indeed difficult to make the economic argument that the media in the United States, in the last quarter of the twentieth century, have operated as a "free" press. It is more likely that, as noted by a disillusioned Ron Nessen when he stepped down as President Ford's press secretary, "Freedom of the press belongs to the one who buys the ink."[73]

While the American public must obviously be concerned with the potential for corporate influence on its press as the U.S. news media process and disseminate information, it must also consider the potential for corporate influence in the gathering of that information. For the democracies of the Western world, determining what is internationally "newsworthy" is for the most part done by four organizations: the Associated Press and the United Press International of the United States, Agence France Presse of France, and Reuters of Great Britain, who, by 1985, operated in 110 countries around the world.[74]

The realities of the business world in a free market system affect freedom of the press within America as summarized by Perdue:

Quite aside from what might be preferred by professional journalists, knowledge and information is a product, like any other, where market share, return on investment, and potential for expansion constitute the bottom line.... Against these considerable forces, broadcast and print journalists have little to offer except a professional code.... In a world where television newspeople survive on the basis of being telegenic, where the audience is asked to judge media personalities rather than the quality of information...the real question of a story is not "does it fairly inform?" but "does it sell?"[75]

A Free Press: Corporate Ownership or Public Subsidies?

In spite of their serious vulnerabilities, the U.S. media cite a preference for press operations within a free market rather than for the public-subsidized media system that exists to some extent in Western Europe.

Perhaps one should consider that in every modern democracy that declares itself a free-enterprise economic system, exceptions to the market system emerge. Some functions simply are too vital to entrust to the market. Evidently education is regarded as too important to leave to the whims of corporate managers and stockholders, thus all modern democracies provide subsidies for their schools. Where private educational institutions stand alongside public educational institutions, one must consider only the difference in the cost to the enrollees to observe the degree to which schools are subsidized.

So also have all democratic nations decided over time that they will provide a subsidized military to defend their borders and support their foreign policies. It is doubtful if any studies have ever been made to determine the possibilities of utilizing free market forces to provide for national defense. However, the salaries paid to mercenary specialists by some emerging Third World countries are indicative of the prohibitive costs that measure would likely involve. In brief, in every democratic nation of the modern world operating with a self-proclaimed free-enterprise economic system, there are key functions that are, for various economic or social reasons, not entrusted to the market but rather are subsidized by the public.

Critics of a public-subsidized press tend to ignore the basic operational philosophy of democratic society. If the population in a school district does not like the way in which its school is being operated, it throws out the old school board and elects a new one. If the duly elected federal government's policies on education are not shared by the majority of voters, those policies will be changed, by either the incumbents or those newly elected. Critics of the partly public-subsidized news media in Western Europe often fail to realize that if the West German or British or Italian publics do not like the performance of their subsidized media, those responsible for overseeing the media will either become enlightened or be replaced. As with the educational system in the United States, the subsidized media in Western Europe are responsible and accountable to the electorate.

In the 1990s, it is perhaps time for dedicated journalists and academicians alike to realistically compare the degree of freedom between a news media that must respond to a giant corporation's profit-seeking board of directors and that of a public-subsidized media.

The Influence of the Competitive Market Place

The intense competition within the news media certainly affects the everyday work of all journalists involved with gathering, analyzing, and presenting information to the public. Since the end of the Walter Cronkite era, with his replacement at CBS by Dan Rather, the Nielsen ratings of the evening news broadcasts of the three major networks have seldom varied more than one point. In May 1990, ABC's Peter Jennings had a 10.1 rating, followed by Dan Rather of CBS with 9.9 and Tom Brokaw of NBC with 9.7. With ratings translating directly into profitability, it is easy to discern the extreme pressure between such closely ranked competitors. In the last few years, another network has emerged to challenge the giants. By November 1990, CNN claimed to be in 40 million American homes, presenting newscasts on a continuing basis. In January 1991, CNN was broadcasting its view of the news of the Persian Gulf conflict to 101 countries.[76]

The extremes of competition are often apparent in the media's coverage of terrorist atrocities. As noted by a participant at an international seminar on terrorism, "most journalists would sell their countries for a headline.... A sensational news story is very hard to resist."[77] CNN's decision to televise Iraqi government-supervised reports from Baghdad during the Persian Gulf war confirms this. It is ironic that a segment of the U.S. media, which have historically stood for a free and totally uncensored press, would agree to daily broadcasts of controlled and supervised information for a dictatorial power at war with the United States. While much research has yet to be done on the possible propaganda results of the CNN broadcasts, it can be noted that CNN achieved a spectacular "scoop" over its competition.

This fiercely competitive character of the U.S. media could be of particular benefit to political terrorists. O'Sullivan considers most damaging the attitude that journalism is "the pursuit of commercial and professional competition, which allows no self-restraint in covering a dramatic story."[78] The intense urge to "break" a story often leads to live coverage of a terrorist atrocity, hence the terrorists are able to communicate directly with their target public. Such an unedited, open dialogue is seldom afforded to individuals or groups in Western democratic politics, with the propaganda potential for terrorists indeed incredible. To observe the media's willingness to grant terrorists this unique advantage, one could recall the jostling between news reporters to gain a better position during the June 1985 live coverage of the Beirut press conferences, staged by the terrorist group responsible for hijacking TWA Flight 847 and murdering U.S. serviceman Robert Stethem.

The seizure of the U.S. embassy in Tehran exemplifies the "overcoverage" of which the U.S. media are capable. Recall that during the 444 days of captivity for the fifty-two American hostages, "there was never a physical threat to the United States itself, nor was the scale of threat to the Americans as great as has been the case in some other circumstances."[79] In retrospect, a media blitz pushed America into what has been termed a "national trauma."[80]

In 1978, when the Ayatollah Khomeini's revolution was changing the face of Iran, ABC, CBS, and NBC each averaged less than one Iranian story per week on their evening news programs. But with the seizure of the embassy in November 1979, these networks televised 721 reports about Iran for the year, or an average of almost five apiece per week.[81] The *Washington Post* coverage of Iran increased from 134 articles in the revolutionary year of 1978 to 801 articles in 1979, with 476 coming in the two months after the hostages were seized. In 1980, it published 916 reports, an average of almost 3 per day.[82] The media frenzy supported Vanocur's observation that "television news can be likened to an omnivorous carnivore which requires fresh meat every day."[83]

A few days after the embassy was seized, ABC began a nightly news show called "America Held Hostage." The show was referred to by one columnist as "the propagation and dissemination of rumor, gossip, and haranguing opinion."[84] In spite of such reviews, the show became so profitable it was turned into the nightly program "Nightline."

After the close of the hostage affair, a noted columnist for the *Washington Post* questioned the relationship between the media and the Iranian captors: "Was the press, in any degree, a party to Iranian tactics.

... Should it have been more cautious? Did it lose its cool? ... Did the press, by writing and broadcasting feverish bits of news, inflame the situation?"[85] A short-term symbiotic relationship developed between the Iranian captors and the U.S. media, as demonstrated by the 10 December 1979 NBC-televised interview of hostage Marine Corporal William Gallegos, which included, as the price of the interview, a five-minute lecture by an Iranian spokeswoman called Mary.

The newly elected Reagan administration appeared politically sensitive to the impact that the media had on the U.S. public's perception of the Ayatollah Khomeini's terrorism. In the first few days of the administration, Secretary of State Alexander Haig indicated that concern with international terrorism would take priority over concern for human rights.[86] It is of course possible that, as noted by Friedlander, Secretary Haig's comments were intended as a deterrent warning in the wake of such statements as journalist William Safire's that the debatable hostage settlement between the United States and Iran had "set a precedent that encourages terrorists, and endangers innocents, everywhere."[87] In retrospect, if Haig's statement was made to deter terrorism, it obviously had little effect, since the 1980s became the decade of hostages. Haig's statement was prophetic to the extent that the Reagan administration did show a turn away from human rights issues.

THE TEDIOUS RELATIONSHIP AMONG
GOVERNMENT, MEDIA, AND PUBLIC

The combination of the U.S. news media's fierce competition and their adversarial attitude toward government has the potential to create severe problems for the nation's security. If not for the incompetence of Iraqi leader Saddam Hussein during the fighting in the Persian Gulf, heavy losses could have been inflicted on coalition forces as a result of sensitive information exposed on a daily basis by the U.S. media. Prior to the commencement of hostilities and during combat operations, former military, Defense Department, and defense industry experts were employed by the media to describe, to the smallest detail, possible coalition-force strategies and tactics as well as weapons' technological capabilities. Those experts were schooled in the same military operations and trained with the same advanced technology weaponry as were commanders in the Persian Gulf. A review of the extensive televised statements by those experts shows a remarkably dangerous similarity to actual offensive combat operations. Apparently only the timing of a potential amphibious operation, which was not necessary because of the quick success of coalition land forces, was misperceived by the media's experts. If Saddam's commanders had been more perceptive planners, and more combat capable, the intelligence made available to them by the U.S. media could have played an important, and likely tragic, role in the conflict. Certainly that situation has been noted by those who might choose a military confrontation with the United States in the future.

The U.S. government and public have apparently not yet realized the severe threat that a competitive and adversarial media, equipped with modern communications technology, can pose to national security during military conflict. While the low casualty rate and euphoric success of the coalition forces in the Persian Gulf war will likely dispel any immediate fears of media disclosure of sensitive information, herein lies the potential for a deeply disturbing relationship among government, press, and public.

The dangers of an overly competitive and adversarial media to America's security against international terrorism were demonstrated in 1985 with the *Washington Post* exposé of a U.S. covert program to preempt terrorist attacks on American targets in the Middle East. As noted earlier in the discussion of press responsibility, the exposé negated the program and placed American citizens in the Middle East at risk.

The media's argumentative coverage of the hijacking of TWA Flight 847 in 1985 also drew much criticism. Congressman Thomas Luken summarized the problem as follows:

The recent American TWA hostage experience in the Middle East suggests that the American media "have yet to learn how to avoid serving as the 'ransom' that is now paid to terrorists who take hostages." Many of the members of the subcommittee are deeply concerned about the astonishing spectacle of T.V. news shows from the Middle East apparently "co-produced by television and the terrorists."[88]

In this adversarial atmosphere, it should be expected that media excesses in the coverage of terrorist events would be quickly criticized. The Deputy Director of the U.S. State Department's Office for Combating Terrorism has been sharply critical of the quality of the media's coverage of terrorism: "It is very shallow reporting.... The American public is not gaining any appreciation for terrorist events and what they mean."[89]

While it could be argued that the increase in targeting of Americans abroad in the 1980s was due to the inconsistency between the Reagan administration's rhetoric and its actions, Steven Anzovin has cited the U.S. media's contribution as well: "Our poor record in antiterrorism... is partly the fault of the news media.... The networks, in their search for marketable programming, have played up stories of hijacking and other attacks in sensational fashion. They have been singularly helpful in publicizing terrorists' demands and providing a stage for their bloody performances."[90]

Members of the U.S. media have expressed dismay at the situation in which they find themselves. A television news director has stated: "We feel that the coverage we give such incidents is partly to blame, for we are glorifying lawbreakers, we are making heroes out of non-heroes. In effect, we are losing control over our news departments. We are being used."[91] The president of NBC News once remarked, "I'm torn, I want to report, but I don't want to help to overdramatize."[92]

In spite of evidence that shows the driving force of competition, some U.S. media representatives claim that loftier goals exist. *Chicago Sun-Times* publisher James Hoge subjugates all media actions to what he regards as the journalist's ultimate responsibility: "to tell the public what is going on."[93] Hoge advocates applying the rules of balance and perspective to the reporting of terrorist acts; "Common sense and sound news judgment should be the prevailing guidelines."[94]

To present a theoretically balanced view, news media analysts would have to possess a superhuman intellect that would allow them to perceive all sides of complex developments as they occur in real time. Hoge's concept, by which the media alone have the task and responsibility of determining what coverage to give terrorists, and how to gather and present that information, assumes that members of the media are both omniscient and omnipotent. Specially trained authorities and well-schooled academicians frequently make errors in the study and analysis of terrorism. How can journalists, with limited knowledge or formal education and training in the subject, possibly fulfill Hoge's expectations? Especially during live coverage of events and in spontaneous situations does the media's lack of familiarity with specific subjects emerge. For example, during the recent liberation of Eastern Europe, when Poland and Hungary were moving rapidly away from communist control, a representative of a leading newspaper in Los Angeles was asked on the "McLaughlin Group" telecast whether he thought that Romania would soon follow the lead of Hungary and Poland. His response included the observation that he was certain that all Romanians were glued to their television sets and were sure to imitate the successes that they viewed. The journalist, with enough status in his profession to participate on such a prestigious panel, apparently had so little familiarity with Romania that he did not realize the scarcity of television sets in that poor and destitute country. Equally as ill-informed was the observation on the evening newscast of a major U.S. network, during the first mass visits of East Germans to West Germany, that the East German government would likely soon restrict those visits because of the vast amount of East Germany money flowing out of the country. (Soviet bloc currencies were never convertible in the West, nor were they ever allowed out of the individual bloc nations.) Such demonstrations of unfamiliarity with newsworthy subjects give one pause before attributing so much capability to the media to make correct decisions about transmitting information on terrorists and their atrocities.

When ABC official George Watson was queried as to whether his network had experts specifically to deal with reporting terrorist activities, his direct reply was, "No. . . . More likely than not when a terrorist episode erupts, the reporters covering it are relatively inexperienced in that field."[95] When challenged that the media should be responsible for providing experts to cover terrorist events, Watson insisted: "The business of journalism doesn't work that way . . . and I am not entirely sure that the volume of the terrorist episodes actually requires it."[96]

The chief counsel for the U.S. Senate's Subcommittee on Security and Terrorism expressed shock at Watson's comments. Joel Lisker noted that media personnel who "interject" themselves into a terrorist operation have responsibilities to others: "If he's going to place the lives of innocent people in possible jeopardy on the strength of some ethereal reason like the public's right to know, . . . then he has responsibilities."[97]

As a profession, and as a democratic institution, the media could indeed be expected to establish and maintain standards of expertise and conduct that lead to responsible self-restraint and discipline in all areas of reporting. In the United States, lawyers must achieve a level of academic expertise for qualification, and their professional conduct is monitored by a national association. So also are standards established and performance monitored for doctors, academicians, military officers, and many other people in public service. Unfortunately, similar qualifications and standards do not apply to the free press. While accepted as a democratic institution, the media operate solely in the private sector where economic survival is the primary standard. It seems an anomaly that a democratic society should look to a free press to keep it fully and accurately informed, while disregarding its professional qualifications and leaving its survival to the whims of the marketplace. Surely members of the media cannot be held responsible for that state of affairs, but as a minimum they should not attempt to impart knowledge they do not possess. To properly analyze a terrorist atrocity takes a team of at least learned psychiatrists, political and social scientists, historians, and law enforcement experts. Members of the news media are well advised to "inform the public" by reporting the basic facts of a terrorist atrocity while carefully avoiding the creation of any image for the perpetrators or any analysis of the intent of their actions.

CONSTITUTIONAL LIMITATIONS ON THE "PUBLIC'S RIGHT TO KNOW"

When challenged with restraint of their exploitation by terrorists, members of the U.S. media frequently refer to what they term "the public's right to know." As acknowledged by Sander Vanocur:

Too many of my colleagues have a tendency to wrap themselves unduly in the First Amendment and solemnly pontificate about "the people's right to know." The First Amendment, as I understand it, simply states that Congress shall make no law abridging freedom of speech or of the press. It says nothing about "the people's right to know."[98]

Indeed, in American democratic society, there seems to be a boundary around the "public's right to know." When that right to know infringes on the formal rights of citizens as proclaimed in the Bill of Rights, set forth by a democratically elected legislature, and interpreted by the duly appointed judicial system, then a clear limitation can be shown to exist. For example, the news media are confronted daily with the boundary between the public's right to know and an individual's right to privacy. While libel laws furnish benchmarks, the media have occasionally infringed upon the rights of others. For instance, during the 1972 presidential election campaign, Senator Thomas Eagleton was forced to withdraw his nomination as the Democratic Party's vice-presidential candidate after the Knight Newspaper Company disclosed confidential medical information. Although that disclosure was clearly a violation of Eagleton's right to privacy, the Pulitzer Committee awarded a 1973 Pulitzer Prize to the Knight Newspaper Company and, in so doing disregarded the illegality and ethics of publishing the senator's private records.

In the coverage of terrorist atrocities, examples have already been offered here to illustrate media actions that have endangered the right to life and freedom of hostages. During a 1974 hostage situation an aggressive reporter conducted lengthy telephone interviews with the hostage-takers in an attempt to gain access to their location. When asked if he had considered the danger of inciting the terrorists to greater violence, he replied: "I never thought about getting them riled up. My primary goal was to . . . get a scoop. My gratification comes from doing something that is worthy of the front page . . . doing a story worth seeing."[99]

Fenyvesi noted that, at the conclusion of a lengthy hostage atrocity, the media demonstrated little sympathy for the hostages and apparently disregarded the severity of their ordeal; rather, they aggressively sought interviews, "pursuing hostages that had to run away to elude them."[100]

In insisting that the public has a right to know, the rhetoric of the American press can be traced to the basic media function: the gathering of information. With profit the overwhelming motivation, gathering marketable information is indeed the media's principal function. But when gathering the material the media deem marketable becomes difficult, and profits are threatened, members of the press immediately and emphatically invoke the public's right to know.

Supreme Court Restraints on Gathering Information

The media generally interpret the First Amendment right to publish as including the right to gather information. They argue that unconstrained coverage of events is both guaranteed within a democracy and vital to its survival. They have anchored their insistence on unrestrained access to information to the words of James Madison: "A popular Government without popular information, or the means of acquiring it, is but a Prologue to a Farce or a Tragedy; or, perhaps both. Knowledge will forever govern ignorance: And a people who mean to be their own Governors, must arm themselves with the power which knowledge gives."[101]

The opposing view warns that the media's right to gather information and publish it must be tempered by the right of all citizens to have their lives and safety protected. In fact, the U.S. Supreme Court, on several occasions during the 1970s, denied that the First Amendment assures the media unrestricted access to information. In 1972, in *Branzburg v. Hayes*, the Supreme Court held that courts could require the testimony of journalists before grand juries, and denied a constitutional right for the media to protect a confidential source.[102]

In 1973, in *Environmental Protection Agency v. Mink*, the Supreme Court ruled that all information in a government file marked "classified" was immune from disclosure.[103] In 1974, in *Pell v. Procunier*, the Supreme Court ruled that the First Amendment does not give the media a constitutional right of access to information that is not also available to the general public; nor do they have a constitutional right to locations of crimes or disasters from which the general public is barred. (At issue was a California Department of Corrections regulation denying journalists special access to interview inmates.) Also in 1974, in *Saxbe v. Washington Post*, the Court again denied a constitutional right of special access for the press.[104]

In 1978, in *Zurcher v. Stanford Daily*, the Supreme Court refused the media immunity from warrants. Police officers had been attacked and injured while removing demonstrators from Stanford University Hospital administration offices. The student newspaper had published photos that led authorities to believe the newspaper held other photos that could help identify the attackers. A warrant was issued that allowed the police to search the newspaper offices. The newspaper brought suit, charging that its rights had been violated under the First, Fourth, and Fourteenth amendments.[105] When balancing the media's right to gather news and law enforcement agencies' right to gather criminal evidence, the Supreme Court chose the latter.

In 1978, in *Houchins v. KQED, Inc.*, the Supreme Court again denied the press special access. The Alameda County sheriff had refused to allow KQED access to photograph prohibited areas of the country jail. Chief Justice Burger's opinion noted that First Amendment rights to speech and publication do not include an unlimited right to gather information.[106] The media were clearly informed that their right of access to information is not different from the right of the general public. Apparently, when the general public is restricted from the scene of a terrorist atrocity, the media may also be denied access.

The Supreme Court actions to restrain the media in its gathering of information in the 1970s did not represent a change in the status quo. Earlier, in *Zemel v. Rusk*, the argument had been made,

There are few restrictions on action which could not be clothed by ingenious argument in the garb of decreased data flow. For example, the prohibition of unauthorized entry into the White House diminishes the citizen's opportunity to gather information he might find relevant to his opinion on the way the country is being run, but that does not make entry into the White House a First Amendment right.[107]

Members of the U.S. Congress, vulnerable to an adversarial news media that consider themselves to be the nation's watchdog, have sometimes supported the press in its quest for unrestrained access to information. After *Environmental Protection Agency v. Mink* denied media access to all contents of a government file marked "classified," the U.S. Congress amended the Freedom of Information Act (Section 552, Title 5, U.S. Code) to permit district courts to allow access to nonclassified information that might be contained in such files.

In 1980, Congress enacted legislation that tended to place the media above the law. After *Zurcher v. Stanford Daily* allowed police search of news rooms, the U.S. Congress passed the Privacy Protection Act of 1980, which "strictly prohibits the use of search and seizure to obtain such materials except under specified circumstances."[108] The exceptions include (1) when the material is possessed by a suspected criminal, (2) when the possession is in violation of espionage laws, (3) when a subpoena might result in the destruction of the material, and (4) when the possessor of the materials has ignored a subpoena.[109] The attorney general's implementation of that law extended it to other professions, such as psychiatry and law, when confidentiality is at stake.

While the Privacy Act of 1980 shields the media from seizure of information by warrant, as prescribed in *Zurcher v. Stanford Daily*, they are not shielded from subpoena, as per *Branzburg v. Hayes*. The use of subpoenas against the press dates back to 1848. *New York Herald* reporter John Nugent was issued a subpoena by the U.S. Senate when he publicized a confidential draft of a treaty to end the Mexican-American war.[110] A form of law to shield the media from subpoenas has been provided by Attorney General John Mitchell's 1970 guidelines, which became part of the Code of Federal Regulations. Direct authorization by the attorney general is required to issue a subpoena against a member of the news media. Neubauer has reported that, between March 1973 and May 1975, seventy-six subpoenas against members of the news media were requested and fifty-four were approved by the attorney general.[111]

Supreme Court Restraints on Freedom of Speech

The U.S. judicial system has acted to strictly interpret limitations on the media under the Constitution. In the written opinion of a 1919 unanimous Supreme Court decision, Justice Holmes indicated that exercise of the freedom of speech,

depends upon the circumstances in which it is done.... The most stringent protection of free speech would not protect a man in falsely shouting fire in a theater, and causing panic.... The question in every case is whether the words used are in such circumstances and are of such a nature as to create a clear and present danger that they will bring about the substantive evils that Congress has the right to prevent.[112]

One editor has chosen to debate that landmark decision with the reply, "But the spirit of the first amendment demands that the press shout 'Fire!' if the crowded theater is burning. Once the warning is given, people can do as they choose."[113] From this rationale one could surmise that the U.S. media feel responsible solely for informing the public, and take no further responsibility for public safety or security.

Bassiouni has interpreted the 1919 Supreme Court decision on freedom of speech to mean: "Thus, despite the strong presumption of unconstitutionality, prior restraints may be constitutionally permissible where specific harm of a grave nature would surely result from media dissemination of certain information."[114]

In *Cox v. New Hampshire*, the Supreme Court further derogated the media's insistence upon a completely unrestrained press by indicating that freedom of the press could not take precedence over public order: "Civil liberties, as guaranteed by the Constitution, imply the existence of an organized society maintaining public order without which liberty itself would be lost in the excesses of unrestrained abuses."[115]

The U.S. media is well advised to note Justice White's caution in *Branz-*

burg v. Hayes: "The prevailing view is that the press is not free to publish with impunity everything and anything it desires to publish."[116]

SUMMATION OF COMPARATIVE FACTORS FOR THE UNITED STATES

The nature of the threat. The threat of political terrorism to the United States has been to its citizens and property abroad. U.S. leadership of the coalition forces in the Persian Gulf war has likely served to significantly increase that threat, as has the 1980s basing of U.S. foreign policy on an anti-Soviet standard while overlooking the excesses of some authoritarian regimes.

Countermeasures to terrorism. U.S. administrations have assigned a relatively low priority to combating terrorism. Consequently, the development of effective countermeasures and the structuring of an efficient antiterrorism organization have suffered. There has been an evolution of counterterrorist policy that has seen an escalation from deterrence by denial to deterrence by punishment with attempts at reprisals. This policy has not proved effective against the major threat originating in the Middle East.

The role of the media. Motivated by corporate requirements for profits, posing as adversaries to government administrations, and operating from the sanctuary of America, the U.S. media have been both easily exploited by international terrorists and particularly disinterested in restraining that exploitation.

The relationship of government, press, and public. The adversarial role taken by the media has resulted in a marked lack of cooperation between the government and the media in many areas. The public has generally sided with the government in criticizing the media for being exploited by terrorists. However, the lack of a domestic terrorist threat has made the issue far less important than other issues that dominate the American agenda.

Vulnerable to the extreme power of the U.S. media, politicians and bureaucrats tend to yield to their demands for special access to information and safeguards for media privacy. The Supreme Court has been the bulwark against the tyranny of the U.S. media, denying them special access to information beyond that accorded to all citizens and clearly stating that freedom of the press and freedom of speech must be balanced against the constitutional rights of all American citizens. In light of media excesses in the coverage of terrorist atrocities in the last decade, challenges to violations by the media of hostages' rights to life and freedom could become a viable issue in the U.S. courts. The increased availability of empirical data on the positive relationship between media coverage and terrorist success, such as that developed in this analysis, enhances that possibility.

NOTES

1. Neil Livingstone and Terrell Arnold, "Democracy under Attack," in *Fighting Back: Winning the War against Terrorism*, eds. Neil Livingstone and Terrell Arnold (Lexington, Mass.: D.C. Heath, 1986), 2.

2. Ibid.

3. Drawn from ibid.

4. Abraham Miller, *Terrorism and Hostage Negotiations* (Boulder: Westview Press, 1980), 103.

5. "Report of the International Task Force on Prevention of Nuclear Terrorism," 25 June 1986, a project of the Nuclear Control Institute, Washington, D.C., 1; quoted in Louis Beres, *Terrorism and Global Security: The Nuclear Threat*, 2d ed. (Boulder: Westview Press, 1987), 15–16.

6. Thomas Davies, "Terrorism's Nuclear Potential: What Might the Means and Targets Be?" Paper presented at the Conference on International Terrorism: The Nuclear Dimension, Nuclear Control Institute, Washington, D.C., June 1985, 2–3; quoted in Beres, *Terrorism and Global Security*, 2d ed., 16–17.

7. Robert Kupperman, "Government Response to Mass-Destruction Threats by Terrorists," in *On Terrorism and Combating Terrorism*, ed. Ariel Merari (Frederick, Md.: University Publications of America, 1985), 157.

8. See the annual publication by the CIA, for example, *International Terrorism in 1978* (Washington, D.C.: Central Intelligence Agency, 1979).

9. Miller, *Terrorism and Hostage Negotiations*, 27.

10. Beres, *Terrorism and Global Security*, 2d ed., 11–12.

11. Ibid., 74.

12. Abu Nidal, quoted in Paul Lewis, "Palestinian Extremist Leader Is Alive, a Paris Journal Says," *New York Times*, 22 February 1985, A3. For more information on Abu Nidal see "Middle East: The Abu Nidal 'Resurrection,' " *Defense and Foreign Affairs Daily*, 13 March 1985.

13. Cited in William Perdue, *Terrorism and the State* (New York: Praeger, 1989), 67.

14. "U.S. 'Appreciation' Expressed," *New York Times*, 6 September 1969, 2.

15. Ernest Evans, *Calling a Truce to Terror: The American Response to International Terrorism* (Westport, Conn.: Greenwood Press, 1979), 128.

16. Alexander George and Richard Smoke, *Deterrence in American Foreign Policy: Theory and Practice* (New York: Columbia University Press, 1974), 48, 58–83.

17. Henry Kissinger, "Secretary Kissinger's News Conference at Vail, Colo., August 17," in *Department of State Bulletin* 73, no. 1890 (15 September 1975): 408.

18. Evans, *Calling a Truce to Terror*, 80.

19. Carol Baumann, *The Diplomatic Kidnappings: A Revolutionary Tactic of Urban Terrorism* (The Hague: Martinus Nijhoff, 1973), 99–100; cited in Evans, *Calling a Truce to Terror*, 84.

20. Ernest Evans, "American Policy Response to International Terrorism: Problems of Deterrence," in *Terrorism: Interdisciplinary Perspectives*, eds. Yonah Alexander and Seymour Maxwell Finger (New York: The John Jay Press, 1977), 110.

21. "American Draft Convention on Terrorism, 25 September 1972," *Survival* 15, no. 1 (January-February 1973): 32.

22. Cyrus Vance, "Terrorism: Scope of the Threat and Need for Effective Legislation," *Department of State Bulletin* 78, no. 2012 (March 1978): 54.

23. Ariel Merari, "Government Policy in Incidents Involving Hostages," in *On Terrorism and Combating Terrorism*, ed. Ariel Merari (Frederick, Md.: University Publications of America, 1985), 167.

24. Noel Koch, quoted in Robert Toth, "Preemptive Anti-Terrorist Raids Allowed," *Washington Post*, 16 April 1984, A19.

25. John Wolf, *Antiterrorist Initiatives* (New York: Plenum Press, 1989), 57–58.

26. Ibid., 58.

27. George Shultz, quoted in Steven Anzovin, "Editor's Introduction," in *Terrorism, The Reference Shelf*, ed. Steven Anzovin, vol. 58, no. 3 (New York: H. W. Wilson, 1986), 90.

28. Drawn from Russell Watson, John Walcott, Kim Willenson, and Zofia Smardz, "Flake or Fox," *Newsweek* 107, no. 3 (20 January 1986): 14–20.

29. Laurent Fabius, quoted in ibid., 15.

30. Polls cited in ibid.

31. Perdue, *Terrorism and the State*, 67.

32. As evaluated in Miller, *Terrorism and Hostage Negotiations*, 108.

33. Kupperman, "Government Response to Mass-Destruction Threats by Terrorists," 160.

34. Ariel Merari, "Introduction," in *On Terrorism and Combating Terrorism*, ed. Ariel Merari (Frederick, Md.: University Publications of America, 1985), x.

35. Drawn from Wolf, *Antiterrorist Initiatives*, 73.

36. Long Commission, quoted in Wolf, *Antiterrorist Initiatives*, 56.

37. Ibid.

38. Caspar Weinberger, quoted in B. Drummond Ayres, Jr., "Pentagon Acts on Report about Marine Bombing," *New York Times*, 9 February 1984, A14.

39. Robert Johnston, quoted in Joel Brinkley, "U.S. Called Ill-Equipped to Fight 'On the Cheap' War by Terrorists," *New York Times*, 29 December 1983, A15.

40. Long Commission, quoted in Wolf, *Antiterrorist Initiatives*, 56.

41. Joel Brinkley, "Report Disputes Marine on Attack," *New York Times*, 22 December 1983, A12.

42. Robert Oakley, "Terrorism: Overview and Developments," in *Department of State Bulletin* 85, no. 2104 (November 1985): 64–65.

43. Ibid., 65.

44. See, for example, Stansfield Turner, *Secrecy and Democracy: The CIA in Transition* (Boston: Houghton Mifflin, 1985), 48–60, 75–89.

45. Drawn from Wolf, *Antiterrorist Initiatives*, 59.

46. John Wolf, "Task Force Urges a Central Agency to Fight Terror," *New York City Tribune*, 17 June 1986, 2; cited in Wolf, *Antiterrorist Initiatives*, 67.

47. Charles Allen, quoted in Wolf, *Antiterrorist Initiatives*, 69.

48. Quoted in Wolf, *Antiterrorist Initiatives*, 170–71.

49. Drawn from Anzovin, *Terrorism*, 79–80.

50. Brian Jenkins, "Statements about Terrorism," *The Annals of the American Academy of Political and Social Science* 463 (September 1982): 11.

51. Hillel Nossek, "The Impact of Mass Media on Terrorists, Supporters, and the Public at Large," in *On Terrorism and Combating Terrorism*, ed. Ariel Merari (Frederick, Md.: University Publications of America, 1985), 94.

52. Walter Jaehnig, "Journalists and Terrorism: Captives of the Libertarian Tradition," *Indiana Law Journal* 53, no. 4 (1977–1978): 720–21.

53. Raymond Copson, "Libya: U.S. Relations," Issue Brief no. IB81152 (Washington, D.C.: Library of Congress, Congressional Research Services, 1982); quoted in Perdue, *Terrorism and the State*, 52.

54. Ronald Reagan, quoted in Perdue, *Terrorism and the State*, 53.

55. Ray Cline and Jeff Gralnick, quoted in ibid., 53.

56. Frank Reynolds, quoted in ibid.

57. Dan Rather, quoted in ibid.

58. Drawn from ibid.

59. Phil Jones, quoted in ibid.

60. Donna Schlagheck, *International Terrorism: An Introduction to the Concepts and Actors* (Lexington, Mass.: Lexington Books, 1988), 77.

61. Quoted in Perdue, *Terrorism and the State*, 57.

62. John O'Sullivan, "Deny Them Publicity," in *Terrorism: How the West Can Win*, ed. Benjamin Netanyahu (New York: Farrar, Straus, Giroux, 1986), 125.

63. Schlagheck, *International Terrorism*, 78.

64. Drawn from *Moody's Industrial Manual* 2 (New York: Moody's Investors Services, 1985): 4326–28.

65. Drawn from *Moody's Industrial Manual* 1 (New York: Moody's Investors Services, 1990): 294, 296.

66. Drawn from *Million Dollar Directory: America's Leading Public and Private Companies* (Parsippany, N.J.: Dun's Marketing Service, 1990): 3023.

67. Drawn from *Moody's Industrial Manual* 1 (New York: Moody's Investors Services, 1990): 2717–18.

68. Drawn from *Ward's Business Directory of U.S. Private and Public Companies* (Detroit: Gale Research, 1991): 578.

69. Drawn from *Moody's Industrial Manual* 1 (New York: Moody's Investors Services, 1990): 2703.

70. Perdue, *Terrorism and the State*, 64.

71. Michael Parenti, *Inventing Reality: The Politics of the Mass Media* (New York: St. Martin's, 1986), 27.

72. Gaye Tuchman, ed., *The TV Establishment: Programming for Power and Profit* (Englewood Cliffs, N.J.: Prentice-Hall, 1974), 3.

73. Ron Nessen, lecture at the Industrial College of the Armed Forces, Washington, D.C., 21 April 1977.

74. Kashi Misra, "The New International Communication Order: An Overview," in *The New International Information and Communication Order*, ed. Hans Köchler (Vienna: Wilhelm Braumüller, 1985), 23.

75. Perdue, *Terrorism and the State*, 65.

76. "NBC Nightly News," 29 January 1991.

77. Quoted in Nossek, "The Impact of Mass Media on Terrorists, Supporters, and the Public at Large," 91.

78. O'Sullivan, "Deny Them Publicity," 125.

79. Don Oberdorfer, "Hostage Seizure: Enormous Consequences," *Washington Post*, 23 January 1981, A1.

80. Robert Friedlander, "Iran: The Hostage Seizure, the Media, and International Law," in *Terrorism, the Media, and the Law*, ed. Abraham Miller (Dobbs Ferry, N.Y.: Transnational Publishers, 1982), 61.

81. Don Oberdorfer, "The Seizure: An Act of Terrorism with Enormous Consequences," *Washington Post*, 23 January 1981, A10.

82. Ibid.

83. Sander Vanocur, quoted in *Northwestern Alumni News*, April-May 1980, 1.

84. Nicholas von Hoffman, "ABC Held Hostage," *New Republic* 182, no. 19 (10 May 1980): 16.

85. Bill Green, "Iran and the Press: First Questions," *Washington Post*, 23 January 1981, A16.

86. *Blade* (Toledo), 29 January 1981, 1; cited in Friedlander, "Iran: The Hostage Seizure, the Media, and International Law," 61.

87. *New York Times*, 19 January 1981, A25; and Friedlander, "Iran: The Hostage Seizure, the Media, and International Law," 66.

88. U.S. Congress, House Committee on Foreign Affairs, Subcommittee on Europe and the Middle East, *Hearings on the Media, Diplomacy and Terrorism in the Middle East*, 99th Cong., 1st sess., 30 July 1985.

89. Frank Perez, quoted in *Terrorism and the Media in the 1980s*, eds. Sarah Midgley and Virginia Rice (Washington, D.C.: The Media Institute, 1984), 19.

90. Anzovin, "Editor's Introduction," 91.

91. Philip Revzin, "A Reporter Looks at Media Role in Terror Threats," *Wall Street Journal*, 14 March 1977, 16.

92. Richard Wald, lecture at the University of California-Riverside, 21 March 1977; quoted in a report to the National News Council, "Paper on Terrorism," in *Terrorism, the Media, and the Law*, ed. Abraham Miller (Dobbs Ferry, N.Y.: Transnational Publishers, 1982), 136.

93. James Hoge, "The Media and Terrorism," in *Terrorism, the Media, and the Law*, ed. Abraham Miller (Dobbs Ferry, N.Y.: Transnational Publishers, 1982), 92.

94. Ibid., 90.

95. George Watson, quoted in *Terrorism and the Media in the 1980s*, eds. Sarah Midgley and Virginia Rice (Washington, D.C.: The Media Institute, 1984), 30.

96. Ibid., 31.

97. Joel Lisker, quoted in *Terrorism and the Media in the 1980s*, eds. Sarah Midgley and Virginia Rice (Washington, D.C.: The Media Institute, 1984), 32.

98. Sander Vanocur, "The Role of the Media," in *Hydra of Carnage*, eds. Uri Ra'anan, Robert Pfaltzgraff, Jr., Richard Shultz, Ernst Halperin, and Igor Lukes (Lexington, Mass.: Lexington Books, 1986), 259.

99. Quoted in Miller, *Terrorism and Hostage Negotiations*, 5.

100. Charles Fenyvesi, remarks to the conference on terrorism sponsored by

the City University of New York, 17 November 1977; quoted in Abraham Miller, "Terrorism, the Media, and the Law: A Discussion of the Issues," in *Terrorism, the Media, and the Law*, ed. Abraham Miller (Dobbs Ferry, N.Y.: Transnational Publishers, 1982), 31.

101. James Madison, letter to W. T. Barry, 4 August 1822; quoted in Justice Brennan, "Separate Opinion," *Environmental Protection Agency v. Patsy Mink*, 410 U.S. 73 (22 January 1973); in *United States Supreme Court Reports* 35 (San Francisco: Lawyers Co-operative Publishing, 1974): 145.

102. Justice White, "Opinion of the Court," *Paul Branzburg v. John Hayes*, 408 U.S. 665 (29 June 1972); in *United States Supreme Court Reports* 33 (San Francisco: Lawyers Co-operative Publishing, 1973): 631, 642.

103. "Summary," *Environmental Protection Agency v. Patsy Mink*, 410 U.S. 73 (22 January 1973); in *United States Supreme Court Reports* 35 (San Francisco: Lawyers Co-operative Publishing, 1974): 119.

104. Drawn from Miller, "Terrorism, the Media, and the Law: A Discussion of the Issues," 42.

105. Ibid., 38–39.

106. *Houchins v. KQED, Inc.*, 438 U.S. 1 (1978); cited in ibid., 43.

107. Chief Justice Warren, "Opinion of the Court," *Louis Zemel v. Dean Rusk*, 381 U.S. 1 (3 May 1965); in *United States Supreme Court Reports* 14 (San Francisco: Lawyers Co-operative Publishing, 1966): 190.

108. U.S. Congress, "Public Law 96–440," *U.S. Code: Congressional and Administrative News* 4 (St. Paul, Minn.: West Publishing, 1981): 3957, 3959–60.

109. U.S. Department of Justice, "Guidelines on Methods of Obtaining Documentary Materials Held by Third Parties," *Code of Federal Regulations*, 28CFR, Part 59 (Washington, D.C.: GPO, 1 July 1990): 604.

110. Miller, "Terrorism, the Media, and the Law: A Discussion of the Issues," 41.

111. Mark Neubauer, "The Newsman's Privilege after *Branzburg*: The Case for a Federal Shield Law," *UCLA Law Review* 24, no. 1 (October 1976): 185–86.

112. Justice Holmes, "Opinion of the Court," *Charles Schenck v. United States of America*, 249 U.S. 47 (3 March 1919); in *Cases Argued and Decided in the Supreme Court of the United States* 63 (Rochester, N.Y.: Lawyers Co-operative Publishing, 1919): 473–74.

113. Hoge, "The Media and Terrorism," 92.

114. M. Cherif Bassiouni, "Terrorism, Law Enforcement, and the Mass Media: Perspectives, Problems, Proposals," *Journal on Criminal Law and Criminology* 72, no. 1 (Spring 1981): 40.

115. Chief Justice Hughes, "Opinion of the Court," *Willis Cox v. State of New Hampshire*, 312 U.S. 569 (31 March 1941); in *Cases Argued and Decided in the Supreme Court of the United States* 85 (Rochester, N.Y.: Lawyers Co-operative Publishing, 1941): 1052.

116. Justice White, "Opinion of the Court," *Paul Branzburg v. John Hayes*, 408 U.S. 665 (29 June 1972); in *United States Supreme Court Reports* 33 (San Francisco: Lawyers Co-operative Publishing, 1973): 641.

11

Conclusions

DEFINING POLITICAL TERRORISM

A universal definition for political terrorism is possible, however its formulation requires movement away from the biases of perpetrator identification and evaluation of cause, which have significantly distorted the existing literature. Concentration on the nonemotional, nonjudgmental, empirical element—the method of violence—can yield a generally acceptable and useful definition. But to proceed in that direction requires that one recognize political terrorism as a subcategory of political violence in general, with its distinguishing characteristic as an act of violence beyond the pale.

All terrorist atrocities committed within the realm of political violence possess the basic elements of political intent and an unacceptable mode of violence. Definition of the basic element of political intent has evolved over time, and is currently expressed in the international covenants for extradition of fugitives. While far from perfect, significant progress has been made toward universal agreement on what constitutes political intent. There is also precedence for evaluating whether certain modes of violence are unacceptable on an international basis. Evolving over time, conventions on *jus in bello* provide a universal framework for establishing whether a specific act of violence committed in war is unacceptable to the civilized world. The progress demonstrated by these conventions on what modes of violence are not acceptable during combat seems to lay the groundwork for eventual agreement on what modes of violence should be classified as terroristic. There is, after all, not great difference among domestic laws as to what violence is unacceptable. All civilized states consider such acts as murder and kidnapping unacceptable, and those atrocities are the basic modes of terrorist violence. Along with international conventions on the clarification of political intent for acts of violence, narrowing the focus to political violence that utilizes modes of violence unacceptable to civilized societies allows for derivation of a universal definition of terrorism.

TERROR AS AN INSTRUMENT OF POLITICS

With a contemporary world order dominated by the threat of nuclear holocaust, lesser forms of political violence short of total war will likely increase. Terrorism as an instrument of politics is well established in the world system. No longer solely a weapon of the weak, it is now also profitably employed by nations large and small.

THE SOURCES OF POLITICAL TERRORISM

In the contemporary violence-prone environment, the search for the causes of terrorism has produced charges and countercharges. Lacking universal agreement on what constitutes terrorism, the literature is mostly concerned with identifying the origins of political violence in general, often debatably labeled as causes of terrorism. The basic issue, which seems to have been avoided, is: "Why do some groups and individuals, and not others, choose to commit terrorist atrocities as a form of violent political expression?" In practically all the categories of the origins of political violence identified in the literature, some perpetrators have chosen terrorism while others have not. When focusing on the contemporary factors involved in such a decision, one common element dominates. Politically motivated violent groups and individuals who perceive that increased publicity is vital to achieve their goals may commit terrorist atrocities to gain that publicity. From the literature's well-researched origins of political violence perpetrated by groups and individuals not in power, political terrorism, as rigorously defined here, emerges primarily when the perpetrators seek publicity.

FUNCTIONS OF THE MEDIA

The principal function that the media perform for terrorists is the transmission of the violence of an atrocity, perpetrated on symbolic victims, to a targeted audience. International terrorists largely depend on the media for that function, which can contribute significantly to their success. It is through the transmission of violence, and the resulting atmosphere of fear, that political terrorists seek to increase their relative power.

The transnational flow of information is a modern phenomenon that serves to inspire others to imitate and emulate the tactics of terrorists. The effective transmission of radicals' thoughts and actions has given an aura of legitimacy to their violence and revolution.

Through casual terminology, semantic labeling, and various modes of propagandizing, whether consciously or otherwise, the media can create images of terrorists and terrorism that lack objectivity and veracity. Especially noteworthy are televised interviews that elevate terrorists to the status of legitimate politicians.

In a democratic society, the free press has absolute power in determining what information is newsworthy and how it will be presented to the public. Hence, the public's perception of terrorism is subject to the operational policies of the media.

The issue of media responsibility in the coverage of terrorism, as reviewed in the literature, can be summarized as: (1) encouragement of violence-prone individuals to become terrorists and inspiration for the commission of atrocities, (2) participation by members of the media, who become closely associated with terrorists through source dependency, and (3) on- and off-scene tactical errors by members of the media that endanger lives.

A symbiotic relationship between the media and terrorists exists only in the short term. In the long term, exploitation of the media by terrorists could contribute to the success of a campaign to destroy the democratic society for whom the existence of the free press is so vital. Such a relationship is more appropriately described as parasitic.

THE QUANTITATIVE ANALYSIS

The lack of a common definition of political terrorism has undermined attempts to form a paradigm for the analysis of terrorism and to accumulate data bases free of estimation and jurisdictional bias. However, consistent application of the definition of political terrorism formulated for this analysis, with focus on the empirical measurements available in certain categories of terrorist atrocities, has allowed a quantitative analysis of the relationship between media coverage and terrorist success. The analysis, utilizing a four-year data base of newspaper coverage of international terrorist barricade and hostage atrocities, demonstrates a significant positive relationship between the level of media coverage and the success of terrorists in obtaining concessions from target governments.

Those barricade and hostage atrocity events, wherein the terrorists were granted concessions, received two to three times as much media coverage as was accorded events that terminated with no concessions. In recognition of the media's attraction to sensationalism, the variable of hostage casualties was examined as a possible antecedent or intervening variable accounting for the dependent variable of concessions to the terrorists. However, when the hostage-casualty variable was held constant, results similar to previous findings emerged. Media coverage retained a strong positive relationship to terrorist success in obtaining concessions.

As demonstrated quantitatively, media coverage of terrorism does, in fact, assist terrorists in achieving success. The issue of limiting terrorist exploitation of the press poses a challenge for democratic societies that come under terrorist attack, and is an important element in considering countermeasures to political terrorism. Threatened democratic societies might ultimately face the choice of restraining their media's coverage of terrorism or allowing an increase in terrorist success achieved through exploitation of the media.

While the results of this quantitative analysis of media coverage and terrorist success add to the relatively few previous reports of empirical research in this particular field, the methodology in the analysis constitutes a more important contribution. The quantifying of terrorist success showed that, when atrocities are analyzed by category, it is possible to select a specific category that possesses the quantifiable characteristics of tangible demands and timely observation of the granting or denial of those demands. In this analysis, the category of barricade and hostage (which included hijackings) provided data that could be operationalized, observed, and measured.

The variable of media coverage of terrorism was operationalized through the coverage of three major Western newspapers. Certainly, coverage by the televised media would have been more interesting and, in terms of results, perhaps more significant. One can sense that, in terrorist barricade and hostage atrocities, media coverage televised at the site carries more weight than events reported in the next day's newspapers. Unfortunately, financial limitations prevented including the international television media in this analysis. It remains a fertile area for future empirical investigation.

It is also quite likely that there are other categories of terrorist atrocities for which unbiased data could be accumulated and similar quantitative analyses performed. Future empirical research to investigate the relationship between media coverage and terrorist success might consider case studies. During the research for this analysis, it became apparent that major cases like the 1979 seizure of the U.S. embassy in Tehran and the 1985 hijacking of TWA Flight 847 offer abundant data for the quantification of the variables both of terrorist success and of media coverage.

If further quantitative research yields results similar to this analysis, a new dimension could be added to the arguments for and against media restraint in the coverage of political terrorism. These arguments, as viewed in the current literature, have involved only one dimension anchored in the freedom of the press, with the basic issue of whether the media should be restrained and, if so, by what methods. However, if a credible body of empirical findings were to emerge that scientifically links media coverage to terrorist success, then a second dimension evolves wherein the rights of terrorist hostages to freedom and life are perceived to be threatened by the media's coverage of terrorist atrocities. One can hypothesize that, in a democratic system similar to the United States, civil damage suits, based on such empirical findings and brought against the media by former hostages or their survivors, could change the arguments about media restraint. That change could introduce a new era in the discussions of the relationship between the media and terrorism.

THE CROSS-NATIONAL COMPARISON

The cross-national comparative analysis of the experiences of four major Western democracies with political terrorism revealed that, when the threat reaches a threshold at which the population is openly exposed to violence and internal stability is disturbed, countermeasures are undertaken that attempt to deny publicity to the terrorists by restraining the media.

The case of the United Kingdom emphasized that (1) the reaction threshold can be breached quickly when the terror erupts from a deep domestic cleavage; (2) when the general population is the target of terrorist choice, legislation leads the way in developing relatively strong countermeasures; and (3) media opposition to restraints is minimal when confronted with government and public unity against terrorist exploitation.

The Federal Republic of Germany's experience demonstrated that (1) a gradual evolution of terror beginning with targets abroad raises the reaction threshold and delays effective countermeasures; (2) when the elite are the initial targets of terrorist choice, the executive branch emerges as the leader in formulating countermeasures, with a strong antiterrorist organization emerging from relatively less legislation; and (3) growing public pressure is more effective in restraining the media than initial government concern.

Italy's decade of terror revealed that (1) the inefficient decision-making process inherent in a multiparty democracy places the reaction threshold at an agonizingly high level; (2) delays in the enactment of countermeasures result in the entrenchment of a terrorist campaign, which ultimately requires drastic legislative and executive actions for suppression; and (3) flagrant and extensive exploitation of the media by terrorists ultimately results in self-restraint on the part of the media, but perhaps only when it reaches a level of absurdity.

The United States' geographical isolation from political terrorism shows that (1) democratic populations that are relatively immune from the violence of terrorism have an extremely high reaction threshold; (2) without public pressure, legislation against international political terrorism has low priority and executive actions generally are initiated only in response to specific incidents of terrorism that may directly challenge elite prestige; and (3) in an environment of general immunity of the populace from terrorist attack, the media have no motivation to restrain their exploitation by international terrorists, but rather capitalize on its profit-making sensationalism.

In sum, the comparative analysis demonstrates that democracies can suppress terrorism, and they can restrain the exploitation of their media by terrorists, but they will normally choose to do so only when their public feels personal danger and the threat to internal stability becomes clear. Perhaps the most important finding is that necessary countermeasures can, and will be, accomplished without serious damage to democratic processes. The experiences of the United Kingdom, the Federal Republic, and Italy have clearly demonstrated that terrorist exploitation of the media can be reduced without destroying democracy, and that restraint on the media is normally accompanied by a decline in terrorism.

THE AMERICAN MEDIA AND THE MARKETPLACE

> That truth is great and will prevail if left to herself; that she is the proper and sufficient antagonist to error, and has nothing to fear from the conflict unless disarmed of her natural weapons, free argument and debate.
>
> Thomas Jefferson

In a utopian democracy, with a totally free and unrestrained media, the truth could be the ultimate power as perceived by Thomas Jefferson. Unfortunately, in a free-enterprise economic system, where the media must struggle for survival in the marketplace, the truth becomes a victim of competition.

The free press in America is subject to all the harsh economic realities of the marketplace. It has become increasingly incorporated and cannot realistically be expected to function without corporate influence. The time is approaching when the American public must consider whether its news media can operate more freely within a corporate structure or with public assistance.

The great American humorist Mark Twain once quipped: "The American people enjoy three blessings: free speech, free press, and a good sense not to use either." Unfortunately, the corporate media in the United States is fiercely motivated by competition for profits. While the quality press recognizes the extreme degree to which this vulnerability allows it to be exploited by international terrorists, proclamations against that exploitation have been mere rhetoric.

The power of the U.S. news media is absolute. Bureaucrats in the executive branch are confronted with a mutually noncooperative and adversarial relationship, while politicians in the legislative branch are tempted to befriend the press with self-serving legislation. On the other hand, the judicial system stands firm against possible tyranny of a fiercely competitive press. The Supreme Court has clearly stated that the power of the press will not be allowed to violate the constitutional rights of citizens.

To this time, no one has directly accused the U.S. news media of violating a hostage's rights to life and freedom by benefiting terrorists with sensational publicity. Such a challenge, supported by empirical data similar to that provided in this analysis, could serve to encourage the U.S. media to restrain their exploitation by terrorists. Certainly civil damage suits, brought by freed hostages or their survivors whose rights to life and freedom were violated, would challenge the media in their most important arena, profitability.

It is unfortunate that a democracy must experience a high level of terrorist atrocities, with numerous victims kidnapped, maimed, and murdered, before its reaction threshold is breached. Perhaps that threshold could be lowered if victims or their survivors would seek remuneration through the judicial system from a media who allow themselves to be exploited by terrorists, and hence contribute directly to the terrorists' success.

Appendix 1

International Terrorist Atrocities: Barricade and Hostage Events, 1978 to 1981

KEY TO PRESS COVERAGE NOTATION

Day = The day of the press coverage in relation to the
day that the terrorist event began, e.g., Day 4 indicates
an article published on the fourth day since the beginning
of the atrocity.

Pg = The page number of the newspaper on which the article
was printed. When the article was separated over more than
one page, the page number indicates the first page on which
the article appeared.

Ph = The number of photographs that were included in the
article.

Col = The length of the article measured in the number
of columns, rounded to the nearest 10th of a column.

Id = Identification of the terrorists. Y indicates that
the affiliation of the terrorists was included in the article.
N indicates that the terrorists were not specifically
identified.

Dmd = Specification of terrorist demands. Y indicates
that the demands of the terrorists were specified in the
article. N indicates that they were not.

EVENT 1

DATE: February 18, 1978
LOCATION: Nicosia, Cyprus
PERPETRATORS:
  NUMBER: 2
  NATIONALITY: Palestinians
  ORGANIZATIONAL AFFILIATION: Black June
VICTIMS:
  NUMBER: 34
  NATIONALITY: Africans and Asians
  STATUS: Delegates to Afro-Asian People's Solidarity
  Organization Conference and an airline crew
PHYSICAL TARGET:
  NATURE: Airliner
  NATIONAL ASSOCIATION: Cypriot
NATURE OF DEMANDS: Airliner and safe passage
TARGET OF DEMANDS: Cypriot government
OUTCOME:
  DURATION AND DESCRIPTION OF INCIDENT: 2 days. After
  assassinating an Egyptian newspaper editor at the conference
  in the Nicosia Hilton, the perpetrators took 30 delegates
  hostage. They demanded an airliner and crew and took off
  from Cyprus. Refused landing by several Arab countries,
  they flew to Djibouti, were refueled, and then flew back
  to Cyprus. Egyptian President Sadat sent commandos to
  Cyprus, who, instead of storming the airliner, had a shoot-out
  with the Greek Cypriot National Guard. The perpetrators
  surrendered after the confrontation between the Egyptians
  and the Cypriots ended.
  SATISFACTION OF DEMANDS: Granted airliner and crew, and
  refueling at Djibouti, but no further concessions.
  FATE OF VICTIMS: Unharmed. Before take-off for Djibouti
  19 were released, the remaining 15 were released upon
  surrender. During the shoot-out, 12 Egyptian commandos
  were killed and 19 wounded, and 7 Greek Cypriot National
  Guardsmen were wounded.
  FATE OF PERPETRATORS: Unharmed. Arrested and sentenced
  to death, commuted to life imprisonment in Cypriot jail.
  PROPERTY DAMAGE: None by perpetrators.
  NATIONS GRANTING OR FACILITATING SAFE HAVEN: None

PRESS COVERAGE

Day	New York Times					London Times					Die Welt				
	Pg	Ph	Col	Id	Dmd	Pg	Ph	Col	Id	Dmd	Pg	Ph	Col	Id	Dmd
1	1	1	2.0	Y	Y	1	0	1.2	Y	Y					
2	1	2	3.0	Y	Y	1	1	1.7	Y	Y	1	1	1.5	Y	Y
3						1	0	0.7	N	N	1	8	3.8	Y	Y

EVENT 1 (continued)

Day	New York Times Pg	Ph	Col	Id	Dmd	London Times Pg	Ph	Col	Id	Dmd	Die Welt Pg	Ph	Col	Id	Dmd
4						1	1	1.2	N	N	1	1	0.7	Y	Y
5											1	0	0.6	Y	Y
6											8	1	1.5	N	N
9											1	0	0.3	Y	N
10											4	0	0.5	Y	Y

EVENT 2

DATE: March 13, 1978
LOCATION: Assen, the Netherlands
PERPETRATORS:
  NUMBER: 3
  NATIONALITY: South Moluccans
  ORGANIZATIONAL AFFILIATION: South Moluccan nationalists
VICTIMS:
  NUMBER: 71
  NATIONALITY: Netherlanders
  STATUS: Government employees
PHYSICAL TARGET:
  NATURE: Government building
  NATIONAL ASSOCIATION: Netherlander
NATURE OF DEMANDS: Release of 21 Moluccan terrorists from
Netherlands jails, $13 million, safe passage and an airliner.
TARGET OF DEMANDS: The Netherlands government
OUTCOME:
  DURATION AND DESCRIPTION OF INCIDENT: 2 days. Ended with
  storming by 60 Netherlands Marines.
  SATISFACTION OF DEMANDS: No reported concessions.
  FATE OF VICTIMS: During captivity, 1 was killed by the
  perpetrators. During the storming by Netherlands Marines,
  1 was killed and 6 were injured, while 63 were rescued
  unharmed.
  FATE OF PERPETRATORS: Unharmed, captured and sentenced
  to 15 years in jail.
  PROPERTY DAMAGE: Minimal
  NATIONS GRANTING OR FACILITATING SAFE HAVEN: None

EVENT 2 (continued)

PRESS COVERAGE

Day	New York Times					London Times					Die Welt				
	Pg	Ph	Col	Id	Dmd	Pg	Ph	Col	Id	Dmd	Pg	Ph	Col	Id	Dmd
1	1	1	1.5	Y	Y	1	1	1.0	Y	Y					
2	1	2	1.3	Y	Y	1	1	1.5	Y	Y	1*	1	1.5	Y	Y
3	8	0	0.2	Y	N	7	0	0.2	Y	N	4*	0	0.6	Y	Y
4	6	0	0.3	Y	N	7	0	0.4	Y	N					

---

* From the International Herald Tribune

EVENT 3

DATE: May 11, 1978
LOCATION: Colombia and the Netherlands Antilles
PERPETRATORS:
  NUMBER: 2
  NATIONALITY: Unknown
  ORGANIZATIONAL AFFILIATION: The Orphans
VICTIMS:
  NUMBER: 119
  NATIONALITY: Various, including 2 Americans
  STATUS: Passengers and crew
PHYSICAL TARGET:
  NATURE: Airliner
  NATIONAL ASSOCIATION: Colombian
NATURE OF DEMANDS: $55,000, food and fuel at stops in Cali,
Colombia, and Aruba and Curacao, the Netherlands Antilles.
TARGET OF DEMANDS: Colombian and the Netherlands Antilles
governments
OUTCOME:
  DURATION AND DESCRIPTION OF INCIDENT: 1 day. Hijacked
  over Colombia, forced to land at Cali, then Aruba, and
  then Curacao. Ended when Curacaoan police stormed the
  airliner.
  SATISFACTION OF DEMANDS: Granted food and fuel, but denied
  the ransom.
  FATE OF VICTIMS: In Aruba, 1 aircrewman was shot and injured
  by the perpetrators. The others were unharmed; 10 were
  released and 11 escaped in Aruba, the others were rescued
  in Curacao.
  FATE OF PERPETRATORS: During the storming, 1 was injured.
  Both were arrested, with disposition unknown.

EVENT 3 (continued)

PROPERTY DAMAGE: Minimal
NATIONS GRANTING OR FACILITATING SAFE HAVEN: None

PRESS COVERAGE

Day	New York Times Pg Ph Col Id Dmd	London Times Pg Ph Col Id Dmd	Die Welt Pg Ph Col Id Dmd
1	3 0 0.8 N Y		
2		4 0 0.3 Y N	

EVENT 4

DATE: August 17, 1978
LOCATION: Chicago
PERPETRATORS:
  NUMBER: 2
  NATIONALITY: Croatian Americans
  ORGANIZATIONAL AFFILIATION: Croatian nationalists
VICTIMS:
  NUMBER: 6
  NATIONALITY: West Germans
  STATUS: Consulate employees
PHYSICAL TARGET:
  NATURE: Consulate
  NATIONAL ASSOCIATION: West German
NATURE OF DEMANDS: Freeing of Croatian prisoner from West
German jail.
TARGET OF DEMANDS: West German government
OUTCOME:
  DURATION AND DESCRIPTION OF INCIDENT: 1 day
  SATISFACTION OF DEMANDS: Granted, comrade in West German
  prison released.
  FATE OF VICTIMS: Unharmed
  FATE OF PERPETRATORS: Unharmed, arrested, jailed in United
  States.
  PROPERTY DAMAGE: None
  NATIONS GRANTING OR FACILITATING SAFE HAVEN: None

EVENT 4 (continued)

PRESS COVERAGE

Day	New York Times					London Times					Die Welt				
	Pg	Ph	Col	Id	Dmd	Pg	Ph	Col	Id	Dmd	Pg	Ph	Col	Id	Dmd
1	1	0	0.8	Y	Y										
2	3	0	0.8	Y	Y	4	0	0.3	Y	Y	1	0	0.1	Y	N
3	6	0	0.3	Y	Y						5	1	2.0	Y	Y

EVENT 5

DATE: September 29, 1978
LOCATION: Guatemala City, Guatemala
PERPETRATORS:
  NUMBER: 60
  NATIONALITY: Guatemalans
  ORGANIZATIONAL AFFILIATION: Cement factory workers
VICTIMS:
  NUMBER: 7
  NATIONALITY: Swiss and Guatemalans
  STATUS: Ambassador and embassy employees
PHYSICAL TARGET:
  NATURE: Embassy
  NATIONAL ASSOCIATION: Swiss
NATURE OF DEMANDS: Reopening of 2 Guatemalan and Swiss cement
factories, and no reprisals from the management.
TARGET OF DEMANDS: Swiss and Guatemalan governments
OUTCOME:
  DURATION AND DESCRIPTION OF INCIDENT: 4 days
  SATISFACTION OF DEMANDS: Concessions granted.
  FATE OF VICTIMS: Released unharmed.
  FATE OF PERPETRATORS: Unharmed, returned to work.
  PROPERTY DAMAGE: None
  NATIONS GRANTING OR FACILITATING SAFE HAVEN: None

PRESS COVERAGE

Day	New York Times					London Times					Die Welt				
	Pg	Ph	Col	Id	Dmd	Pg	Ph	Col	Id	Dmd	Pg	Ph	Col	Id	Dmd
4	14	0	0.1	Y	Y						5	0	0.1	Y	Y

EVENT 6

DATE: January 12, 1979
LOCATION: Tunisia and Libya
PERPETRATORS:
  NUMBER: 3
  NATIONALITY: Tunisians
  ORGANIZATIONAL AFFILIATION: Opposition political party
VICTIMS:
  NUMBER: 83
  NATIONALITY: Various, including 25 West Germans
  STATUS: Passengers and crew
PHYSICAL TARGET:
  NATURE: Airliner
  NATIONAL ASSOCIATION: Tunisian
NATURE OF DEMANDS: Release of 2 political prisoners from
Tunisian jails.
TARGET OF DEMANDS: Tunisian government
OUTCOME:
  DURATION AND DESCRIPTION OF INCIDENT: 2 days. Hijacked
  over Tunisia, denied landing at Malta, landed at Tripoli,
  refueled and departed to return later.
  SATISFACTION OF DEMANDS: No reported concessions.
  FATE OF VICTIMS: Released unharmed.
  FATE OF PERPETRATORS: Unharmed, surrendered to Libyan
  authorities, disposition unknown.
  PROPERTY DAMAGE: None
  NATIONS GRANTING OR FACILITATING SAFE HAVEN: Libya

PRESS COVERAGE

Day	New York Times					London Times					Die Welt				
	Pg	Ph	Col	Id	Dmd	Pg	Ph	Col	Id	Dmd	Pg	Ph	Col	Id	Dmd
1	2	0	0.3	N	N										
2	8	0	0.3	Y	Y										
3						2*	0	0.2	Y	Y	5	0	0.5	Y	Y

---

*   From the International Herald Tribune

EVENT 7

DATE: January 16, 1979
LOCATION: San Salvador, El Salvador
PERPETRATORS:
  NUMBER: 30

EVENT 7 (continued)

NATIONALITY: Salvadorans
ORGANIZATIONAL AFFILIATION: FAPU, United Popular Action Front
VICTIMS:
  NUMBER: 7
  NATIONALITY: 3 Mexicans and 4 Salvadorans
  STATUS: Mexican Embassy employees
PHYSICAL TARGET:
  NATURE: Mexican Embassy
  NATIONAL ASSOCIATION: Mexican
NATURE OF DEMANDS: Political asylum
TARGET OF DEMANDS: Mexican government
OUTCOME:
  DURATION AND DESCRIPTION OF INCIDENT: 2 days
  SATISFACTION OF DEMANDS: Concessions granted.
  FATE OF VICTIMS: Released unharmed.
  FATE OF PERPETRATORS: Unharmed, moved to asylum in Mexico.
  PROPERTY DAMAGE: Minimal
  NATIONS GRANTING OR FACILITATING SAFE HAVEN: Mexico

PRESS COVERAGE

Day	New York Times					London Times					Die Welt				
---	Pg	Ph	Col	Id	Dmd	Pg	Ph	Col	Id	Dmd	Pg	Ph	Col	Id	Dmd
2	4	0	0.3	Y	Y						7	0	0.1	Y	N
3											8	0	0.2	Y	Y
4											7	0	0.1	Y	Y

EVENT 8

DATE: January 16, 1979
LOCATION: San Salvador, El Salvador
PERPETRATORS:
  NUMBER: 11
  NATIONALITY: Salvadorans
  ORGANIZATIONAL AFFILIATION: FAPU, United Popular Action Front
VICTIMS:
  NUMBER: 15
  NATIONALITY: Unknown
  STATUS: OAS employees
PHYSICAL TARGET:
  NATURE: OAS office buildings
  NATIONAL ASSOCIATION: International

EVENT 8 (continued)

NATURE OF DEMANDS: Release of political prisoners from
Salvadoran jails and immunity from prosecution.
TARGET OF DEMANDS: Salvadoran government
OUTCOME:
  DURATION AND DESCRIPTION OF INCIDENT: 3 days
  SATISFACTION OF DEMANDS: No prisoners released, ended
  with storming by Salvadoran National Guard troops.
  FATE OF VICTIMS: Rescued unharmed.
  FATE OF PERPETRATORS: Unharmed, arrested, disposition
  unknown.
  PROPERTY DAMAGE: Minimal
  NATIONS GRANTING OR FACILITATING SAFE HAVEN: None

PRESS COVERAGE

| | New York Times | | | | | London Times | | | | | Die Welt | | | | |
Day	Pg	Ph	Col	Id	Dmd	Pg	Ph	Col	Id	Dmd	Pg	Ph	Col	Id	Dmd
2	4	0	0.3	Y	Y						7	0	0.1	Y	N
3											8	0	0.2	Y	Y
4											7	0	0.1	Y	Y

EVENT 9

DATE: January 16, 1979
LOCATION: San Salvador, El Salvador
PERPETRATORS:
  NUMBER: 21
  NATIONALITY: Salvadorans
  ORGANIZATIONAL AFFILIATION: FAPU, United Popular Action Front
VICTIMS:
  NUMBER: 39
  NATIONALITY: Unknown
  STATUS: Red Cross employees
PHYSICAL TARGET:
  NATURE: Red Cross office building
  NATIONAL ASSOCIATION: International
NATURE OF DEMANDS: Release of political prisoners from
Salvadoran jails and immunity from prosecution.
TARGET OF DEMANDS: Salvadoran government
OUTCOME:
  DURATION AND DESCRIPTION OF INCIDENT: 1 day
  SATISFACTION OF DEMANDS: No prisoners released, ended
  with storming by Salvadoran National Guard troops.

EVENT 9 (continued)

FATE OF VICTIMS: Rescued unharmed.
FATE OF PERPETRATORS: Unharmed, arrested, disposition
unknown.
PROPERTY DAMAGE: Minimal
NATIONS GRANTING OR FACILITATING SAFE HAVEN: None

PRESS COVERAGE

Day	New York Times					London Times					Die Welt				
	Pg	Ph	Col	Id	Dmd	Pg	Ph	Col	Id	Dmd	Pg	Ph	Col	Id	Dmd
2	4	0	0.3	Y	Y						7	0	0.1	Y	N
3											8	0	0.2	Y	Y
4											7	0	0.1	Y	Y

EVENT 10

DATE: January 16, 1979
LOCATION: Beirut, Lebanon
PERPETRATORS:
  NUMBER: 6
  NATIONALITY: Lebanese
  ORGANIZATIONAL AFFILIATION: Shiite Muslims
VICTIMS:
  NUMBER: 81
  NATIONALITY: Unknown
  STATUS: Passengers and crew
PHYSICAL TARGET:
  NATURE: Airliner
  NATIONAL ASSOCIATION: Lebanese
NATURE OF DEMANDS: Press conference to publicize the
disappearance of their religious leader, whom they claimed
was a prisoner in Libya.
TARGET OF DEMANDS: Lebanese government
OUTCOME:
  DURATION AND DESCRIPTION OF INCIDENT: 2 days. Hijacked
  over Lebanon enroute to Jordan, denied landing by Cyprus,
  returned to Beirut.
  SATISFACTION OF DEMANDS: Granted press conference.
  FATE OF VICTIMS: Released unharmed.
  FATE OF PERPETRATORS: Unharmed, arrested, disposition
  unknown.
  PROPERTY DAMAGE: None
  NATIONS GRANTING OR FACILITATING SAFE HAVEN: None

EVENT 10 (continued)

PRESS COVERAGE

Day	New York Times Pg	Ph	Col	Id	Dmd	London Times Pg	Ph	Col	Id	Dmd	Die Welt Pg	Ph	Col	Id	Dmd
1	6	0	0.5	Y	Y										
2						2*	0	0.2	Y	Y	7	0	0.4	Y	Y

*   From the International Herald Tribune

EVENT 11

DATE: February 14, 1979
LOCATION: Kabul, Afghanistan
PERPETRATORS:
  NUMBER: 4
  NATIONALITY: Afghans
  ORGANIZATIONAL AFFILIATION: Afghan right-wing Muslims
VICTIMS:
  NUMBER: 1
  NATIONALITY: American
  STATUS: Ambassador
PHYSICAL TARGET:
  NATURE: None
  NATIONAL ASSOCIATION: None
NATURE OF DEMANDS: Release of Muslim religious figures from
Afghan jails.
TARGET OF DEMANDS: Afghan government
OUTCOME:
  DURATION AND DESCRIPTION OF INCIDENT: 1 day. Kidnapped
  ambassador was held in hotel room. Stormed by security
  forces over objections of American authorities (reportedly
  upon advice of KGB).
  SATISFACTION OF DEMANDS: No reported concessions.
  FATE OF VICTIMS: Killed during storming.
  FATE OF PERPETRATORS: During the storming, 1 was killed
  and 2 were injured. Disposition unknown.
  PROPERTY DAMAGE: Minimal
  NATIONS GRANTING OR FACILITATING SAFE HAVEN: None

EVENT 11 (continued)

PRESS COVERAGE

Day	New York Times Pg	Ph	Col	Id	Dmd	London Times Pg	Ph	Col	Id	Dmd	Die Welt Pg	Ph	Col	Id	Dmd
1	1	1	1.8	Y	Y	1*	1	1.2	Y	Y	1	1	0.3	Y	Y
2	1	0	1.0	N	N	1*	0	0.8	Y	N	1	0	0.7	Y	Y
3						1*	0	0.1	Y	N					
4						1*	0	1.5	Y	Y					

* From the International Herald Tribune

EVENT 12

DATE: February 27, 1979
LOCATION: Norway and Sweden
PERPETRATORS:
  NUMBER: 4
  NATIONALITY: 1 Swede, 1 Indian, 1 Brazilian, and 1 German
  ORGANIZATIONAL AFFILIATION: Unidentified religious sect
VICTIMS:
  NUMBER: 34
  NATIONALITY: Unknown
  STATUS: Passengers and crew
PHYSICAL TARGET:
  NATURE: Airliner
  NATIONAL ASSOCIATION: Soviet
NATURE OF DEMANDS: Publicity to focus world attention on
religious conditions in the USSR. One perpetrator asked
for political asylum.
TARGET OF DEMANDS: Swedish government
OUTCOME:
  DURATION AND DESCRIPTION OF INCIDENT: 1 day. Hijacked
  the Norway to USSR flight, landed at Stockholm, overpowered
  by the crew.
  SATISFACTION OF DEMANDS: Publicity achieved, but asylum
  not granted.
  FATE OF VICTIMS: Unharmed
  FATE OF PERPETRATORS: Unharmed, arrested and jailed in
  Sweden.
  PROPERTY DAMAGE: None
  NATIONS GRANTING OR FACILITATING SAFE HAVEN: None

EVENT 12 (continued)

PRESS COVERAGE

	New York Times					London Times					Die Welt				
Day	Pg	Ph	Col	Id	Dmd	Pg	Ph	Col	Id	Dmd	Pg	Ph	Col	Id	Dmd
1						2*	0	0.4	Y	Y	1	0	0.2	Y	Y
2	7	0	0.3	Y	Y										

---

* From the International Herald Tribune

EVENT 13

DATE: May 4, 1979
LOCATION: San Salvador, El Salvador
PERPETRATORS:
  NUMBER: 16
  NATIONALITY: Salvadorans
  ORGANIZATIONAL AFFILIATION: BPR, Popular Revolutionary Bloc
VICTIMS:
  NUMBER: 6
  NATIONALITY: Frenchmen
  STATUS: Ambassador and embassy employees
PHYSICAL TARGET:
  NATURE: Embassy
  NATIONAL ASSOCIATION: French
NATURE OF DEMANDS: Release of 5 of their leaders from
Salvadoran jails. On 12 May, demands were increased to include
the release of 5 more members newly imprisoned in Salvadoran
jails, the repatriation of 3 of their members previously
granted asylum in Costa Rica, safe passage, and asylum in
Mexico.
TARGET OF DEMANDS: Salvadoran and Mexican governments
OUTCOME:
  DURATION AND DESCRIPTION OF INCIDENT: 29 days
  SATISFACTION OF DEMANDS: Safe passage and asylum were
  granted, and 2 leaders were released from jail.
  FATE OF VICTIMS: Released unharmed.
  FATE OF PERPETRATORS: Unharmed, flown to Mexico.
  PROPERTY DAMAGE: None
  NATIONS GRANTING OR FACILITATING SAFE HAVEN: Mexico

EVENT 13 (continued)

PRESS COVERAGE

Day	New York Times					London Times					Die Welt				
	Pg	Ph	Col	Id	Dmd	Pg	Ph	Col	Id	Dmd	Pg	Ph	Col	Id	Dmd
1	5	0	0.5	Y	Y										
2											1	0	0.2	Y	Y
3						6*	0	0.6	Y	Y					
4	2	0	0.1	Y	Y	2*	0	0.2	Y	Y					
5	3	1	1.0	Y	Y	2*	0	0.2	Y	Y					
6	3	1	0.5	Y	Y	2*	1	0.6	Y	Y	1	0	0.1	Y	Y
7	3	0	0.3	Y	Y	3*	0	0.3	Y	Y	7	0	0.8	Y	Y
8	16	1	0.2	Y	Y	5*	0	0.5	Y	Y	7	0	0.3	Y	Y
9	5	0	0.5	Y	Y	5*	0	0.4	Y	N					
10											7	1	0.2	Y	Y
11											9	0	0.1	Y	Y
12						2*	0	0.1	Y	N					
14	5	0	0.2	Y	Y	5*	0	0.2	Y	Y	5	0	0.1	Y	N
16											5	0	0.1	Y	N
17	4	0	0.3	Y	Y	5*	0	0.5	Y	Y					
18											8	0	0.1	Y	N
19	8	0	0.1	Y	Y										
20						2*	0	0.5	Y	Y					
21	4	0	0.1	Y	Y	2*	1	0.3	Y	Y					
22						2*	0	0.1	Y	Y					
25						2*	0	0.1	Y	N					
26	7	0	0.2	Y	Y										
27	2	0	0.3	Y	Y						7	0	0.1	Y	Y
29						1*	0	0.6	Y	Y					

*   From the International Herald Tribune

EVENT 14

DATE: May 4, 1979
LOCATION: San Salvador, El Salvador
PERPETRATORS:
  NUMBER: 3
  NATIONALITY: Salvadorans
  ORGANIZATIONAL AFFILIATION: BPR, Popular Revolutionary Bloc
VICTIMS:
  NUMBER: 5
  NATIONALITY: Costa Ricans
  STATUS: Ambassador and embassy employees

EVENT 14 (continued)

PHYSICAL TARGET:
  NATURE: Embassy
  NATIONAL ASSOCIATION: Costa Rican
NATURE OF DEMANDS: Release of 5 of their leaders from
Salvadoran jails, safe passage and asylum in Costa Rica.
TARGET OF DEMANDS: Salvadoran and Costa Rican governments
OUTCOME:
  DURATION AND DESCRIPTION OF INCIDENT: 6 days. Hostages
  escaped on 7 May, building was held until 9 May.
  SATISFACTION OF DEMANDS: Safe passage and asylum were
  granted, and 2 leaders were released from jail.
  FATE OF VICTIMS: Escaped unharmed.
  FATE OF PERPETRATORS: Unharmed
  PROPERTY DAMAGE: None
  NATIONS GRANTING OR FACILITATING SAFE HAVEN: Costa Rica

PRESS COVERAGE

| Day | New York Times | | | | | London Times | | | | | Die Welt | | | | |
	Pg	Ph	Col	Id	Dmd	Pg	Ph	Col	Id	Dmd	Pg	Ph	Col	Id	Dmd
1	5	0	0.5	Y	Y										
2											1	0	0.2	Y	Y
3						6*	0	0.6	Y	Y					
4	2	0	0.1	Y	Y	2*	0	0.2	Y	Y					
5	3	1	1.0	Y	Y	2*	0	0.2	Y	Y					
6	3	1	0.5	Y	Y	2*	1	0.6	Y	Y	1	0	0.1	Y	Y
7	3	0	0.2	Y	Y	3*	0	0.1	Y	N	7	0	0.8	Y	Y
8	16	1	0.1	Y	Y	5*	0	0.2	Y	Y	7	0	0.8	Y	Y
14	5	0	0.1	Y	Y										
17	4	0	0.3	Y	Y										
19	8	0	0.1	Y	Y										
26	7	0	0.1	Y	Y										
27	2	0	0.1	Y	Y										

---

*   From the International Herald Tribune

EVENT 15

DATE: May 11, 1979
LOCATION: San Salvador, El Salvador
PERPETRATORS:
  NUMBER: 9
  NATIONALITY: Salvadorans

EVENT 15 (continued)

ORGANIZATIONAL AFFILIATION: BPR, Popular Revolutionary Bloc
VICTIMS:
  NUMBER: 8
  NATIONALITY: Venezuelans
  STATUS: Ambassador and embassy employees
PHYSICAL TARGET:
  NATURE: Embassy
  NATIONAL ASSOCIATION: Venezuelan
NATURE OF DEMANDS: Release of 3 of their members from
Salvadoran jails and immunity from prosecution.
TARGET OF DEMANDS: Salvadoran government
OUTCOME:
  DURATION AND DESCRIPTION OF INCIDENT: 20 days
  SATISFACTION OF DEMANDS: No charges pressed and 2 of their
  members released from jail.
  FATE OF VICTIMS: Unharmed, escaped on 9th day.
  FATE OF PERPETRATORS: Unharmed, not arrested.
  PROPERTY DAMAGE: Minimal
  NATIONS GRANTING OR FACILITATING SAFE HAVEN: Offered by
  Venezuela but refused.

PRESS COVERAGE

Day	New York Times					London Times					Die Welt				
---	Pg	Ph	Col	Id	Dmd	Pg	Ph	Col	Id	Dmd	Pg	Ph	Col	Id	Dmd
1	3	0	0.5	Y	Y										
2	16	1	0.2	Y	Y										
3	5	0	0.5	Y	Y	5*	0	0.3	Y	N					
4											7	0	0.2	Y	Y
5						2*	0	0.1	Y	N	8	0	0.1	Y	Y
7	5	0	0.2	Y	Y	5*	0	0.2	Y	Y	5	0	0.1	Y	Y
9											5	0	0.1	Y	N
10	4	0	0.3	Y	Y	5*	0	0.8	Y	Y	1	0	0.1	Y	N
11											8	0	0.1	Y	N
12	8	0	0.2	Y	Y	2*	0	0.4	Y	Y					
13						2*	0	0.5	Y	Y	1	0	0.1	Y	N
14	4	0	0.1	Y	Y	2*	1	0.2	Y	Y					
16						2*	0	0.1	Y	Y					
18						2*	0	0.1	Y	N					
19	7	0	0.2	Y	Y										
20	2	0	0.3	Y	Y	1*	0	0.4	Y	Y					

---

*   From the International Herald Tribune

EVENT 16

DATE: June 20, 1979
LOCATION: United States and Ireland
PERPETRATORS:
  NUMBER: 1
  NATIONALITY: Serbian American
  ORGANIZATIONAL AFFILIATION: Serbian nationalist
VICTIMS:
  NUMBER: 135
  NATIONALITY: Unknown
  STATUS: Passengers and crew
PHYSICAL TARGET:
  NATURE: Airliner
  NATIONAL ASSOCIATION: American
NATURE OF DEMANDS: Release of a Serbian jailed in the U.S.
and safe passage to Peru.
TARGET OF DEMANDS: American and Peruvian governments
OUTCOME:
  DURATION AND DESCRIPTION OF INCIDENT: 2 days. Hijacked
  over Michigan, 128 passengers and 5 crew released after
  landing in Chicago. Flew on to New York with 3 crew members
  and a negotiator. Got another airliner and flew to Ireland.
  SATISFACTION OF DEMANDS: No reported concessions.
  FATE OF VICTIMS: Released unharmed.
  FATE OF PERPETRATORS: Unharmed. Surrendered in Ireland,
  returned to U.S. and jailed for 60 years for previous crime.
  PROPERTY DAMAGE: None
  NATIONS GRANTING OR FACILITATING SAFE HAVEN: None

PRESS COVERAGE

Day	New York Times					London Times					Die Welt				
	Pg	Ph	Col	Id	Dmd	Pg	Ph	Col	Id	Dmd	Pg	Ph	Col	Id	Dmd
1	1	2	2.0	Y	Y	1*	0	0.1	Y	Y					
2	3	0	1.5	Y	Y	1*	1	0.9	Y	Y	8	0	0.2	Y	Y
3	6	1	1.0	Y	Y	2*	0	0.2	Y	Y					
4						3*	0	0.4	Y	Y					

---

* From the International Herald Tribune

EVENT 17

DATE: June 26, 1979
LOCATION: Guatemala City, Guatemala

EVENT 17 (continued)

PERPETRATORS:
  NUMBER: 20
  NATIONALITY: Guatemalans
  ORGANIZATIONAL AFFILIATION: Textile workers
VICTIMS:
  NUMBER: 38
  NATIONALITY: Mexicans
  STATUS: Ambassador and embassy employees
PHYSICAL TARGET:
  NATURE: Embassy
  NATIONAL ASSOCIATION: Mexican
NATURE OF DEMANDS: Release of labor leaders jailed in
Guatemala, rights for workers, and immunity from prosecution.
TARGET OF DEMANDS: Guatemalan government
OUTCOME:
  DURATION AND DESCRIPTION OF INCIDENT: 5 days
  SATISFACTION OF DEMANDS: Concessions granted.
  FATE OF VICTIMS: Released unharmed.
  FATE OF PERPETRATORS: Unharmed, not arrested.
  PROPERTY DAMAGE: Minimal
  NATIONS GRANTING OR FACILITATING SAFE HAVEN: None

PRESS COVERAGE

Day	New York Times Pg	Ph	Col	Id	Dmd	London Times Pg	Ph	Col	Id	Dmd	Die Welt Pg	Ph	Col	Id	Dmd
2											5	0	0.1	Y	Y

EVENT 18

DATE: July 13, 1979
LOCATION: Ankara, Turkey
PERPETRATORS:
  NUMBER: 4
  NATIONALITY: Palestinians
  ORGANIZATIONAL AFFILIATION: Eagles of the Palestinian
  Revolution
VICTIMS:
  NUMBER: 17
  NATIONALITY: Egyptians and Turks
  STATUS: Ambassador and embassy employees
PHYSICAL TARGET:
  NATURE: Embassy

EVENT 18 (continued)

NATIONAL ASSOCIATION: Egyptian
NATURE OF DEMANDS: Release of two of their organization
from Egyptian jails, an airliner, and safe passage. Turkey
should sever diplomatic relations with Egypt and Israel,
recognize the PLO, and denounce the Egyptian-Israeli peace
treaty.
TARGET OF DEMANDS: Turkish and Egyptian governments
OUTCOME:
  DURATION AND DESCRIPTION OF INCIDENT: 3 days. Ended with
  PLO mediation and surrender.
  SATISFACTION OF DEMANDS: Turkish government reported no
  concessions. However, it was immediately announced that
  the PLO would be allowed to set up an official mission
  in Ankara, and a special message recognizing Turkish support
  of the Palestinian struggle was sent to Arafat by the Turkish
  Foreign Ministry.
  FATE OF VICTIMS: When attempting to escape by jumping
  off the building, 1 was killed and 1 was injured, while
  2 escaped unharmed through a window. During the siege,
  4 were released unharmed, and 9 were released unharmed
  upon surrender of the perpetrators. During the take-over,
  2 policemen were killed and 1 was wounded.
  FATE OF PERPETRATORS: Surrendered unharmed, arrested,
  sentenced to death.
  PROPERTY DAMAGE: Minimal
  NATIONS GRANTING OR FACILITATING SAFE HAVEN: None

PRESS COVERAGE

Day	New York Times					London Times					Die Welt				
	Pg	Ph	Col	Id	Dmd	Pg	Ph	Col	Id	Dmd	Pg	Ph	Col	Id	Dmd
1	1	1	1.5	Y	Y	1*	1	1.5	Y	Y	1	0	0.5	Y	Y
2	1	1	1.5	Y	Y										
3	1	0	1.8	Y	Y	1*	1	1.0	Y	Y	1	1	2.0	Y	Y
4	6	0	0.3	Y	N										
5											5	0	0.3	Y	Y
16	6	0	0.2	Y	Y						5	1	0.1	Y	N

---

* From the International Herald Tribune

EVENT 19

DATE: July 25, 1979
LOCATION: Bangladesh and India

EVENT 19 (continued)

PERPETRATORS:
  NUMBER: 3
  NATIONALITY: Bangladeshis
  ORGANIZATIONAL AFFILIATION: Unknown
VICTIMS:
  NUMBER: 40
  NATIONALITY: Bangladeshis and others
  STATUS: A member of the Bangladeshi Parliament, passengers
  and crew
PHYSICAL TARGET:
  NATURE: Airliner
  NATIONAL ASSOCIATION: Bangladeshi
NATURE OF DEMANDS: $1 million from the Bangladeshi government
and safe conduct out of India.
TARGET OF DEMANDS: Bangladeshi and Indian governments
OUTCOME:
  DURATION AND DESCRIPTION OF INCIDENT: 1 day. Hijacked
  over Bangladesh, diverted to Calcutta. Ended with surrender
  to Indian authorities.
  SATISFACTION OF DEMANDS: No reported concessions.
  FATE OF VICTIMS: Released unharmed.
  FATE OF PERPETRATORS: Unharmed, arrested by Indian
  authorities, deported to Bangladesh, disposition unknown.
  PROPERTY DAMAGE: Unknown
  NATIONS GRANTING OR FACILITATING SAFE HAVEN: None

PRESS COVERAGE

Day	New York Times					London Times					Die Welt				
	Pg	Ph	Col	Id	Dmd	Pg	Ph	Col	Id	Dmd	Pg	Ph	Col	Id	Dmd
1	4	0	0.3	N	Y	1*	0	0.2	Y	Y					

---

* From the International Herald Tribune

EVENT 20

DATE: August 5, 1979
LOCATION: Spain, Portugal, and Switzerland
PERPETRATORS:
  NUMBER: 3
  NATIONALITY: 2 Frenchmen and a Chilean
  ORGANIZATIONAL AFFILIATION: Spanish Foreign Legion deserters

EVENT 20 (continued)

VICTIMS:
  NUMBER: 23
  NATIONALITY: Unknown
  STATUS: Passengers and crew
PHYSICAL TARGET:
  NATURE: Airliner
  NATIONAL ASSOCIATION: Spanish
NATURE OF DEMANDS: Refueling, safe passage, and flight to Rhodesia.
TARGET OF DEMANDS: Portuguese and Rhodesian governments
OUTCOME:
  DURATION AND DESCRIPTION OF INCIDENT: 2 days. Hijacked from Canary Islands, denied landing in Morocco, landed in Lisbon. Refueled and flew on to Geneva to surrender to Swiss authorities.
  SATISFACTION OF DEMANDS: Refueled in Lisbon, all else denied.
  FATE OF VICTIMS: Unharmed, 10 were released in Lisbon and the remainder in Geneva.
  FATE OF PERPETRATORS: Unharmed, arrested in Switzerland, disposition unknown.
  PROPERTY DAMAGE: None
  NATIONS GRANTING OR FACILITATING SAFE HAVEN: None

PRESS COVERAGE

Day	New York Times					London Times					Die Welt				
	Pg	Ph	Col	Id	Dmd	Pg	Ph	Col	Id	Dmd	Pg	Ph	Col	Id	Dmd
1	7	0	0.2	Y	Y	1*	0	0.1	Y	N					
2	9	0	0.2	Y	Y	1*	0	0.3	Y	Y					

---

* From the International Herald Tribune

EVENT 21

DATE: August 24, 1979
LOCATION: Libya and Cyprus
PERPETRATORS:
  NUMBER: 1
  NATIONALITY: Libyan
  ORGANIZATIONAL AFFILIATION: Unknown
VICTIMS:
  NUMBER: 69

EVENT 21 (continued)

NATIONALITY: Unknown
STATUS: Passengers and crew
PHYSICAL TARGET:
  NATURE: Airliner
  NATIONAL ASSOCIATION: Libyan
NATURE OF DEMANDS: Political asylum
TARGET OF DEMANDS: Cypriot government
OUTCOME:
  DURATION AND DESCRIPTION OF INCIDENT: 1 day. Hijacked
  from over Libya to Cyprus.
  SATISFACTION OF DEMANDS: Denied political asylum.
  FATE OF VICTIMS: Released unharmed.
  FATE OF PERPETRATORS: Unharmed, arrested, disposition
  unknown.
  PROPERTY DAMAGE: None
  NATIONS GRANTING OR FACILITATING SAFE HAVEN: None

PRESS COVERAGE

| Day | New York Times | | | | | London Times | | | | | Die Welt | | | | |
	Pg	Ph	Col	Id	Dmd	Pg	Ph	Col	Id	Dmd	Pg	Ph	Col	Id	Dmd
1						2*	0	0.2	Y	Y					

---

*   From the International Herald Tribune

EVENT 22

DATE: November 23, 1979
LOCATION: Japan
PERPETRATORS:
  NUMBER: 1
  NATIONALITY: Japanese
  ORGANIZATIONAL AFFILIATION: Unknown
VICTIMS:
  NUMBER: 356
  NATIONALITY: Various
  STATUS: Passengers and crew
PHYSICAL TARGET:
  NATURE: Airliner
  NATIONAL ASSOCIATION: Japanese
NATURE OF DEMANDS: Safe passage and flight to the USSR
TARGET OF DEMANDS: Japanese and Soviet governments

EVENT 22 (continued)

OUTCOME:
  DURATION AND DESCRIPTION OF INCIDENT: 1 day. Hijacked
  over Japan, landed at Narita, overpowered by the pilot.
  SATISFACTION OF DEMANDS: No reported concessions.
  FATE OF VICTIMS: Rescued unharmed.
  FATE OF PERPETRATORS: Unharmed, arrested, disposition
  unknown.
  PROPERTY DAMAGE: None
  NATIONS GRANTING OR FACILITATING SAFE HAVEN: None

PRESS COVERAGE

Day	New York Times Pg Ph Col Id Dmd	London Times Pg Ph Col Id Dmd	Die Welt Pg Ph Col Id Dmd
1	5 0 0.1 Y Y	3* 1 0.3 Y Y	

---

* From the International Herald Tribune

EVENT 23

DATE: January 7, 1980
LOCATION: Bastelica, Corsica
PERPETRATORS:
  NUMBER: 30
  NATIONALITY: Corsicans
  ORGANIZATIONAL AFFILIATION: Front for the Liberation of
  National Corsica
VICTIMS:
  NUMBER: 3
  NATIONALITY: Corsicans
  STATUS: Leaders of anti-separationist organization
PHYSICAL TARGET:
  NATURE: Town hall
  NATIONAL ASSOCIATION: Corsican
NATURE OF DEMANDS: Punishment of anti-separationist terrorists
by France.
TARGET OF DEMANDS: French government
OUTCOME:
  DURATION AND DESCRIPTION OF INCIDENT: 3 days
  SATISFACTION OF DEMANDS: No concessions granted.
  FATE OF VICTIMS: Escaped unharmed.
  FATE OF PERPETRATORS: Escaped unharmed.

EVENT 23 (continued)

PROPERTY DAMAGE: None
NATIONS GRANTING OR FACILITATING SAFE HAVEN: None

PRESS COVERAGE

| Day | New York Times | | | | | London Times | | | | | Die Welt | | | | |
	Pg	Ph	Col	Id	Dmd	Pg	Ph	Col	Id	Dmd	Pg	Ph	Col	Id	Dmd
1						4	0	0.3	Y	Y					
8	5	1	1.2	Y	Y										

EVENT 24

DATE: January 9, 1980
LOCATION: Ajaccio, Corsica
PERPETRATORS:
  NUMBER: 30
  NATIONALITY: Corsicans
  ORGANIZATIONAL AFFILIATION: Front for the Liberation of
  National Corsica
VICTIMS:
  NUMBER: 10
  NATIONALITY: 9 Frenchmen and 1 Corsican
  STATUS: 9 hotel guests and 1 Corsican anti-separatist
PHYSICAL TARGET:
  NATURE: Hotel
  NATIONAL ASSOCIATION: Corsican
NATURE OF DEMANDS: Punishment of anti-separatist terrorists
by France, news conference, and a parade through town to
the police station.
TARGET OF DEMANDS: French government
OUTCOME:
  DURATION AND DESCRIPTION OF INCIDENT: 3 days
  SATISFACTION OF DEMANDS: Granted the news conference and
  the parade.
  FATE OF VICTIMS: Released unharmed.
  FATE OF PERPETRATORS: Surrendered unharmed, arrested and
  jailed.
  PROPERTY DAMAGE: None
  NATIONS GRANTING OR FACILITATING SAFE HAVEN: None

EVENT 24 (continued)

PRESS COVERAGE

Day	New York Times Pg	Ph	Col	Id	Dmd	London Times Pg	Ph	Col	Id	Dmd	Die Welt Pg	Ph	Col	Id	Dmd
1	7	0	0.2	Y	Y	6	0	0.2	Y	Y	5	0	0.1	Y	Y
2	5	0	0.2	Y	N	1	1	1.0	Y	Y					
3						4	1	1.0	Y	Y	7	0	0.6	Y	Y
6	5	1	1.6	Y	Y										

EVENT 25

DATE: January 11, 1980
LOCATION: San Salvador, El Salvador
PERPETRATORS:
  NUMBER: 58
  NATIONALITY: Salvadorans
  ORGANIZATIONAL AFFILIATION: LP-28, February 28 Popular
  League
VICTIMS:
  NUMBER: 6
  NATIONALITY: Panamanians and Costa Ricans
  STATUS: 2 Ambassadors and 4 embassy employees
PHYSICAL TARGET:
  NATURE: Embassy
  NATIONAL ASSOCIATION: Panamanian
NATURE OF DEMANDS: . Release of 7 members of their organization
from Salvadoran jails, and immunity from prosecution.
TARGET OF DEMANDS: Salvadoran government
OUTCOME:
  DURATION AND DESCRIPTION OF INCIDENT: 4 days
  SATISFACTION OF DEMANDS: All demands granted.
  FATE OF VICTIMS: Released unharmed.
  FATE OF PERPETRATORS: Unharmed, allowed to leave.
  PROPERTY DAMAGE: None
  NATIONS GRANTING OR FACILITATING SAFE HAVEN: None

PRESS COVERAGE

Day	New York Times Pg	Ph	Col	Id	Dmd	London Times Pg	Ph	Col	Id	Dmd	Die Welt Pg	Ph	Col	Id	Dmd
1	5	0	0.2	Y	Y	1	0	0.2	Y	Y					

EVENT 25 (continued)

PRESS COVERAGE

	New York Times					London Times					Die Welt				
Day	Pg	Ph	Col	Id	Dmd	Pg	Ph	Col	Id	Dmd	Pg	Ph	Col	Id	Dmd
2						5*	0	0.6	Y	Y					
4	14	0	0.2	Y	Y	7	0	0.3	Y	Y					

* From the International Herald Tribune

EVENT 26

DATE: January 14, 1980
LOCATION: Italy and Sicily
PERPETRATORS:
  NUMBER: 1
  NATIONALITY: Tunisian
  ORGANIZATIONAL AFFILIATION: Opposition political party
VICTIMS:
  NUMBER: 89
  NATIONALITY: Tunisians and Italians
  STATUS: Passengers and crew
PHYSICAL TARGET:
  NATURE: Airliner
  NATIONAL ASSOCIATION: Italian
NATURE OF DEMANDS: Release of 25 political prisoners from
Tunisian jails.
TARGET OF DEMANDS: ' Tunisian government
OUTCOME:
  DURATION AND DESCRIPTION OF INCIDENT: 2 days. Hijacked
  over Italy, could not land in Libya due to sandstorm, landed
  in Palermo.
  SATISFACTION OF DEMANDS: No concessions granted.
  FATE OF VICTIMS: Released unharmed.
  FATE OF PERPETRATORS: Surrendered unharmed, jailed in
  Sicily.
  PROPERTY DAMAGE: None
  NATIONS GRANTING OR FACILITATING SAFE HAVEN: None

EVENT 26 (continued)

PRESS COVERAGE

Day	New York Times Pg Ph Col Id Dmd	London Times Pg Ph Col Id Dmd	Die Welt Pg Ph Col Id Dmd
1		1 0 0.1 N N	
2	9 0 0.2 Y Y	5 0 0.3 Y Y	5 0 0.1 Y Y

EVENT 27

DATE: January 25, 1980
LOCATION: United States and Cuba
PERPETRATORS:
  NUMBER: 2
  NATIONALITY: Americans
  ORGANIZATIONAL AFFILIATION: Black Muslims
VICTIMS:
  NUMBER: 65
  NATIONALITY: Americans
  STATUS: Passengers and crew
PHYSICAL TARGET:
  NATURE: Airliner
  NATIONAL ASSOCIATION: American
NATURE OF DEMANDS: Safe passage and flight to Iran
TARGET OF DEMANDS: Cuban and Iranian governments
OUTCOME:
  DURATION AND DESCRIPTION OF INCIDENT: 2 days. Hijacked
  over the U.S., landed at Havana. While perpetrators were
  negotiating in the cockpit, the passengers escaped from
  the rear of the aircraft. Perpetrators then surrendered
  to the crew.
  SATISFACTION OF DEMANDS: No reported concessions.
  FATE OF VICTIMS: Escaped unharmed.
  FATE OF PERPETRATORS: Unharmed, turned over to Cuban
  authorities, disposition unknown.
  PROPERTY DAMAGE: None
  NATIONS GRANTING OR FACILITATING SAFE HAVEN: None

EVENT 27 (continued)

PRESS COVERAGE

Day	New York Times Pg Ph Col Id Dmd	London Times Pg Ph Col Id Dmd	Die Welt Pg Ph Col Id Dmd
1	8 2 1.2 Y Y	4 0 0.3 Y Y	
2	18 0 0.3 Y Y		

EVENT 28

DATE: January 31, 1980
LOCATION: Guatemala City, Guatemala
PERPETRATORS:
  NUMBER: 27
  NATIONALITY: Guatemalans
  ORGANIZATIONAL AFFILIATION: Quiche Indians
VICTIMS:
  NUMBER: 14
  NATIONALITY: 12 Spaniards and 2 Guatemalans
  STATUS: Ambassador and embassy employees
PHYSICAL TARGET:
  NATURE: Embassy
  NATIONAL ASSOCIATION: Spanish
NATURE OF DEMANDS: Conference with government concerning
army repression of the Quiche Indians.
TARGET OF DEMANDS: Guatemalan government
OUTCOME:
  DURATION AND DESCRIPTION OF INCIDENT: 1 day. Embassy
  stormed by police. Ensuing fire from a perpetrator's gasoline
  bomb killed all but the Ambassador and one perpetrator.
  SATISFACTION OF DEMANDS: No reported concessions.
  FATE OF VICTIMS: During the storming, 13 were killed and
  1 was unharmed.
  FATE OF PERPETRATORS: During the storming, 26 were killed.
  The 1 survivor was later kidnapped from a hospital and killed.
  PROPERTY DAMAGE: Embassy destroyed.
  NATIONS GRANTING OR FACILITATING SAFE HAVEN: None

EVENT 28 (continued)

PRESS COVERAGE

Day	New York Times					London Times					Die Welt				
	Pg	Ph	Col	Id	Dmd	Pg	Ph	Col	Id	Dmd	Pg	Ph	Col	Id	Dmd
1	2	0	0.5	Y	Y	1	0	0.1	Y	N					
2	2	0	0.5	Y	N	4	0	0.4	Y	Y	1	0	0.6	Y	Y
4						6	0	0.5	Y	Y	5	0	0.1	Y	Y
5											7	0	0.1	N	N
7											5	0	0.1	Y	N
8						7	0	0.1	Y	N					
9						4	0	0.6	Y	Y					
11						4	0	0.4	Y	N					

EVENT 29

DATE: February 5, 1980
LOCATION: San Salvador, El Salvador
PERPETRATORS:
  NUMBER: 7
  NATIONALITY: Salvadorans
  ORGANIZATIONAL AFFILIATION: LP-28, February 28 Popular
  League
VICTIMS:
  NUMBER: 16
  NATIONALITY: Spaniards and Salvadorans
  STATUS: Ambassador and embassy employees
PHYSICAL TARGET:
  NATURE: Embassy
  NATIONAL ASSOCIATION: Spanish
NATURE OF DEMANDS: Release of 16 of their members from
Salvadoran jails, Spain to break diplomatic relations with
El Salvador, inquiry by the OAS and the Red Cross into human
rights violations in El Salvador, and immunity from prosecution.
TARGET OF DEMANDS: Salvadoran and Spanish governments, the
OAS, and the Red Cross
OUTCOME:
  DURATION AND DESCRIPTION OF INCIDENT: 14 days
  SATISFACTION OF DEMANDS: Partially granted, 11 prisoners
  were released from Salvadoran jails.
  FATE OF VICTIMS: Unharmed, 3 released on the 1st day,
  7 on the 2nd day, 2 on the 6th day, 2 on the 10th day,
  and 2 on the last day.
  FATE OF PERPETRATORS: Unharmed, left embassy unmolested.

EVENT 29 (continued)

PROPERTY DAMAGE: Minor
NATIONS GRANTING OR FACILITATING SAFE HAVEN: None

PRESS COVERAGE

Day	New York Times					London Times					Die Welt				
	Pg	Ph	Col	Id	Dmd	Pg	Ph	Col	Id	Dmd	Pg	Ph	Col	Id	Dmd
1	3	0	0.5	Y	Y										
2	5	0	0.2	N	Y	7	0	0.1	Y	N	4	0	0.2	Y	Y
3						5	0	0.1	N	Y	7	0	0.1	N	Y
4						1*	0	0.6	Y	Y					
5											5	0	0.2	Y	Y
6	13	0	0.2	Y	Y	4	0	0.1	Y	N	7	0	0.1	N	Y
8											7	0	0.2	Y	Y
9						8	0	0.1	Y	Y					
10						9	0	0.1	Y	N					
11	5	0	0.1	Y	N										
12											4	0	0.2	Y	Y
13											4	0	0.5	Y	Y
14	6	0	0.1	Y	Y						8	0	0.1	Y	N

---

* From the International Herald Tribune

EVENT 30

DATE: February 13, 1980
LOCATION: San Salvador, El Salvador
PERPETRATORS:
  NUMBER: 50
  NATIONALITY: Salvadorans
  ORGANIZATIONAL AFFILIATION: LP-28, February 28 Popular
  League
VICTIMS:
  NUMBER: 3
  NATIONALITY: Panamanian and Salvadoran
  STATUS: Ambassador and embassy employees
PHYSICAL TARGET:
  NATURE: Embassy
  NATIONAL ASSOCIATION: Panamanian
NATURE OF DEMANDS: Release of 23 LP-28 and BPR members from
Salvadoran jails, and immunity from prosecution.
TARGET OF DEMANDS: Salvadoran government

EVENT 30 (continued)

OUTCOME:
  DURATION AND DESCRIPTION OF INCIDENT: 2 days
  SATISFACTION OF DEMANDS: Concessions granted.
  FATE OF VICTIMS: Released unharmed.
  FATE OF PERPETRATORS: Unharmed, left embassy unmolested.
  PROPERTY DAMAGE: None
  NATIONS GRANTING OR FACILITATING SAFE HAVEN: None

PRESS COVERAGE

Day	New York Times					London Times					Die Welt				
	Pg	Ph	Col	Id	Dmd	Pg	Ph	Col	Id	Dmd	Pg	Ph	Col	Id	Dmd
1	11	0	0.2	Y	Y										
2	5	0	0.2	Y	Y	9	0	0.1	Y	N					
5	6	0	0.2	Y	N										

EVENT 31

DATE: February 27, 1980
LOCATION: Bogotá, Colombia
PERPETRATORS:
  NUMBER: 17
  NATIONALITY: Colombians
  ORGANIZATIONAL AFFILIATION: M-19, April 19th Movement
VICTIMS:
  NUMBER: 58
  NATIONALITY: Austrian, American, Brazilian, Colombian,
  Costa Rican, Dominican Republican, Egyptian, Salvadoran,
  Guatemalan, Haitian, Israeli, Mexican, Swiss, Uruguayan,
  and Venezuelan
  STATUS: 13 Ambassadors and 45 embassy employees
PHYSICAL TARGET:
  NATURE: Embassy
  NATIONAL ASSOCIATION: Dominican Republican
NATURE OF DEMANDS: Release of 311 M-19 members from Colombian
jails (later reduced to OAS observation of trials), $50 million
from hostage ambassadors' governments (later reduced to $2.5
million), publication of M-19 manifesto in newspapers of
hostage ambassadors' nations, safe passage, and flight from
Colombia.
TARGET OF DEMANDS: All governments listed above

EVENT 31 (continued)

OUTCOME:
  DURATION AND DESCRIPTION OF INCIDENT: 62 days. Embassy
  seized during independence day dinner celebration. Ended
  with flight of terrorists and hostages to Cuba.
  SATISFACTION OF DEMANDS: Colombian presidential agreement
  with OAS Human Rights Commission observation of M-19 trials,
  $2.5 million paid by private businesses in Colombia and
  Venezuela, extensive publicity received, safe passage,
  and asylum in Cuba.
  FATE OF VICTIMS: During the take-over, 3 were injured
  in the embassy and 1 was injured while escaping. The others
  were unharmed; 13 released on 2nd day, 5 on 3rd day, 1
  on 9th day, 3 on 29th day, 2 on 34th day, 2 on 38th day,
  2 on 39th day, 3 on 41st day, 1 on 54th day, 1 on 57th
  day, 6 freed at Colombian airport on last day, and 12 released
  after flight to Havana. During the take-over, 1 soldier
  was killed and 4 were injured.
  FATE OF PERPETRATORS: During the take-over, 1 was killed
  and 1 was injured. The others were unharmed and flown
  to asylum in Cuba.
  PROPERTY DAMAGE: Minimal
  NATIONS GRANTING OR FACILITATING SAFE HAVEN: Cuba

PRESS COVERAGE

Day	New York Times					London Times					Die Welt				
	Pg	Ph	Col	Id	Dmd	Pg	Ph	Col	Id	Dmd	Pg	Ph	Col	Id	Dmd
1	1	3	2.0	Y	Y	1	0	0.1	N	N					
2	1	2	1.5	Y	Y	1	1	0.4	Y	Y	1	1	1.3	Y	Y
3	1	3	1.2	Y	Y	1*	1	1.0	Y	Y	1	0	0.2	Y	Y
4	5	0	1.0	Y	Y	6	0	0.5	Y	Y					
5	1	1	1.5	Y	Y	6	0	0.3	N	N	1	0	0.5	Y	Y
6	1	1	1.0	Y	N	8	0	0.2	N	N	7	0	0.1	Y	Y
7	3	1	0.7	N	N	7	0	0.6	Y	N	7	0	0.8	Y	Y
8	13	0	1.0	Y	Y						8	0	0.1	N	N
9	4	1	0.7	Y	Y						8	1	0.2	Y	Y
10	5	0	0.6	N	Y						1	0	0.1	Y	Y
11	8	0	0.6	Y	Y										
12	1	0	1.6	Y	Y						1	0	0.1	Y	N
13	6	0	0.5	Y	Y	7	0	0.1	N	N					
14	10	1	0.5	Y	Y										
15	4	0	0.7	Y	Y	9	0	0.4	Y	Y	7	0	0.1	Y	Y
16	6	0	0.6	Y	Y						7	0	0.3	Y	Y
17						2*	0	0.6	Y	Y	7	0	0.1	Y	Y
18	3	1	0.8	N	Y										
19						8	0	0.5	Y	Y	5	0	0.3	Y	Y
20	3	0	0.3	Y	N	8	0	0.4	Y	Y	7	0	0.3	N	N

EVENT 31 (continued)

PRESS COVERAGE

Day	New York Times					London Times					Die Welt				
	Pg	Ph	Col	Id	Dmd	Pg	Ph	Col	Id	Dmd	Pg	Ph	Col	Id	Dmd
21	1	0	1.3	Y	N						8	0	0.2	Y	Y
22	4	0	0.5	Y	Y						7	0	0.1	N	Y
23	3	1	1.0	Y	Y										
24						2*	0	0.2	Y	Y					
27	9	0	0.8	Y	Y										
28	9	0	1.0	Y	Y						7	1	0.1	Y	Y
29	5	0	0.8	Y	N	10	0	1.0	Y	Y					
30	12	0	0.6	Y	Y										
31	4	0	0.3	N	N										
33	11	0	0.2	N	Y						4	0	0.1	Y	N
34	12	0	0.4	Y	Y										
36	4	0	0.4	Y	Y										
38	6	1	0.3	N	Y	2	0	0.1	Y	N	7	0	0.1	N	Y
39	2	1	0.6	Y	Y										
40	3	1	0.7	Y	Y										
41	5	0	0.5	N	Y	6	0	0.2	N	N	5	0	0.1	Y	Y
44	3	1	0.6	Y	Y						7	1	0.2	Y	Y
45											7	0	0.1	Y	Y
47	5	0	0.2	N	N										
48	7	0	0.2	Y	N										
49	12	0	0.4	Y	N						9	0	0.1	Y	Y
51	4	0	0.2	N	Y	9	0	0.5	Y	N	8	0	0.1	Y	Y
53	6	0	0.3	Y	Y										
54	11	0	0.4	Y	Y	8	0	0.1	Y	N	7	0	0.1	Y	Y
57	5	0	0.2	N	N						7	0	0.1	Y	Y
60	4	0	0.7	Y	Y										
61	6	0	1.0	Y	Y	1	0	0.3	Y	Y	1	0	0.3	Y	Y
62	1	3	3.5	Y	Y	9	1	1.0	Y	Y	5	2	0.7	Y	Y
63	8	0	0.4	Y	Y										
64	8	1	0.6	Y	N										

*   From the International Herald Tribune

EVENT 32

DATE: April 7, 1980
LOCATION: Misgav Am, Israel
PERPETRATORS:
  NUMBER: 5
  NATIONALITY: Palestinians

EVENT 32 (continued)

ORGANIZATIONAL AFFILIATION: ALF, Arab Liberation Front
VICTIMS:
  NUMBER: 7
  NATIONALITY: Israelis
  STATUS: Kibbutz children and babysitter
PHYSICAL TARGET:
  NATURE: Kibbutz
  NATIONAL ASSOCIATION: Israeli
NATURE OF DEMANDS: Release of Palestinians from Israeli
jails.
TARGET OF DEMANDS: Israeli government
OUTCOME:
  DURATION AND DESCRIPTION OF INCIDENT: 2 days.   Ended with
  storming by Israeli soldiers.
  SATISFACTION OF DEMANDS: No reported concessions.
  FATE OF VICTIMS: The perpetrators killed 1 and injured
  1, and 4 were injured during the storming.   Also, 1 kibbutz
  resident was killed during the take-over, and 1 soldier
  was killed and 11 wounded during the storming.
  FATE OF PERPETRATORS: All 5 were killed.
  PROPERTY DAMAGE: Building destroyed.
  NATIONS GRANTING OR FACILITATING SAFE HAVEN: None

PRESS COVERAGE

	New York Times					London Times					Die Welt				
Day	Pg	Ph	Col	Id	Dmd	Pg	Ph	Col	Id	Dmd	Pg	Ph	Col	Id	Dmd
1	1	0	0.7	Y	Y	1	1	0.6	Y	Y	1	0	1.0	Y	Y
2	1	1	1.5	Y	Y	6	0	0.7	Y	Y					
3											5	1	0.2	Y	Y

EVENT 33

DATE: April 30, 1980
LOCATION: London
PERPETRATORS:
  NUMBER: 6
  NATIONALITY: Khuzistanis
  ORGANIZATIONAL AFFILIATION: Group of the Martyr
VICTIMS:
  NUMBER: 26
  NATIONALITY: Iranian, Syrian, and British

EVENT 33 (continued)

STATUS: 23 embassy employees, 2 journalists, and 1
policeman
PHYSICAL TARGET:
  NATURE: Embassy
  NATIONAL ASSOCIATION: Iranian
NATURE OF DEMANDS: Autonomy for Khuzistan, release of 91
political prisoners from Iranian jails, airliner and safe
passage.
TARGET OF DEMANDS: Iranian and British governments
OUTCOME:
  DURATION AND DESCRIPTION OF INCIDENT: 6 days. Ended with
  storming by British SAS troops.
  SATISFACTION OF DEMANDS: No reported concessions.
  FATE OF VICTIMS: An embassy employee was released on the
  1st day, a BBC producer on the 2nd day, 2 employees on
  the 4th day, and a Syrian journalist on the 5th day. The
  perpetrators shot and killed 2 employees on the last day,
  and 2 were injured when rescued by the SAS.
  FATE OF PERPETRATORS: The SAS killed 5 and arrested 1,
  who was later sentenced to life imprisonment.
  PROPERTY DAMAGE: Embassy destroyed.
  NATIONS GRANTING OR FACILITATING SAFE HAVEN: None

PRESS COVERAGE

Day	New York Times					London Times					Die Welt				
	Pg	Ph	Col	Id	Dmd	Pg	Ph	Col	Id	Dmd	Pg	Ph	Col	Id	Dmd
1	1	2	2.0	Y	Y	1	4	3.5	Y	Y					
2	12	1	1.0	Y	Y	1	0	1.5	Y	Y	1	0	1.0	Y	Y
3	4	0	0.7	Y	Y										
4	5	0	1.0	Y	Y										
5	3	2	1.0	Y	Y	1	0	1.3	Y	Y	5	0	1.2	Y	Y
6	1	4	2.0	Y	Y	1	0	1.3	Y	Y	7	0	0.1	Y	N
7	1	1	1.6	Y	Y	1	2	2.2	Y	Y	1	6	3.5	Y	Y
8	18	0	1.0	Y	Y	2	0	1.0	Y	Y					
9	3	1	0.6	Y	N	1	1	0.8	Y	Y	7	0	0.1	Y	N
10						3	0	1.1	Y	N					

EVENT 34

DATE: September 17, 1980
LOCATION: San Salvador, El Salvador
PERPETRATORS:
  NUMBER: 25

EVENT 34 (continued)

NATIONALITY: Salvadorans
ORGANIZATIONAL AFFILIATION: FDR, Democratic Revolutionary
Front
VICTIMS:
  NUMBER: 11
  NATIONALITY: Unknown
  STATUS: OAS employees
PHYSICAL TARGET:
  NATURE: OAS offices
  NATIONAL ASSOCIATION: International
NATURE OF DEMANDS: Release of 55 political prisoners from
Salvadoran jails, freedom of organization for labor unions,
an end to Salvadoran government repression, an end to the
state of siege, and immunity from prosecution.
TARGET OF DEMANDS: Salvadoran government
OUTCOME:
  DURATION AND DESCRIPTION OF INCIDENT: 21 days
  SATISFACTION OF DEMANDS: Agreement to investigate political
  prisoner status, and immunity from prosecution.
  FATE OF VICTIMS: Unharmed, 1 released on 12th day, and
  the remainder on the last day. During the take-over, 5
  security guards were injured.
  FATE OF PERPETRATORS: Unharmed, went free.
  PROPERTY DAMAGE: None
  NATIONS GRANTING OR FACILITATING SAFE HAVEN: None

PRESS COVERAGE

Day	New York Times					London Times					Die Welt				
---	Pg	Ph	Col	Id	Dmd	Pg	Ph	Col	Id	Dmd	Pg	Ph	Col	Id	Dmd
1	10	0	0.4	Y	Y										
2	7	0	0.3	Y	Y						7	0	0.1	Y	Y
3						6	0	0.1	Y	N					
12	7	0	0.2	Y	Y										
21	11	0	1.0	Y	Y										
22											7	0	0.5	Y	Y

EVENT 35

DATE: October 13, 1980
LOCATION: West Germany and Turkey
PERPETRATORS:
  NUMBER: 6

EVENT 35 (continued)

NATIONALITY: Turks
ORGANIZATIONAL AFFILIATION: Unknown
VICTIMS:
  NUMBER: 148
  NATIONALITY: 140 Turks, 6 Iranians, 1 American, and 1
  Italian
  STATUS: Passengers and crew
PHYSICAL TARGET:
  NATURE: Airliner
  NATIONAL ASSOCIATION: Turkish
NATURE OF DEMANDS: Flight and safe passage to Saudi Arabia,
other demands kept secret by Turkish authorities.
TARGET OF DEMANDS: Saudi and Turkish governments
OUTCOME:
  DURATION AND DESCRIPTION OF INCIDENT: 2 days. Hijacked
  out of Munich, landed at Diyarbakir, Turkey. Ended with
  storming by Turkish security force.
  SATISFACTION OF DEMANDS: No reported concessions.
  FATE OF VICTIMS: Before the storming, 39 were released
  unharmed. During the storming, 1 was killed and 6 injured.
  FATE OF PERPETRATORS: During the storming, 2 were injured.
  All were arrested, disposition unknown.
  PROPERTY DAMAGE: Aircraft damaged by the rescuers.
  NATIONS GRANTING OR FACILITATING SAFE HAVEN: None

PRESS COVERAGE

Day	New York Times Pg	Ph	Col	Id	Dmd	London Times Pg	Ph	Col	Id	Dmd	Die Welt Pg	Ph	Col	Id	Dmd
1	8	1	0.7	N	Y	1	0	0.1	N	N					
2						6	0	0.2	Y	N	26	0	0.4	Y	Y

EVENT 36

DATE: December 9, 1980
LOCATION: Havana
PERPETRATORS:
  NUMBER: 14
  NATIONALITY: Cubans
  ORGANIZATIONAL AFFILIATION: Dissidents
VICTIMS:
  NUMBER: 5
  NATIONALITY: 3 Canadians, 1 Spaniard, and 1 Cuban

EVENT 36 (continued)

STATUS: 4 Nuns and a porter
PHYSICAL TARGET:
  NATURE: Church, Apostolic Nunciature
  NATIONAL ASSOCIATION: Vatican
NATURE OF DEMANDS: Safe passage out of Cuba
TARGET OF DEMANDS: Cuban government
OUTCOME:
  DURATION AND DESCRIPTION OF INCIDENT: 1 day. Ended with
  storming by police.
  SATISFACTION OF DEMANDS: No reported concessions.
  FATE OF VICTIMS: Unharmed, 1 employee was killed during
  take-over.
  FATE OF PERPETRATORS: During the storming, 1 was injured.
  All were arrested, disposition unknown.
  PROPERTY DAMAGE: None
  NATIONS GRANTING OR FACILITATING SAFE HAVEN: None

PRESS COVERAGE

Day	New York Times					London Times					Die Welt				
	Pg	Ph	Col	Id	Dmd	Pg	Ph	Col	Id	Dmd	Pg	Ph	Col	Id	Dmd
1	3	0	0.2	Y	N						1	0	0.1	Y	Y
2						7	0	0.3	Y	Y					

EVENT 37

DATE: December 15, 1980
LOCATION: Colombia and Cuba
PERPETRATORS:
  NUMBER: 8
  NATIONALITY: Colombians
  ORGANIZATIONAL AFFILIATION: M-19, April 19th Movement
VICTIMS:
  NUMBER: 122
  NATIONALITY: Unknown
  STATUS: Passengers and crew
PHYSICAL TARGET:
  NATURE: Airliner
  NATIONAL ASSOCIATION: Colombian
NATURE OF DEMANDS: Refueling and food, publicity to disrupt
Conference of Latin American Presidents convening in Colombia.
TARGET OF DEMANDS: Colombian, Panamanian, and Mexican
governments

EVENT 37 (continued)

OUTCOME:
DURATION AND DESCRIPTION OF INCIDENT: 2 days. Hijacked
out of Bogotá, landed first in Santa Marta and Barranquilla,
Colombia, then Panama City and Mexico City. Ended with
landing and surrender in Havana.
SATISFACTION OF DEMANDS: Concessions granted.
FATE OF VICTIMS: Unharmed, 7 released in Santa Marta,
47 in Barranquilla, 24 in Panama City, and 54 in Havana.
FATE OF PERPETRATORS: Unharmed, remained in Cuba, disposition
unknown.
PROPERTY DAMAGE: None
NATIONS GRANTING OR FACILITATING SAFE HAVEN: None

PRESS COVERAGE

	New York Times					London Times					Die Welt				
Day	Pg	Ph	Col	Id	Dmd	Pg	Ph	Col	Id	Dmd	Pg	Ph	Col	Id	Dmd
1	9	0	0.2	Y	N						1	0	0.5	Y	Y
2	10	1	0.4	Y	Y	6	0	0.5	Y	Y	8	0	0.1	Y	N
3						6	0	0.3	Y	Y					

EVENT 38

DATE: February 13, 1981
LOCATION: Havana
PERPETRATORS:
NUMBER: 29
NATIONALITY: Cubans
ORGANIZATIONAL AFFILIATION: Dissidents
VICTIMS:
NUMBER: 4
NATIONALITY: 3 Ecuadoreans and 1 Cuban
STATUS: Ambassador and embassy employees
PHYSICAL TARGET:
NATURE: Embassy
NATIONAL ASSOCIATION: Ecuadorean
NATURE OF DEMANDS: Safe passage out of Cuba and asylum in
Ecuador.
TARGET OF DEMANDS: Cuban and Ecuadorean governments
OUTCOME:
DURATION AND DESCRIPTION OF INCIDENT: 8 days. Ended with
storming by Cuban troops after all hostages were released.

EVENT 38 (continued)

SATISFACTION OF DEMANDS: No reported concessions.
FATE OF VICTIMS: Unharmed, 1 released on 2nd day, remainder
released on 7th day.
FATE OF PERPETRATORS: Unharmed, arrested, disposition unknown.
PROPERTY DAMAGE: Unknown
NATIONS GRANTING OR FACILITATING SAFE HAVEN: None

PRESS COVERAGE

Day	New York Times					London Times					Die Welt				
	Pg	Ph	Col	Id	Dmd	Pg	Ph	Col	Id	Dmd	Pg	Ph	Col	Id	Dmd
1	5	0	0.2	Y	Y	1	0	0.2	Y	N					
2	4	0	0.2	Y	Y	4	0	0.2	Y	N	1	0	0.1	Y	Y
6	7	0	0.2	Y	Y										
8	7	0	0.2	Y	Y						7	0	0.1	Y	N
9	10	0	0.3	Y	Y						8	0	0.2	Y	Y
12											7	1	0.2	Y	Y

EVENT 39

DATE: March 2, 1981
LOCATION: Pakistan, Afghanistan, and Syria
PERPETRATORS:
  NUMBER: 3
  NATIONALITY: Pakistanis
  ORGANIZATIONAL AFFILIATION: Al Zulfikar
VICTIMS:
  NUMBER: 147
  NATIONALITY: 126 Pakistanis, 11 Afghans, 5 Americans,
  1 South African, 1 Swede, 2 Nigerians, and 1 Canadian
  STATUS: Pakistani diplomat, other passengers, and crew
PHYSICAL TARGET:
  NATURE: Airliner
  NATIONAL ASSOCIATION: Pakistani
NATURE OF DEMANDS: Release of 92 political prisoners from
Pakistani jails, flight and safe passage to Libya. Safe
passage for perpetrators' families out of Pakistan.
TARGET OF DEMANDS: Pakistani government
OUTCOME:
  DURATION AND DESCRIPTION OF INCIDENT: 14 days. Hijacked
  out of Karachi, landed in Kabul. Flew to Syria on 9 March.
  Surrendered to Syrian authorities on 15 March.

EVENT 39 (continued)

SATISFACTION OF DEMANDS: 54 prisoners released from Pakistani
jails and flown to asylum in Syria. 25 of those joined the
perpetrators and were flown to the Al Zulfikar base in Kabul
by the Syrians on 20 April.
FATE OF VICTIMS: On the 2nd day, 27 were released unharmed.
The Pakistani diplomat was shot and killed on the 4th day.
On the 5th day, 4 were released. Another was released on
the 7th day and the remainder were released unharmed on the
last day.
FATE OF PERPETRATORS: Unharmed, went free.
PROPERTY DAMAGE: None
NATIONS GRANTING OR FACILITATING SAFE HAVEN: Syria and
Afghanistan

PRESS COVERAGE

Day	New York Times					London Times					Die Welt				
	Pg	Ph	Col	Id	Dmd	Pg	Ph	Col	Id	Dmd	Pg	Ph	Col	Id	Dmd
1	5	0	0.2	N	Y	5	0	0.2	Y	N					
2											5	0	0.1	Y	Y
3						6	0	0.1	N	N	8	0	0.1	Y	Y
4	5	0	0.2	N	Y	7	0	0.8	Y	Y					
5	3	1	0.6	Y	Y	1	0	0.3	Y	Y					
6	3	0	0.8	Y	Y	1	0	1.0	Y	Y	1	0	0.3	Y	Y
7	1	1	1.2	Y	Y	1	0	1.0	Y	Y	8	0	0.1	Y	Y
8	3	0	0.6	N	Y	8	1	1.0	Y	Y	1	0	0.5	Y	Y
9	3	1	0.6	Y	Y	9	1	0.7	Y	Y	1	1	0.5	Y	Y
10	6	0	1.0	N	Y	1	0	0.8	Y	Y					
11	1	0	1.6	N	Y	1	0	1.5	Y	Y					
12	1	0	1.2	N	Y										
13	1	1	1.3	N	Y										
14	1	3	1.2	Y	Y	1	1	2.0	Y	Y	7	0	0.6	Y	Y
15	11	0	1.0	Y	Y	5	0	0.3	Y	Y					
16						6	0	0.6	N	N					
17						6	0	0.8	Y	Y					
18						6	0	0.1	N	N					
19						6	0	0.1	Y	N					
20						5	0	0.1	Y	Y					

EVENT 40

DATE: March 27, 1981
LOCATION: Honduras and Panama
PERPETRATORS:
  NUMBER: 4
  NATIONALITY: Salvadorans
  ORGANIZATIONAL AFFILIATION: MLP, Popular Liberation Front
VICTIMS:
  NUMBER: 87
  NATIONALITY: Various, including 11 Americans
  STATUS: Passengers and crew
PHYSICAL TARGET:
  NATURE: Airliner
  NATIONAL ASSOCIATION: Honduran
NATURE OF DEMANDS: Release of 16 Salvadorans from Honduran
jails.   Refueling, flight and safe passage, with asylum in
Cuba.
TARGET OF DEMANDS: Honduran, Nicaraguan, Panamanian, and
Cuban governments
OUTCOME:
  DURATION AND DESCRIPTION OF INCIDENT: 2 days.   Hijacked
  over Honduras, landed at Managua, continued to Panama City
  and finally to Havana.
  SATISFACTION OF DEMANDS: 15 prisoners released from Honduran
  jails, flown to Panama City, and on to Cuba with the
  perpetrators.
  FATE OF VICTIMS: Unharmed, 34 released in Nicaragua,
  remainder in Panama City.
  FATE OF PERPETRATORS: Unharmed, flown to asylum in Cuba.
  PROPERTY DAMAGE: None
  NATIONS GRANTING OR FACILITATING SAFE HAVEN: Cuba

PRESS COVERAGE

Day	New York Times					London Times					Die Welt				
	Pg	Ph	Col	Id	Dmd	Pg	Ph	Col	Id	Dmd	Pg	Ph	Col	Id	Dmd
1	6	0	0.2	N	Y	2*	0	0.2	Y	Y					
2	17	0	0.8	Y	Y	1*	1	0.4	Y	Y					
3	4	0	0.3	Y	Y										
4	9	0	0.2	N	Y										

---

*   From the International Herald Tribune

EVENT 41

DATE: March 28, 1981
LOCATION: Indonesia and Thailand
PERPETRATORS:
  NUMBER: 5
  NATIONALITY: Indonesians
  ORGANIZATIONAL AFFILIATION: IIRB, Jihad Command
VICTIMS:
  NUMBER: 58
  NATIONALITY: Various, including 3 Americans, 1 Japanese,
  1 Netherlander, and 1 Briton
  STATUS: Passengers and crew
PHYSICAL TARGET:
  NATURE: Airliner
  NATIONAL ASSOCIATION: Indonesian
NATURE OF DEMANDS: Release of 84 political prisoners from
Indonesian jails, expulsion of all Jewish officials and Israeli
militarists from Indonesia, refueling, another airliner and
crew, and safe passage to Sri Lanka.
TARGET OF DEMANDS: Indonesian, Thai, Malaysian, and Sri
Lankan governments
OUTCOME:
  DURATION AND DESCRIPTION OF INCIDENT: 3 days. Hijacked
  over Indonesia to Malaysia, refueled, and continued to
  Bangkok. Ended with storming by Indonesian Red Beret
  Commandos.
  SATISFACTION OF DEMANDS: No reported concessions.
  FATE OF VICTIMS: During the stop in Malaysia, 1 was released
  unharmed. A British passenger escaped and an American
  passenger was shot and seriously wounded by the perpetrators
  while escaping on the 2nd day. During the storming, the
  pilot and 1 commando were killed, the others were rescued
  unharmed.
  FATE OF PERPETRATORS: During the storming, 4 were killed
  and 1 was arrested, disposition unknown.
  PROPERTY DAMAGE: Airliner damaged by rescuers.
  NATIONS GRANTING OR FACILITATING SAFE HAVEN: None

PRESS COVERAGE

	New York Times					London Times					Die Welt				
Day	Pg	Ph	Col	Id	Dmd	Pg	Ph	Col	Id	Dmd	Pg	Ph	Col	Id	Dmd
1	16	0	0.5	N	Y						1	0	0.6	Y	Y
2	1	0	0.8	N	Y	1	1	0.4	N	Y	1	1	0.5	Y	Y
3	8	1	1.0	Y	Y	1	0	0.3	N	Y	4	0	0.5	Y	Y
4						8	1	1.0	Y	Y					

EVENT 42

DATE: May 24, 1981
LOCATION: Turkey and Bulgaria
PERPETRATORS:
  NUMBER: 4
  NATIONALITY: Turks
  ORGANIZATIONAL AFFILIATION: Dev-Sol
VICTIMS:
  NUMBER: 119
  NATIONALITY: 110 Turks, 5 Americans, 1 Frenchman, 2
  Japanese, and 1 Iranian
  STATUS: Passengers and crew
PHYSICAL TARGET:
  NATURE: Airliner
  NATIONAL ASSOCIATION: Turkish
NATURE OF DEMANDS: $500,000 and release of 47 prisoners
from Turkish jails.
TARGET OF DEMANDS: Turkish government
OUTCOME:
  DURATION AND DESCRIPTION OF INCIDENT: 2 days. Hijacked
  out of Istanbul, diverted to Burgas. Ended when perpetrators
  were overpowered by passengers and crew.
  SATISFACTION OF DEMANDS: No reported concessions.
  FATE OF VICTIMS: On the 1st day, 17 were released and
  2 escaped unharmed. While overpowering the perpetrators,
  5 were injured and the remainder were rescued unharmed.
  FATE OF PERPETRATORS: During the overpowering, 1 was injured.
  All were sentenced to 3 years in Bulgarian jail.
  PROPERTY DAMAGE: None
  NATIONS GRANTING OR FACILITATING SAFE HAVEN: None

PRESS COVERAGE

Day	New York Times					London Times					Die Welt				
	Pg	Ph	Col	Id	Dmd	Pg	Ph	Col	Id	Dmd	Pg	Ph	Col	Id	Dmd
1	4	0	1.2	Y	Y	1	0	0.2	Y	Y	1	0	0.1	Y	N
2	12	0	2.5	Y	Y	1	1	0.4	Y	Y	1	0	0.5	Y	Y
3	11	0	0.5	Y	Y	5	0	0.4	Y	Y					
4						4	0	0.3	Y	Y					

EVENT 43

DATE: August 13, 1981
LOCATION: Spain, Morocco, and France

EVENT 43 (continued)

PERPETRATORS:
  NUMBER: 22
  NATIONALITY: Iranians
  ORGANIZATIONAL AFFILIATION: Azadegan
VICTIMS:
  NUMBER: 30
  NATIONALITY: Iranians
  STATUS: Boat crew
PHYSICAL TARGET:
  NATURE: Gunboat
  NATIONAL ASSOCIATION: Iranian
NATURE OF DEMANDS: Food, water, and refueling, with asylum
in France.
TARGET OF DEMANDS: Moroccan and French governments
OUTCOME:
  DURATION AND DESCRIPTION OF INCIDENT: 6 days. Hijacked
  gunboat off Spain, replenished in Morocco, surrendered
  in Marseille.
  SATISFACTION OF DEMANDS: Granted replenishment by Morocco
  and asylum by France.
  FATE OF VICTIMS: Released unharmed.
  FATE OF PERPETRATORS: Unharmed, remained in France.
  PROPERTY DAMAGE: None
  NATIONS GRANTING OR FACILITATING SAFE HAVEN: France

PRESS COVERAGE

Day	New York Times					London Times					Die Welt				
	Pg	Ph	Col	Id	Dmd	Pg	Ph	Col	Id	Dmd	Pg	Ph	Col	Id	Dmd
2						4	0	1.5	Y	Y	1	0	0.6	Y	Y
3	14	0	0.6	Y	N										
4	6	0	0.1	Y	N						7	0	0.4	Y	Y
5	3	0	0.2	N	N	1	1	1.0	Y	Y	1	0	0.1	Y	Y
6	9	1	1.0	Y	Y	1	0	0.7	Y	Y	1	0	0.5	Y	Y
7	3	1	1.0	Y	Y	5	0	0.4	Y	Y	5	0	0.6	Y	N
8	9	0	0.5	Y	N										

EVENT 44

DATE: September 24, 1981
LOCATION: Paris
PERPETRATORS:
  NUMBER: 4

EVENT 44 (continued)

NATIONALITY: Lebanese Armenians
ORGANIZATIONAL AFFILIATION: ASALA, Armenian Secret Army for
the Liberation of Armenia
VICTIMS:
  NUMBER: 60
  NATIONALITY: Turks and Frenchmen
  STATUS: Consulate employees
PHYSICAL TARGET:
  NATURE: Consulate
  NATIONAL ASSOCIATION: Turkish
NATURE OF DEMANDS: Release of all Armenian prisoners in
Turkish jails.
TARGET OF DEMANDS: Turkish government
OUTCOME:
  DURATION AND DESCRIPTION OF INCIDENT: 1 day. Ended with
  surrender of perpetrators.
  SATISFACTION OF DEMANDS: No reported concessions.
  FATE OF VICTIMS: During the take-over, 4 were injured.
  The others were released unharmed. Also, 1 guard was killed
  and 1 was injured during the take-over.
  FATE OF PERPETRATORS: During the take-over, 1 was injured.
  All were arrested and charged with murder.
  PROPERTY DAMAGE: Minimal
  NATIONS GRANTING OR FACILITATING SAFE HAVEN: None

PRESS COVERAGE

Day	New York Times					London Times					Die Welt				
	Pg	Ph	Col	Id	Dmd	Pg	Ph	Col	Id	Dmd	Pg	Ph	Col	Id	Dmd
1	1	2	0.8	Y	Y	1	1	0.5	Y	Y	1	0	0.1	Y	N
2						1	0	0.6	Y	Y					
3	7	0	1.0	Y	N	1*	1	0.5	Y	Y					

---

* From the International Herald Tribune

EVENT 45

DATE: September 26, 1981
LOCATION: Yugoslavia and Cyprus
PERPETRATORS:
  NUMBER: 3
  NATIONALITY: Croatian Yugoslavs
  ORGANIZATIONAL AFFILIATION: Croatian nationalist

EVENT 45 (continued)

VICTIMS:
  NUMBER: 107
  NATIONALITY: Unknown
  STATUS: Passengers and crew
PHYSICAL TARGET:
  NATURE: Airliner
  NATIONAL ASSOCIATION: Yugoslav
NATURE OF DEMANDS: Refueling and political asylum
TARGET OF DEMANDS: Greek and Cypriot governments
OUTCOME:
  DURATION AND DESCRIPTION OF INCIDENT: 2 days. Hijacked
  over Yugoslavia, denied landing in Israel, landed in Athens
  and refueled, then continued on to Cyprus. Ended when
  passengers and crew staged a fake fire alarm and escaped.
  SATISFACTION OF DEMANDS: Refueled by Greece, but no further
  reported concessions.
  FATE OF VICTIMS: Escaped unharmed.
  FATE OF PERPETRATORS: Unharmed, surrendered to Cypriot
  authorities. Extradited to Yugoslavia, disposition unknown.
  PROPERTY DAMAGE: None
  NATIONS GRANTING OR FACILITATING SAFE HAVEN: None

PRESS COVERAGE

| Day | New York Times | | | | | London Times | | | | | Die Welt | | | | |
	Pg	Ph	Col	Id	Dmd	Pg	Ph	Col	Id	Dmd	Pg	Ph	Col	Id	Dmd
1	38	0	0.4	N	N						6	0	0.2	Y	N
2	5	0	0.3	Y	Y										

EVENT 46

DATE: September 29, 1981
LOCATION: India and Pakistan
PERPETRATORS:
  NUMBER: 5
  NATIONALITY: Indians
  ORGANIZATIONAL AFFILIATION: Sikh, Society of the Pure
VICTIMS:
  NUMBER: 117
  NATIONALITY: Unknown
  STATUS: Passengers and crew
PHYSICAL TARGET:
  NATURE: Airliner

EVENT 46 (continued)

NATIONAL ASSOCIATION: Indian
NATURE OF DEMANDS: Release of Sikh militants from Indian
jails, and $11,000 to the families of 9 Sikhs killed by Indian
police.
TARGET OF DEMANDS: Indian government
OUTCOME:
  DURATION AND DESCRIPTION OF INCIDENT: 2 days. Hijacked
  over India, landed at Lahore. Ended with storming by
  Pakistani commandos.
  SATISFACTION OF DEMANDS: No reported concessions.
  FATE OF VICTIMS: Unharmed, 61 released by perpetrators
  on 1st day, remainder rescued by the commandos.
  FATE OF PERPETRATORS: Captured unharmed by the commandos,
  disposition unknown.
  PROPERTY DAMAGE: None
  NATIONS GRANTING OR FACILITATING SAFE HAVEN: None

PRESS COVERAGE

| Day | New York Times | | | | | London Times | | | | | Die Welt | | | | |
	Pg	Ph	Col	Id	Dmd	Pg	Ph	Col	Id	Dmd	Pg	Ph	Col	Id	Dmd
1	7	0	1.0	Y	Y										
2	8	0	0.4	Y	N	6	0	0.6	Y	Y	1	0	0.1	Y	N

EVENT 47

DATE: October 29, 1981
LOCATION: Costa Rica
PERPETRATORS:
  NUMBER: 5
  NATIONALITY: Nicaraguans
  ORGANIZATIONAL AFFILIATION: Right-wing exiles
VICTIMS:
  NUMBER: 21
  NATIONALITY: Various, including 3 Americans
  STATUS: Passengers and crew
PHYSICAL TARGET:
  NATURE: Airliner
  NATIONAL ASSOCIATION: Costa Rican
NATURE OF DEMANDS: Release of 7 Nicaraguans from Costa Rican
jails, an airliner, and safe passage to El Salvador.
TARGET OF DEMANDS: Costa Rican government

EVENT 47 (continued)

OUTCOME:
  DURATION AND DESCRIPTION OF INCIDENT: 2 days. Hijacked
  over Costa Rica, landed at San Jose, and continued on to
  El Salvador with released prisoners. Surrendered to
  Salvadoran authorities.
  SATISFACTION OF DEMANDS: 6 Nicaraguan exiles released
  from jail and flown to El Salvador with perpetrators.
  FATE OF VICTIMS: Unharmed, 4 released on 1st day, 15 released
  in San Jose, and 2 released in El Salvador.
  FATE OF PERPETRATORS: Unharmed, remained in El Salvador.
  PROPERTY DAMAGE: None
  NATIONS GRANTING OR FACILITATING SAFE HAVEN: El Salvador

PRESS COVERAGE

| Day | New York Times | | | | | London Times | | | | | Die Welt | | | | |
---	Pg	Ph	Col	Id	Dmd	Pg	Ph	Col	Id	Dmd	Pg	Ph	Col	Id	Dmd
1	5	0	0.2	Y	Y	6	0	0.1	N	N	5	0	0.1	Y	Y
2	7	0	0.3	Y	Y										

EVENT 48

DATE: December 7, 1981
LOCATION: Venezuela and Cuba
PERPETRATORS:
  NUMBER: 11
  NATIONALITY: Venezuelans, Puerto Ricans, and Salvadorans
  ORGANIZATIONAL AFFILIATION: Red Flag
VICTIMS:
  NUMBER: 225
  NATIONALITY: Unknown
  STATUS: Passengers and crew
PHYSICAL TARGET:
  NATURE: 3 airliners
  NATIONAL ASSOCIATION: Venezuelan
NATURE OF DEMANDS: Release of 12 prisoners from Venezuelan
jails, $30 million, publicity for the solidarity of 3 terrorist
groups, and refuelings.
TARGET OF DEMANDS: Venezuelan, Colombian, Honduran, Guatemalan,
Panamanian, and Netherlands Antilles governments

EVENT 48 (continued)

OUTCOME:
  DURATION AND DESCRIPTION OF INCIDENT: 2 days. 3 airliners
  were hijacked simultaneously over Venezuela. Landings
  were made in Colombia, Honduras, Guatemala, Panama, and
  the Netherlands Antilles before the final stop in Havana.
  SATISFACTION OF DEMANDS: Refueled, and publicity achieved,
  but no further reported concessions.
  FATE OF VICTIMS: Unharmed, 22 released in the Netherlands
  Antilles, 67 released in Colombia, 23 released in Guatemala,
  23 released in Honduras, 2 released in Panama, and 108
  released in Havana.
  FATE OF PERPETRATORS: Unharmed, surrendered to Cuban
  authorities, disposition unknown.
  PROPERTY DAMAGE: None
  NATIONS GRANTING OR FACILITATING SAFE HAVEN: None

PRESS COVERAGE

	New York Times					London Times					Die Welt				
Day	Pg	Ph	Col	Id	Dmd	Pg	Ph	Col	Id	Dmd	Pg	Ph	Col	Id	Dmd
1	1	2	0.9	Y	Y	6	0	0.2	Y	Y	1	0	0.1	N	N
2	1	1	1.0	Y	Y	6	0	0.4	Y	Y	1	0	0.1	Y	Y
3	14	0	0.2	Y	Y	8	0	0.1	N	N	5	0	0.7	Y	Y

EVENT 49

DATE: December 7, 1981
LOCATION: Libya and Lebanon
PERPETRATORS:
  NUMBER: 5 (original 3 hijackers joined by 2 more during
  first Beirut refueling)
  NATIONALITY: Lebanese
  ORGANIZATIONAL AFFILIATION: Lebanese Shiite Muslim
VICTIMS:
  NUMBER: 38
  NATIONALITY: Various, including 4 Britons
  STATUS: Passengers and crew
PHYSICAL TARGET:
  NATURE: Airliner
  NATIONAL ASSOCIATION: Libyan
NATURE OF DEMANDS: Investigation into the disappearance
of Imam Sadr in Libya, and refueling.

EVENT 49 (continued)

TARGET OF DEMANDS: Libyan, Greek, Italian, Lebanese, and
Iranian governments
OUTCOME:
   DURATION AND DESCRIPTION OF INCIDENT: 4 days. Hijacked
   out of Switzerland, landed at Beirut, Athens, Rome, Beirut,
   Tehran, and finally back to Beirut. Ended with surrender
   to Syrian peace-keeping troops in Lebanon.
   SATISFACTION OF DEMANDS: Refuelings and agreement to
   investigate the Imam's disappearance.
   FATE OF VICTIMS: Unharmed, 3 released during first Beirut
   refueling, 3 released in Iran, remainder released on last
   Beirut stop.
   FATE OF PERPETRATORS: Unharmed, disposition unknown.
   PROPERTY DAMAGE: None
   NATIONS GRANTING OR FACILITATING SAFE HAVEN: Lebanon

PRESS COVERAGE

Day	New York Times					London Times					Die Welt				
	Pg	Ph	Col	Id	Dmd	Pg	Ph	Col	Id	Dmd	Pg	Ph	Col	Id	Dmd
1	1	0	0.2	Y	Y	6	0	0.1	N	N					
2	1	0	0.5	Y	Y	6	0	0.1	Y	N	1	0	0.2	Y	Y
3	14	0	0.3	Y	Y	8	0	0.4	Y	Y					
4											6	0	0.3	Y	Y

Appendix 2

Tabular Displays of Media Coverage: Accumulations and Comparisons

KEY TO NOTATION

Evt = The cumulative number of events in the subject category.

Evt # = The identifying number of the particular event as it is listed in Appendix 1.

Day = The duration of events expressed in the number of days.

Art = The number of articles published.

Ph = The number of photographs that were included with the published articles.

Col = The length of the published articles measured by the number of columns, rounded to the nearest 10th of a column.

Id = Identification of the terrorists. Y indicates that the affiliations of the terrorists were included in the articles. N indicates that the terrorists were not specifically identified.

Dmd = Specification of terrorist demands. Y indicates that the demands of the terrorists were specified in the articles. N indicates that they were not.

Mean Pg # = The calculated mean value of the page numbers on which the articles appeared.

TABLE 10
MEDIA COVERAGE vs. GRANTING OF CONCESSIONS
ALL EVENTS

	Coverage During Event							No. of Participants
Evt	Day	Art	Ph	Col	Id %	Dmd %	Mean Pg #	Hostages/Terrorists
Concessions								
23	212	295	72	142.9	88	81	4.8	983/397
No Concessions								
26	55	96	38	61.8	89	81	4.3	1,804/198
Combined								
49	267	391	110	204.7	88	81	4.7	2,787/595

Mean Values Per Event				Median Values Per Event			
Day	Art	Ph	Col	Day	Art	Ph	Col
Concessions							
9.2	12.8	3.1	6.2	4.0	6.0	1.0	2.1
No Concessions							
2.1	3.7	1.5	2.4	2.0	3.0	0.0	0.8

TABLE 11
MEDIA COVERAGE vs. CASUALTIES
ALL EVENTS

	Coverage During Event							No. of Participants
Evt	Day	Art	Ph	Col	Id %	Dmd %	Mean Pg #	Hostages/Terrorists
Hostage Casualties								
13	100	179	79	128.1	81	83	4.3	843/90
No Hostage Casualties								
36	167	212	31	76.6	94	80	5.0	1,944/505
Combined								
49	267	391	110	204.7	88	81	4.7	2,787/595

TABLE 11 (continued)

Mean Values Per Event				Median Values Per Event			
Day	Art	Ph	Col	Day	Art	Ph	Col
Hostage Casualties							
7.7	13.8	6.1	9.9	2.0	5.0	3.0	4.6
No Hostage Casualties							
4.6	5.9	0.9	2.1	2.0	4.0	0.0	1.0

TABLE 12
MEDIA COVERAGE vs. GRANTING OF CONCESSIONS
CASUALTY EVENTS

	Coverage During Event							No. of Participants
Evt	Day	Art	Ph	Col	Id %	Dmd %	Mean Pg #	Hostages/Terrorists
Concessions								
3	79	129	47	82.2	79	81	4.7	222/24
No Concessions								
10	21	50	32	45.9	86	88	3.3	621/66
Combined								
13	100	179	79	128.1	81	83	4.3	843/90

Mean Values Per Event				Median Values Per Event			
Day	Art	Ph	Col	Day	Art	Ph	Col
Concessions							
26.3	43.0	15.7	27.4	14.0	30.0	11.C	23.1
No Concessions							
2.1	5.0	3.2	4.6	2.0	4.5	2.5	3.9

Appendix 2

TABLE 13

MEDIA COVERAGE vs. GRANTING OF CONCESSIONS
NO CASUALTY EVENTS

	Coverage During Event						No. of Participants
Evt	Day	Art	Ph	Col	Id %	Dmd %	Mean Pg #	Hostages/Terrorists

Concessions
| 20 | 133 | 166 | 25 | 60.7 | 95 | 82 | 4.9 | 761/373 |

No Concessions
| 16 | 34 | 46 | 6 | 15.9 | 91 | 74 | 5.3 | 1,183/132 |

Combined
| 36 | 167 | 212 | 31 | 76.6 | 94 | 80 | 5.0 | 1,944/505 |

Mean Values Per Event				Median Values Per Event			
Day	Art	Ph	Col	Day	Art	Ph	Col

Concessions
| 6.7 | 8.3 | 1.3 | 3.0 | 3.0 | 5.0 | 0.0 | 1.7 |

No Concessions
| 2.1 | 2.9 | 0.4 | 1.0 | 2.0 | 3.0 | 0.0 | 0.6 |

TABLE 14

MEDIA COVERAGE vs. CASUALTIES
CONCESSIONS GRANTED

	Coverage During Event						No. of Participants
Evt	Day	Art	Ph	Col	Id %	Dmd %	Mean Pg #	Hostages/Terrorists

Hostage Casualties
| 3 | 79 | 129 | 47 | 82.2 | 79 | 81 | 4.7 | 222/24 |

No Hostage Casualties
| 20 | 133 | 166 | 25 | 60.7 | 95 | 82 | 4.9 | 761/373 |

Combined
| 23 | 212 | 295 | 72 | 142.9 | 88 | 81 | 4.8 | 983/397 |

TABLE 14 (continued)

Mean Values Per Event				Median Values Per Event			
Day	Art	Ph	Col	Day	Art	Ph	Col
Hostage Casualties							
26.3	43.0	15.7	27.4	14.0	30.0	11.0	23.1
No Hostage Casualties							
6.7	8.3	1.3	3.0	3.0	5.0	0.0	1.7

TABLE 15
MEDIA COVERAGE vs. CASUALTIES
NO CONCESSIONS GRANTED

Coverage During Event								No. of Participants
Evt	Day	Art	Ph	Col	Id %	Dmd %	Mean Pg #	Hostages/Terrorists
Hostage Casualties								
10	21	50	32	45.9	86	88	3.3	621/66
No Hostage Casualties								
16	34	46	6	15.9	91	74	5.3	1,183/132
Combined								
26	55	96	38	61.8	89	81	4.3	1,804/198

Mean Values Per Event				Median Values Per Event			
Day	Art	Ph	Col	Day	Art	Ph	Col
Hostage Casualties							
2.1	5.0	3.2	4.6	2.0	4.5	2.5	3.9
No Hostage Casualties							
2.1	2.9	0.4	1.0	2.0	3.0	0.0	0.6

TABLE 16
MEDIA COVERAGE OF CASUALTY EVENTS
CONCESSIONS GRANTED

Evt #	Day	Art	Ph	Col	Id	Dmd	Mean Pg #	Hostages/Terrorists
	Coverage During Event							No. of Participants
#18	3	7	5	9.8	Y7	Y7	1.0	17/4

1 victim killed while attempting to escape and 1 injured while escaping

| #31 | 62 | 92 | 31 | 49.3 | Y73 | Y69 | 5.4 | 58/17 |
| | | | | | N19 | N23 | | |

3 victims injured in take-over and 1 injured while escaping

| #39 | 14 | 30 | 11 | 23.1 | Y22 | Y28 | 3.5 | 147/3 |
| | | | | | N8 | N2 | | |

1 victim killed by perpetrators

Combined								
3	79	129	47	82.2	Y102	Y104	4.7	222/24
					N27	N25		

Mean days per event = 26.3
Median days per event = 14.0
Mean articles per event = 43.0
Median articles per event = 30.0
Mean photos per event = 15.7
Median photos per event = 11.0
Mean columns per event = 27.4
Median columns per event = 23.1
Perpetrators identified in 79% of the articles
Perpetrators demands specified in 81% of the articles

TABLE 17
MEDIA COVERAGE OF CASUALTY EVENTS
NO CONCESSIONS GRANTED

Evt #	Day	Art	Ph	Col	Id	Dmd	Mean Pg #	Hostages/Terrorists
	Coverage During Event							No. of Participants
#2	2	5	6	6.8	Y5	Y5	1.0	71/3

1 victim killed by perpetrators, 1 killed and 6 injured during rescue

TABLE 17 (continued)

| | Coverage During Event | | | | | | No. of Participants |
Evt #	Day	Art	Ph	Col	Id	Dmd	Mean Pg #	Hostages/Terrorists
#3	1	1	0	0.8	N1	Y1	3.0	119/2

1 victim injured by perpetrators

#11	1	3	3	3.3	Y3	Y3	1.0	1/4

1 victim killed during rescue attempt

#28	1	2	0	0.6	Y2	Y1 N1	1.5	14/27

13 victims killed during rescue

#32	2	5	2	4.5	Y5	Y5	2.0	7/5

1 victim killed and 1 injured by perpetrators, 4 injured during rescue

#33	6	13	13	17.6	Y13	Y12 N1	3.3	26/6

2 victims killed by perpetrators, 2 injured during rescue

#35	2	4	1	1.4	Y2 N2	Y2 N2	10.3	146/6

1 victim killed and 6 injured during rescue

#41	3	8	3	4.6	Y4 N4	Y8	4.1	58/5

1 victim injured while escaping, 1 injured during rescue

#42	2	6	1	4.9	Y6	Y5 N1	3.7	119/4

5 victims injured during rescue

#44	1	3	3	1.4	Y3	Y2 N1	1.0	60/4

4 victims injured during take-over

Combined								
10	21	50	32	45.9	Y43 N7	Y44 N6	3.3	621/66

Mean days per event = 2.1
Median days per event = 2.0
Mean articles per event = 5.0
Median articles per event = 4.0
Mean photos per event = 3.2
Median photos per event = 3.0

TABLE 17 (continued)

Mean columns per event = 4.6
Median columns per event = 3.3
Perpetrators identified in 86% of the articles
Perpetrators demands specified in 88% of the articles

TABLE 18
MEDIA COVERAGE OF NO CASUALTY EVENTS
CONCESSIONS GRANTED

	Coverage During Event						No. of Participants
Evt #	Day	Art	Ph	Col	Id	Dmd	Mean Pg #	Hostages/Terrorists
#1	2	5	5	9.4	Y5	Y5	1.0	34/2
#4	1	1	0	0.8	Y1	Y1	1.0	6/2
#5	4	2	0	0.2	Y2	Y2	9.5	7/60
#7	2	2	0	0.4	Y2	Y2	5.5	7/30
#10	2	3	0	1.1	Y3	Y3	5.0	81/6
#13	29	38	6	11.6	Y38	Y32 N6	4.5	6/16
#14	6	10	3	4.0	Y10	Y10	2.7	5/3
#15	20	26	2	6.4	Y26	Y19 N7	4.5	8/9
#17	5	1	0	0.1	Y1	Y1	5.0	38/20
#24	3	7	2	3.3	Y7	Y6 N1	5.0	10/30
#25	4	5	0	1.5	Y5	Y5	6.4	6/58
#29	14	19	0	3.8	Y15 N4	Y14 N5	5.9	16/7
#30	2	3	0	0.5	Y3	Y2 N1	8.3	3/50
#34	21	6	0	2.1	Y6	Y5 N1	8.0	11/25
#37	2	5	1	1.7	Y5	Y3 N2	6.8	122/8
#40	2	4	1	1.6	Y3 N1	Y4	6.5	87/4
#43	6	11	2	6.7	Y10 N1	Y8 N3	4.4	30/22
#47	2	4	0	0.7	Y3 N1	Y3 N1	5.8	21/5
#48	2	6	3	2.7	Y5 N1	Y5 N1	2.7	225/11
#49	4	8	0	2.1	Y7 N1	Y6 N2	5.4	38/5

TABLE 18 (continued)

	Coverage During Event						No. of Participants
Evt #	Day	Art	Ph	Col	Id	Dmd	Mean Pg #	Hostages/Terrorists

Combined

Evt #	Day	Art	Ph	Col	Id	Dmd	Mean Pg #	Hostages/Terrorists
20	133	166	25	60.7	Y157 N9	Y136 N30	4.9	761/373

Mean days per event = 6.7
Median days per event = 3.0
Mean articles per event = 8.3
Median articles per event = 5.0
Mean photos per event = 1.3
Median photos per event = 0.0
Mean columns per event = 3.0
Median columns per event = 1.7
Perpetrators identified in 95% of the articles
Perpetrators demands specified in 82% of the articles

TABLE 19
MEDIA COVERAGE OF NO CASUALTY EVENTS
NO CONCESSIONS GRANTED

	Coverage During Event							No. of Participants
Evt #	Day	Art	Ph	Col	Id	Dmd	Mean Pg #	Hostages/Terrorists
#6	2	2	0	0.6	Y1 N1	Y1 N1	5.0	83/3
#8	3	3	0	0.6	Y3	Y2 N1	6.3	15/11
#9	1	0	0	0.0				38/21
#12	1	2	0	0.6	Y2	Y2	1.5	34/4
#16	2	5	3	4.7	Y5	Y5	2.8	135/1
#19	1	2	0	0.5	Y1 N1	Y2	2.5	40/3
#20	2	4	0	0.8	Y4	Y3 N1	4.5	23/3
#21	1	1	0	0.2	Y1	Y1	2.0	69/1
#22	1	2	1	0.4	Y2	Y2	4.0	356/1
#23	3	1	0	0.3	Y1	Y1	4.0	3/30
#26	2	4	0	0.7	Y3 N1	Y3 N1	5.0	89/1
#27	2	3	2	1.8	Y3	Y3	10.0	65/2

TABLE 19 (continued)

Evt #	Day	Art	Ph	Col	Id	Dmd	Mean Pg #	No. of Participants Hostages/Terrorists
	Coverage During Event							
#36	1	2	0	0.3	Y2	Y1 N1	2.0	5/14
#38	8	8	0	1.4	Y8	Y5 N3	4.5	4/29
#45	2	3	0	0.9	Y2 N1	Y1 N2	16.3	107/3
#46	2	4	0	2.1	Y4	Y2 N2	5.5	117/5
Combined								
16	34	46	6	15.9	Y42 N4	Y34 N12	5.3	1,183/132

Mean days per event = 2.1
Median days per event = 2.0
Mean articles per event = 2.9
Median articles per event = 3.0
Mean photos per event = 0.4
Median photos per event = 0.0
Mean columns per event = 1.0
Median columns per event = 0.6
Perpetrators identified in 91% of the articles
Perpetrators demands specified in 74% of the articles

TABLE 20
HOSTAGE CASUALTIES AND GRANTING OF CONCESSIONS
vs.
PHASE OF ATROCITY

	Hostage Casualties					
	Concessions		No Concessions		Combined Events	
Phase	Killed	Injured	Killed	Injured	Killed	Injured
Take-over	0	3	0	4	0	7
Captivity	1	0	4	2	5	2
Escape	1	2	0	1	1	3
Rescue	0	0	16	24	16	24
Totals	2	5	20	31	22	36

TABLE 20 (continued)

Phase	Concessions (N = 983)		No Concessions (N = 1,804)		Combined Events (N = 2,787)	
	Killed	Injured	Killed	Injured	Killed	Injured
Take-over	0.00	0.31	0.00	0.22	0.00	0.25
Captivity	0.10	0.00	0.22	0.11	0.18	0.07
Escape	0.10	0.20	0.00	0.06	0.04	0.11
Rescue	0.00	0.00	0.89	1.33	0.57	0.86
Combined	0.20	0.51	1.11	1.72	0.79	1.29

Hostage Casualties
(as a percent of total hostages)

TABLE 21
DURATION OF BARRICADE AND HOSTAGE EVENTS
vs.
MEAN PAGE NUMBER OF ARTICLE

Mean Page Number	Duration of Event (days)			
	0 – 2	3 – 4	5 – 6	7 and over
0.0 – 2.9	4	1	1	0
3.0 – 4.9	4	2	2	4
5.0 – 6.9	8	4	1	2
7.0 and over	4	1	0	1

Somer's d = 0.18 Tau_b = 0.16

Selected Bibliography

Alexander, Yonah, ed. *International Terrorism: National, Regional and Global Perspectives*. New York: Praeger Publishers, 1976.

Alexander, Yonah, David Carlton, and Paul Wilkinson, eds. *Terrorism: Theory and Practice*. Boulder: Westview Press, 1979.

Alexander, Yonah, and John Gleason, eds. *Behavioral and Quantitative Perspectives on Terrorism*. New York: Pergamon Press, 1981.

Alexander, Yonah, and Seymour Maxwell Finger, eds. *Terrorism: Interdisciplinary Perspectives*. New York: The John Jay Press, 1977.

Anderson, R. H., and J. J. Gillogly. *Rand Intelligent Terminal Agent (R.I.T.A.): Design Philosophy*. Santa Monica: Rand Corporation, R–1809-ARPA, 1976.

Andropov, Yuri. *Speeches and Writings*. Trans. by *VAAP Moscow*. New York: Pergamon Press, 1983.

Anzovin, Steven, ed. *Terrorism. The Reference Shelf*. 58, no. 3. New York: H.W. Wilson Company, 1986.

Arendt, Hannah. *On Violence*. New York: Harcourt, Brace and World, 1970.

Aron, Raymond. *Peace and War*. London: Weidenfeld and Nicolson, 1966.

Ayad, Abu. *Le'lo Moledet*. Jerusalem: Mifras, 1978.

Barron, John. *KGB: The Secret Work of Soviet Secret Agents*. New York: Bantam Books, 1974.

Bassiouni, M. Cherif, ed. *International Terrorism and Political Crimes*. Springfield, Ill.: Charles C. Thomas, 1975.

Baumann, Carol. *The Diplomatic Kidnappings: A Revolutionary Tactic of Urban Terrorism*. The Hague: Martinus Nijhoff, 1973.

Becker, Jillian. *Hitler's Children: The Story of the Baader-Meinhof Terrorist Gang*. Philadelphia: J. B. Lippincott, 1977.

Bell, J. Bowyer. "Assassination in International Politics: Lord Moyne, Count Bernadotte and the Lehi." *International Studies Quarterly* 16 (March 1972): 59–82.

———. *Transnational Terror.* AEI-Hoover Policy Study 17. Washington, D.C.: American Enterprise Institute for Public Policy Research, 1975.

Beres, Louis. *Terrorism and Global Security: The Nuclear Threat.* Boulder: Westview Press, 1979.

———. *Terrorism and Global Security: The Nuclear Threat,* 2d ed. Boulder: Westview Press, 1987.

Bryson, Lyman, ed. *The Communication of Ideas.* New York: Cooper Square, 1964.

Central Intelligence Agency, National Foreign Assessment Center. *International Terrorism in 1977: A Research Paper.* Washington, D.C.: Government Printing Office, RP–78–102554, 1978.

Chomsky, Norm. *The Fateful Triangle: The United States, Israel, and the Palestinians.* Boston: South End Press, 1983.

Cline, Ray, and Yonah Alexander. *Terrorism: The Soviet Connection.* New York: Crane, Russak, 1984.

Commission on Freedom of the Press. *A Free and Responsible Press.* Chicago: University of Chicago, 1947.

Crenshaw, Martha. *Terrorism and International Cooperation.* Boulder: Westview Press, 1989.

Crozier, Brian. *A Theory of Conflict.* London: Hamish Hamilton, 1974.

Dekmejian, R. Hrair. *Islam on Revolution.* Syracuse, N.Y.: Syracuse University Press, 1985.

Deutsch, Karl. *Nationalism and Social Communication: An Inquiry into the Foundation of Nationality,* 2d ed. Cambridge, Mass.: The MIT Press, 1966.

Eckstein, Harry, ed. *Internal War.* New York: Free Press of Glencoe, 1964.

Enloe, Cynthia. *Ethnic Conflict and Political Development.* Boston: Little, Brown and Company, 1973.

Epstein, Edward. *Between Fact and Fiction: The Problem of Journalism.* New York: Vintage Press, 1975.

Esposito, John. *Islam and Politics.* Syracuse, N.Y.: Syracuse University Press, 1984.

Eulau, Heinz. *The Behavior Persuasion in Politics.* New York: Random House, 1963.

Evans, Ernest. *Calling a Truce to Terror: The American Response to International Terrorism.* Westport, Conn.: Greenwood Press, 1979.

Friedlander, Robert. *Terror—Violence: Aspects of Social Control.* New York: Oceana Publications, 1983.

George, Alexander, and Richard Smoke. *Deterrence in American Foreign Policy: Theory and Practice.* New York: Columbia University Press, 1974.

Guggenberger, Bernd. "What Motivates the Urban Guerrilla?" *German Tribune-Political Affairs Review* 28 (3 October 1976): 16.

Gurr, Ted Robert. *Why Men Rebel.* Princeton: Princeton University Press, 1971.

Harkabi, Y. *Fedayeen Action and Arab Strategy.* London: Institute for Strategic Studies, 1968.

Hayakawa, Samuel. *Language in Thought and Action.* New York: Harcourt, Brace, Jovanovich, 1972.

Hull, Roger. *The Irish Triangle: Conflict in Northern Ireland.* Princeton, N.J.: Princeton University Press, 1976.

Ingraham, Barton. *Political Crime in Europe: A Comparative Study of France, Germany, and England.* Berkeley: University of California Press, 1979.

Institute for the Study of Conflict. *Annual of Power and Conflict: 1978–79.* London: Institute for the Study of Conflict, 1979.

———. *Annual of Power and Conflict: 1979–80.* London: Institute for the Study of Conflict, 1980.

———. *Annual of Power and Conflict: 1980–81.* London: Institute for the Study of Conflict, 1981.

———. *Annual of Power and Conflict: 1981–82.* London: Institute for the Study of Conflict, 1982.

Jeahnig, Walter. "Journalists and Terrorism: Captives of the Libertarian Tradition." *Indiana Law Journal* 53 (1978): 720.

Jenkins, Brian. "International Terrorism: A Balance Sheet." *Survival* 17, no. 4 (July-August 1975): 158.

———. "Statements about Terrorism." *Annals of American Academy of Political and Social Science* 463 (September 1982).

Jenkins, Brian, and Janera Johnson. *International Terrorism: A Chronology, 1968–1974.* Santa Monica: Rand Corporation, R–1597-DOS/ARPA, 1975.

Köchler, Hans, ed. *The New International Information and Communication Order.* Vienna: Wilhelm Braumüller, 1985.

Kupperman, Robert, and Darrell Trent. *Terrorism: Threat, Reality, Response.* Stanford, Calif.: Hoover Institute Press, 1979.

Laqueur, Walter, ed. *The Terrorism Reader: A Historical Anthology.* Philadelphia: Temple University Press, 1978.

Lasky, Melvin. "Ulrike Meinhof and the Baader-Meinhof Gang." *Encounter* 44 (June 1975): 15–16.

Lasswell, Harold. *Politics: Who Gets What, When and How.* New York: Meridian, 1958.

Lee, Alfred, and Elizabeth Lee, eds. *The Fine Art of Propaganda: A Study of Father Coughlin's Speeches.* New York: Harcourt, Brace, 1939.

Livingstone, Neil, and Terrell Arnold, eds. *Fighting Back: Winning the War against Terrorism.* Lexington, Mass.: D.C. Heath, 1986.

Lodge, Juliet, ed. *Terrorism: A Challenge to the State.* New York: St. Martin's, 1981.

McGuffin, John. *Internment.* Tralee, Ireland: Anvil Books, 1973.

McGuire, Maria. *To Take Arms: A Year in the Provisional IRA.* London: MacMillian, 1973.

Merari, Ariel, ed. *On Terrorism and Combating Terrorism.* Frederick, Md.: University Publications of America, 1985.

Methvin, Eugene. *The Rise of Radicalism: The Social Psychology of Messianic Extremism.* New Rochelle, N.Y.: Arlington House, 1973.

Midgley, Sarah, and Virginia Rice, eds. *Terrorism and the Media in the 1980's.* Washington, D.C.: The Media Institute, 1984.

Miller, Abraham. "Negotiations for Hostages: Implications from the Police Experience." *Terrorism: An International Journal* 1, no. 2 (1978).

———. *Terrorism and Hostage Negotiations.* Boulder: Westview Press, 1980.

————, ed. *Terrorism, the Media, and the Law.* Dobbs Ferry, N.Y.: Transnational Publishers, 1982.

Moss, Robert. *Urban Guerrillas.* London: Maurice Temple Smith, 1972.

National Advisory Committee on Criminal Justice Standards and Goals. *Disorders and Terrorism: Report of the Task Force on Disorders and Terrorism.* Washington, D.C.: Law Enforcement Assistance Administration, 1976.

Netanyahu, Benjmain, ed. *Terrorism: How the West Can Win.* New York: Farrar, Straus, Giroux, 1986.

Neubauer, Mark. "The Newsman's Privilege *Branzburg*: The Case for a Federal Shield Law." *U.C.L.A. Law Review* 24 (1976): 185–86.

Nieburg, Harold. *Political Violence: The Behavioral Process.* New York: St. Martin's, 1969.

Nye, Joseph Jr., and Robert Keohane, eds. *Transnational Relations and World Politics.* Cambridge, Mass.: Harvard University Press, 1972.

O'Brien, Conor Cruise. *Herod: Reflections on Political Violence.* London: Hutchinson, 1978.

Parenti, Michael. *Inventing Reality: The Politics of the Mass Media.* New York: St. Martin's, 1986.

Perdue, William. *Terrorism and the State.* New York: Praeger Publishers, 1989.

Pridham, Geoffrey. *Christian Democracy in Western Germany.* London: Croom Helm, 1977.

Ra'anan, Uri, Robert Pfaltzgraff, Jr., Richard Shultz, Ernst Halperin, and Igor Lukes, eds. *Hydra of Carnage.* Lexington, Mass.: Lexington Books, 1986.

Schlagheck, Donna. *International Terrorism: An Introduction to the Concepts and Actors.* Lexington, Mass.: Lexington Books, 1988.

Schlesinger, Philip. *Putting "Reality" Together.* London: Constable, 1978.

Schmid, Alex. *Political Terrorism: A Research Guide.* New Brunswick, N.J.: Transaction, 1984.

Schramm, Wilbur, and Donald Roberts, eds. *The Processes and Effects of Mass Communication,* 2d ed. Urbana: University of Illinois Press, 1971.

Stavrianos, Leften. *The Balkans Since 1453.* New York: Rinehart, 1958.

Sterling, Claire. *The Terror Network: The Secret War of International Terrorism.* New York: Reader's Digest Press, 1981.

Taheri, Amir. *The Spirit of Allah: Khomeini and the Islamic Revolution.* Bethesda, Md.: Adler and Adler, 1986.

Taylor, Peter, ed. *The British Media and Ireland.* London: Constable, 1978.

Tessandori, V. *Br, imputazione: banda armata.* Milan: Aldo Garzanti Editore, 1977.

Tophoven, Rolf. *German Response to Terrorism.* Koblenz: Bernhard & Gräfe Verlag, 1984.

Tuchman, Gaye. *The T.V. Establishment: Programming for Power and Profit.* Englewood Cliffs, N.J.: Prentice-Hall, 1974.

Turner, Stansfield. *Secrecy and Democracy: The CIA in Transition.* Boston: Houghton Mifflin, 1985.

von Hoffman, Nicholas. "ABC Held Hostage." *New Republic,* 10 May 1980, 15–16.

Waters, Harry. "Gomorrah Revisited." *Newsweek,* 5 April 1976, 61.

Weinberg, Leonard, and William Eubank. *The Rise and Fall of Italian Terrorism.* Boulder: Westview Press, 1987.

Welch, Susan, and John Comer. *Quantitative Methods for Public Administration: Techniques and Applications*, 2d ed. Chicago: The Dorsey Press, 1988.

Wilkinson, Paul. *Political Terrorism*. London: MacMillian, 1974.

————. "Terrorism versus Liberal Democracy—The Problem of Response." *Conflict Studies*, no. 67. London: Institute for the Study of Conflict, 1976.

————. *Terrorism and the Liberal State*, 2d ed. New York: New York University Press, 1986.

Wolf, John. *Fear of Fear: A Survey of Terrorist Operations and Controls in Open Societies*. New York: Plenum Press, 1981.

————. *Antiterrorist Initiatives*. New York: Plenum Press, 1989.

Index

ABOUT THE AUTHOR

RICHARD W. SCHAFFERT's interest in political terrorism stems from his participation in the development of counterterror policies while serving as a liaison officer at the U.S. embassy in Manila in 1980–81. From 1981 to 1983, he served as Director of Policy Studies at NATO military headquarters in Belgium. Dr. Schaffert is a retired U.S. Navy Captain, and he continues private research and consultation on Eastern European politics and international terrorism.